Good Governance and Modern International Financial Institutions

AIIB Yearbook of International Law

General Editor

Gerard J. Sanders

VOLUME 1

The titles published in this series are listed at *brill.com/aiib*

Good Governance and Modern International Financial Institutions

AIIB Yearbook of International Law 2018

Edited by

Peter Quayle
Xuan Gao

BRILL
NIJHOFF

LEIDEN | BOSTON

Typeface for the Latin, Greek, and Cyrillic scripts: "Brill". See and download: brill.com/brill-typeface.

ISSN 2590-2822
ISSN 978-90-04-39801-6 (hardback)
ISSN 978-90-04-40832-6 (e-book)

This book is printed on acid-free paper and produced in a sustainable manner.

Contents

Preface

This book is the first edition of the *AIIB Yearbook of International Law*, a publication of the Asian Infrastructure Investment Bank, an international financial institution fostering growth, development and infrastructure connectivity in Asia. Its content springs from activity sponsored by the Office of the General Counsel in 2017, the first complete year of operations of the Bank. Although the treaty establishing the institution became effective almost a year earlier, the legal function was set on a permanent footing only in August 2016 with the first staff appointment of a lawyer, followed quickly by the recruitment of several other counsel.

These lawyers, working within the Office of the General Counsel, provide advice to the new organization primarily on institutional and operational matters, a conventional role of many in-house legal departments. However, it was always understood that the legal function would also look outwards and embrace the larger responsibilities that befall a modern organization owned primarily by states, substantially supported by public funds and with the potential to impact on the lives of many. Those responsibilities include the obligation to share what we learn, the successes we celebrate and the failures we suffer, so that others may benefit from that experience. Because it is not only experience that informs knowledge the Bank will also wish to offer, for the critical consideration of others, new ways of thinking about difficult issues with which international organizations and the wider legal community must contend. Some of those issues will be recurrent, sometimes being seemingly intractable. Doubtless, as yet unknown challenges also lie ahead, about what role law does, can and ought to play in empowering and constraining international organizations and others in the pursuit of societal objectives. The search for answers, in the international legal sphere as elsewhere, will always draw us forwards together; an impulse of the human condition as much as the need for law itself.

For its part, AIIB hopes to make some modest contribution to legal knowledge and understanding, not only by drawing on its own experiences and insights, but by offering a platform for others to develop ideas on matters of common interest and for the Bank to disseminate them. We all stand to gain with the enlargement of public goods. In this spirit, 2017 saw AIIB host its inaugural international Legal Conference, on *Good Governance and Modern International Financial Institutions*, which is also the title of this first edition of the *AIIB Yearbook of International Law*. The conference drew together, at the AIIB's headquarters in Beijing, general counsel of international financial institutions and leading international law practitioners and academics to examine the benchmarks of good governance, such as transparency, stakeholder participation, the rule of law, accountability and efficiency. Complementing the conference, the inaugural AIIB Law Lecture was given by the United Nations Under-Secretary-General for Legal Affairs and UN Legal Counsel on "The Necessity of Cooperation between International Organizations." The papers that emerged from the conference and the law lecture together form the basis of this, the inaugural, edition of the *AIIB Yearbook of International Law*.

*Gerard Sanders**

---

* General Counsel, AIIB, General Editor, AIIB Yearbook of International Law, Visiting Professorial Fellow at Queen Mary, University of London, and Founding Editor of *Law in Transition*.

Introduction: Good Governance and Modern International Financial Institutions

Peter Quayle and Xuan Gao***

In accordance with its Articles of Agreement, one of the reasons that the Asian Infrastructure Investment Bank (AIIB) exists is of course to "improve infrastructure connectivity in Asia." From the outset, this is to be understood in its broadest sense as the entire sustaining context of successful major infrastructure projects. With the 2017 AIIB Legal Conference, this mandate was to the fore, bringing together and connecting an unrivalled range of diverse experiences and expertise to help the AIIB, as the newest International Financial Institution (IFI), examine and understand the challenges and possibilities of good governance of multilateral development institutions. This debate and discourse surrounding the good governance of IFIs and the broader standards set by intergovernmental institutions was of pressing relevance given how, in today's era a commitment to globalized trade, investment and interconnectedness comes under pressure.

This first edition of the *AIIB Yearbook of International Law* (AYIL) pursues this theme, to examine the benchmarks of good governance, such as transparency and stakeholder participation, utilizing the insights shared and dialogue begun by the 2017 AIIB Legal Conference. Drawing upon expertise from other IFIs, international law practitioners and eminent academics, this edition of AYIL is divided into three parts to reflect a series of overarching themes. Firstly, the role of the membership of IFIs as expressed through their executive governance organs. Second, the legal basis of governance of IFIs. Third, the interaction around governance between IFIs and external stakeholders.

In his chapter that begins the first part of this edition of AYIL, Stilpon Nestor examines data from a peer group of international and private financial institutions and whilst identifying important distinctive governance features of IFI boards, concludes that IFIs share with private sector governance bodies the same key drivers of superior performance. Next, Marie-Anne Birken and Gian

* Peter Quayle, Chief Counsel, Corporate at Asian Infrastructure Investment Bank, Editor of the *AIIB Yearbook of International Law* and Visiting Professor of International Organizations Law at Peking University Law School, peter.quayle@aiib.org.

** Xuan Gao, Chief Counsel, Institutional at Asian Infrastructure Investment Bank, Editor of the *AIIB Yearbook of International Law* and Deputy Editor-in-Chief of the *Manchester Journal of International Economic Law*, xuan.gao@aiib.org.

Piero Cigna turn to a specific component of all governance boards—gender diversity—to argue for the deserved prominence of this feature in good governance, drawing upon the experience of private financial institutions and, in turn, IFIs. Lastly this first part concludes with the unrivalled vantage point of Whitney Debevoise on the role of member states, given voice and weighted votes on the governance board of IFIs, to contributing to the good governance of multilateral development institutions and their broader operational success, and sometime shortcomings. The chapter does not shy away from arguing for a particularly essential governance role of an IFI's leading and largest shareholder.

In the second part of this edition, Yan Liu begins with the case study of the International Monetary Fund, its time tested but evolving purpose, and examines the way in which the Fund's legal office contributes to the rule of law and so to the effectiveness and independence of this essential global institution. From one of the longest established, to the most recently founded IFI, Natalie Lichtenstein places the recently formed AIIB into a legal comparative context, highlighting the important areas of constitutional continuity and contrast of this newest institution to its IFI peers. This part concludes with an examination by Joan Powers of the only routine judicial oversight of the governance of IFIs, namely that afforded by international administrative tribunals which adjudicate employment disputes in accordance with international administrative law, the law of employment relations of the international civil service. This chapter considers whether the jurisprudence of multiple international administrative tribunals intends towards fragmentation or synthesis, and the resulting implications upon the governance of IFIs.

The third and last part of this edition considers how the good governance of IFIs implicates broader concerns about interactions with, and influence upon, third parties. Catherine Weaver examines the way in which the World Bank led the way in making its operations more open and transparent, with significant ramifications for its own governance, its influence on other IFIs and ultimately with consequences for the operational efficiency and effectiveness of the Bank. Yifeng Chen traces the expanding role that employment standards have had in the conditionality of IFI projects and whether or not this has led to a distinct body of IFI labor standards or transposed existing standards expounded by the International Labour Organization. Lastly Pascale Hélène Dubois, David Fielder, Robert Delonis, Frank Fariello and Kathleen Peters co-author a chapter that studies the role of the World Bank Group's sanctions system and considers its contribution to global efforts to promote good governance and thwart the misuse of public monies.

This edition concludes with the text of the 2017 AIIB Law Lecture, delivered by the United Nations Under-Secretary-General for Legal Affairs and Legal Counsel, Miguel de Serpa Soares on the subject of "The Necessity of Cooperation between International Organizations" and a summary report on the proceedings of the 2017 AIIB Legal Conference.

Running through this inaugural edition of AYIL is a constant thread: that whilst rules, regulations, systems and processes are essential to the good governance of modern IFIs, they are not altogether sufficient. Rather, what animates multilateral development institutions are not procedures, but people and their principles. For IFIs to succeed, to entrench and expand their relevance, to deliver upon their high purposes, is to depend everyday upon the professionalism, good conscience and seriousness of purpose of the international civil servants who staff these essential institutions. It is these servants whom are called upon to apply themselves to the constant task and toil of good governance, with a fidelity to the principles of professionalism and a public trust and duty, dependent upon the rule of law, that governs and enables the mandates of IFIs.

PART 1

The Governance Role of the Boards of International Financial Institutions

CHAPTER 1

Board Effectiveness in International Financial Institutions: A Comparative Perspective on the Effectiveness Drivers in Constituency Boards

*Stilpon Nestor**

Abstract

Using comparative data from a peer group of international and private financial institutions, this chapter explores what drives effectiveness in International Financial Institution (IFI) boards. It starts by identifying their overarching constituency nature and the dual role of directors as representative of shareholder governments and "fiduciaries" of the institution. It also underlines their somewhat contradictory power structure, with a high concentration of decision-making at board level, performed by non-professionals, whose nomination as "executives" belies the absence of any personal executive responsibilities in the organization even when these directors are full-time "residents"—another particularity of IFI boards. The main argument of the chapter is that, while these particularities are important, IFI boards resemble all other boards, especially those of private financial institutions, when it comes to the key drivers of their performance. These consists of their size, composition, leadership, diversity; the competencies and tenure of their directors; the quality of the support they get from management and the tools they use to maintain their effectiveness over time. The chapter concludes with some preliminary ideas on improving IFI board effectiveness.

* Stilpon Nestor, LL.M (Harv.), is the Managing Director, Nestor Advisors Ltd. and the Chairman of AKTIS Ltd. He has advised the boards of numerous private financial institutions as well as international financial institutions and organizations on governance issues. From 2010 to 2014 he sat on the board of the European Investment Bank. In the earlier part of his career he was the head of the OECD's corporate Affairs division. E-mail address: snestor@nestoradvisors.com. The author would like to thank Konstantina Tsilipira, Analyst at Nestor Advisors, and Lisa Andersson, Senior Analyst at AKTIS for their research support. My gratitude also goes also to Emmanuel Maurice, Enery Quinones and George Papakonstantinou, all senior advisors at Nestor Advisors, for their extremely valuable comments and insights.

 | DOI:10.1163/9789004408326_002

1 Introduction

The focus of this paper is the effectiveness of the boards of International Financial Institutions (IFIs). Its perspective is that of a practitioner.

Underpinning the discussion of IFI board effectiveness are two sets of elements: Firstly, the idiosyncratic nature of IFI boards, mostly due to their overarching constituency nature, which is addressed in Part 2 of the paper. Second, the key drivers of effectiveness of *any* board—that is, of any team that is supposed to direct and control an organization, as per Sir Adrian Cadbury's definition of governance.[1]

The analysis of the drivers, i.e., of the second element, is often based on comparisons between IFI and private Financial Institutions (FIs). The empirical research quoted throughout this chapter focuses on two different peer groups: a selected group of 11 large global and regional IFIs, analyzed internally at Nestor Advisors,[2] and data from private banks collected and analyzed by AKTIS a company that specializes in bank governance data.[3] This paper uses AKTIS governance data pertaining to the 25 largest European commercial banks. In some noted instances the data used pertain to the 24 globally significant banks (G-SIBs), not including Chinese banks.

2 The Idiosyncrasy of IFIs and its Impact on Board Effectiveness

2.1 *Constituency Boards*

At the heart of this discussion, and common to all IFIs, is what is often referred to as "a constituency board." This is a board in which directors are not appointed as individual "fiduciaries" of all shareholders/members; rather they are representatives of a "constituency," i.e., a single shareholder/stakeholder or of a group of them. The difference to the typical board as anticipated by company laws throughout the world, centers on the loyalty of board members, both as a psychological attribute and as an actual duty. Under most company laws, the members of the board are not there to serve the interest of the shareholders

1 "Corporate Governance is the system by which companies are directed and controlled." Committee on the Financial Aspects of Corporate Governance, *The Code of Best Practice on Corporate Governance* 6 (Gee 1992).

2 The data date from end-August 2017.

3 Stilpon Nestor and Lisa Andersson, "Ten Years on: Governance of the 25 largest European Banks a Decade After the Crisis" (AKTIS and Nestor Advisors, 2018) (forthcoming). The data date from end-2016.

that helped elect them but those of the company as a whole. In the US, the duty is a "fiduciary" one to the shareholders but courts interpret this to be to the shareholders, not to a current shareholder.[4] While there might be the occasional shareholder representative on an FI board, current practice and, most importantly, regulatory requirements and supervisory expectations make this a rare occurrence.[5]

In contrast, all IFI boards are constituency boards and their members have a "dual role": all members are shareholder representatives by design,[6] with the exception of some individual independent experts.[7] On the other hand, most IFIs explicitly postulate a duty of loyalty to the institution. For instance, the Code of Conduct for World Bank Board officials provides that "Board Officials shall hold the interests of the Organizations paramount..." while the EIB Code of Conduct states that "in discharging their duties to the Bank, members of the Board of Directors shall...endeavor to only act in the interest of the Bank...."

The loyalty tension in such boards is palpable, almost schizophrenic: member country representatives, usually civil servants who are legally bound to serve the interests of their country, are also expected to somehow transcend these interests and act in the interests of the organization as a whole. It is of course easy to hide behind "what is good for my country is good for the world." But this is hardly defendable when, for example, a director finds themselves in a minority of one in important matter that affects their country. Or comes in possession of important, confidential but not yet distributed documents that affect the interests of their country.

The IFI board thus looks much more like a general meeting of shareholders, a place where the synthesis of shareholder interests is to be negotiated rather than assumed. One would think that the Boards of Governors, the higher instance of shareholder decision making in most IFIs, should be playing this

4 Robert Clark, *Corporate Law* (*Textbook Treatise Series*) (2nd edn, AA Balkema 1986).

5 European Parliament and Council Directive 2013/36/EU on access to the activity of credit institutions and the prudential supervision of credit institutions and investment firms, amending Directive 2002/87/EC and repealing Directives 2006/48/EC and 2006/49/EC [2013] OJ L176/338 (Capital Requirements Directive 2013) art 88 2 b.

6 The dual role might be less pronounced for directors who represent multi-country constituencies. In some organizations, there exist internal constituency arrangements to address divergence of opinion among constituency members in determining the constituency position.

7 In some cases, there may be a relatively small number of directors appointed by all shareholders due to their expertise in the matters dealt with by the board. The board of EIB includes 6 such directors. European Investment Bank, *EIB Group Corporate Governance Report 2016* (EIB 2016) <www.eib.org/attachments/general/reports/eib_group_corporate_governance_report_2016_en.pdf> accessed 24 January 2018.

synthesizing role given their stature and seniority of the Governors, usually Ministers in their respective countries. In practice, it works the other way around. The IFI boards spend a lot of time negotiating the common denominators on strategy and governance from the perspective of individual constituencies and prepare the formal statements endorsed by governors;[8] instead of focusing on directing and controlling the institution, as per Sir Adrian's definition.

2.2 *Board Effectiveness*

What is an effective board? The answer is deceptively simple: an effective board is one that is composed, organized and functions in a way that optimizes the delivery of its mandate. Note that this discussion is not about the effectiveness of the organization but of its *board*. There is an obvious relationship between the two, but they are not the same. The effectiveness of the organization will be linked to optimizing governance. Optimal governance will depend on the effectiveness of the board but also on the adequate distribution of responsibility and authority in the organization, i.e., the mandate and power of various principals and agents[9]—including, most importantly, the mandate and retained powers of the board.

This chapter does not focus on the discussion of the board's mandate as such. However, it is important to note that IFI boards do have significantly different mandates than private sector FIs. The most important difference consists in the vastly more expansive authorities that IFI boards retain compared to their commercial counterparts that tend to delegate much more to professional management.[10] Despite a post crisis push by regulators for bank boards to assume more direct responsibility in certain areas, private FI mandates still cannot be compared to those of most IFI boards. The latter typically retain most credit/financial decision-making authority,[11] a function that has been delegated to management credit committees a long time ago.[12] This has an important impact on the agendas of IFI boards that are disproportionately tilted towards operational decision making. This constraint seems even more counterproductive if one takes into consideration the profile of the large majority of

8 High-Level Commission on Modernization of World Bank Group Governance, *Repowering the World Bank for the 21st Century* (2009) 22.

9 Michael Jensen and William Meckling, "Theory of the Firm: Managerial Behaviour, Agency Costs and Ownership Structure" (1976) 3 J. Financial Econ 305, 309.

10 Domenico Lombardi, "The Governance of the World Bank: Lessons from the Corporate Sector" (2008) 3 Rev Int Organ 5.

11 For example, this is the case in the WBG, the EBRD and the EIB.

12 In a few cases, private FI boards retain credit authority for very large credit transactions.

TABLE 1.1

	IFI	Resident/ Non-Resident	Number of Meetings
1	International Bank for Reconstruction and Development (IBRD)	Yes	>Twice/week
2	International Monetary Fund (IMF)	Yes	Several times/week
3	European Investment Bank (EIB)	No	10 / year
4	European Bank for Reconstruction and Development (EBRD)	Yes	2–3/month
5	International Fund for Agricultural Development (IFAD)	No	3/ year
6	Black Sea Trade and Development Bank (BSTDB)	No	N/D
7	Asian Development Bank (ADB)	Yes	Several times/ month
8	Asian Infrastructure Investment Bank (AIIB)	No	5 / year
9	African Development Bank (AfDB)	Yes	As often as required
10	Inter-American Development Bank Group (IADB)	Yes	1/ week
11	Nordic Investment Bank (NIB)	No	8 / year

IFI board members: civil servants with limited financial experience—a point this article will return to.

Extensive retained authorities explain, at least partly, one more IFI characteristic: a significant majority of them are run by resident boards who meet much more often than private FI boards. Table 1.1 identifies the boards that are resident and compares the frequency of board meeting among the IFI peer group.

What is interesting in the typical IFI board is that while the directors are "executive"[13] in the sense that they are full time and partake in extensive collective board authorities, none of them have individual executive responsibilities in the running of the institution, as is usually the case in private FI

13 In many IFIs, like IBRD, IMF, IADB, AfDB, their actual title is "executive director."

management boards—the lower tier in a two-tier board system[14]—or among executive directors in one tier systems. Their personal responsibility resembles those of Non-Executive Directors ("NEDs") in one-tier systems or supervisory board directors in two-tier ones. Just like in the case of NEDs, their accountability for adequately discharging their responsibilities is collective, not individual.[15] Moreover, this extensive authority is of an ambiguous nature as identified in the Zedillo committee's report on World Bank governance, which I believe speaks to the issue in many IFI boards:

> The division of labor between Board and Management in the WBG is ambiguous. In some instances, disputes emerge over whether a decision is Management's to recommend and the Board's to approve or turn down, or whether it falls under the Board's prerogative to direct the President. This ambiguity makes it difficult to ascertain who is responsible and who should be held accountable.[16]

In contrast to their extensive transactional authority, IFI boards seem to have little say in the appointment of the top teams in the institutions they lead. The executive leader (i.e., president, managing director, etc.) of the institution is usually appointed by the shareholders (usually, the Governors), typically in a quite non-transparent way. In the case of EIB, a management board is appointed directly by the Governors, on a constituency basis. In many IFIs, the top team around the institution's leader is appointed by him/herself with only information provided to the board on such appointments.[17] This contrast sharply with private FI practice, where the board and its nomination committee would be closely associated with all top management hiring

14 In a one-tier board structure, both supervisory and managerial duties are discharged by a unified board of directors. In contrast, a two-tier board structure consists of a management board and a supervisory board that both act on an autonomous basis; the management board comprises senior management while the supervisory board consists of non-executive members, that have different responsibilities and tasks. David Kershaw, *Company Law in Context: Text and Materials* (OUP 2012) 216.

15 This refers to governance accountability rather than personal liability of a criminal or civil nature, a related but quite distinct subject which is not be discussed in this paper. For a comprehensive review of liability regimes in private companies in Europe see Carsten Gerner—Beuerle and others, "Study on Directors' Duties and Liability" (2013) LSE Enterprise <http://ec.europa.eu/internal_market/company/docs/board/2013-study-analysis_en.pdf> accessed 22 December 2017.

16 Committee on the Financial Aspects of Corporate Governance (n 2) 13.

17 Lombardi (n 11) 18.

decisions and would be well informed on the performance of the senior executive team.[18]

3 The Individual Drivers of Effectiveness

Based on years of working with boards, I would distinguish nine individual drivers of board effectiveness that are relevant to all organizations:

A. Size of the board.
B. Board leadership.
C. Knowledge, skills and experience of board members.
D. Board diversity.
E. Tenure of board members.
F. Personal commitment of board members.
G. Board workload and its distribution through committees.
H. Board "maintenance."
I. Board support.

It is also important to note that these board drivers can be categorized under two broad headings: people-related and structure-related—and some belong to both categories. In general, IFI boards are much more about structure than other organizations, especially as compared to commercial boards. The reason is simple: given the constituency nature of these boards, appointments are completely shareholder-driven—and there are many shareholders. Unlike private FIs, IFI boards have practically no say on the profile and quality of their members. They have no mandate to control them for fit and proper aspects that are now a litmus test for board membership in the private sector.[19] On the other hand, IFI boards usually have more elaborate rules on (weighted) voting, on the board's formal authorities, and on the ways boards connect and get information from management. Usually they also have a fairly developed committee structure, although committees are staffed less on the basis of expertise and more on representation imperatives. Such imperatives also explain the fact that, in contrast to private FIs, in almost all IFIs committee attendance is often open to all board members.[20]

---

18 All the banks of our private FI (European) peer group appoint all top management at executive committee level. Nestor and Andersson (n 3) 19.

19 See below page 10.

20 An exception is the non-resident board of the EIB that restricts committee attendance to committee members only. Also, Ethics committees in several IFIs have more restrictive attendance rules given the sensitivity of the issues in their purview.

Another important point to note is that there is always a degree of tension among the different effectiveness drivers. For example, consider diversity: a degree of diversity is very welcome as it allows for out-of-the-box thinking; but too much diversity might compete at the margin with director knowledge, skills and experience (KSE). Workload is another example: while boards need to work harder as they have more and more responsibilities and tasks in the eyes of supervisors and other stakeholders, an overly heavy workload might result in boards becoming rubber stamping machines, thus lowering effectiveness. We are, as ever, looking for the golden middle.

3.1 *The Size of the Board*

Clearly size impacts effectiveness because it impacts the dynamics of board discussions:[21] too small a board limits perspective and might amplify group think. But too large a board inhibits discussion and thereby limits challenge. Is there a "magic" number? Our experience suggests that there is significant pressure by supervisors for private FIs with larger boards to bring them down to anywhere between 13–15 members. Hence the average size in our private FI peer group is currently approximately 14, down from approximately 16 in 2007.[22]

IFIs have much larger boards, as per Table 1.2. The mean among our 11 IFI peers is approximately 18 members. Furthermore, this relatively high number significantly underestimates the number of people in the board room—and hence the negative impact on board dynamics. In most IFIs, board meetings always include senior management (which is also the case in many private FIs) and, usually, many alternate directors as well as board advisors.[23]

It might be that limiting the number of people in the room even without lowering the number of seats might actually play a positive role in board dynamics. This might not be possible in all, even most, board meetings. But it is important that, from time to time, the board has the opportunity to meet without all the other attendees. Limiting the right to take the floor to directors only might also help. Finally, some IFI boards[24] have adopted rules that limit the time available to participants for oral interventions while others[25] encourage directors to prepare written statements on agenda issues and look down

21 Colin Carter and J. William Lorsch, *Back to the Drawing Board: Designing Corporate Boards for a Complex World* (HBSP 2003) 88.

22 Nestor and Andersson (n 3) 4.

23 For example, the WBG has 24 alternate EDs in addition to its 25 EDs, the EIB 19 alternate directors in addition to its 29 EDs and the EBRD 23 alternate EDs in addition to its 23 EDs.

24 For example, the World bank.

25 For example, the IMF.

TABLE 1.2

	IFI	Board Size
1	IBRD	25
2	IMF	24
3	EIB	29
4	EBRD	23
5	IFAD	18
6	BSTDB	11
7	ADB	12
8	AIIB	12
9	AfDB	20
10	IADB	14
11	NIB	8
	Average	17.9

on "read" statements during board minutes. The results on board effectiveness seem to be rather mixed from such limitations.

3.2 *Board Leadership*

Every team needs a leader and the quality of the leader clearly impacts both on the capacity of the team to deliver on its mandate as well as on the culture that drives team dynamics. When it comes to boards, the quality of the leader impacts directly on the quality and openness of the discussion and therefore the robustness of challenge it offers to management. As Sir Adrian Cadbury highlighted, "The job of the chairman is to encourage board members to give of their individual best in a cooperative cause."[26]

On the issue of board leadership things could not be more different between private FIs and IFIs. In the latter, the leader of the board is almost always the leader of the institution.[27] In corporate governance terms, we always have a Chairman/CEO. In contrast, the great majority of G-SIBs (more than 80 percent) have now separated the position of the Chairman of the Board from that of the CEO.[28] The rationale is obvious: the leader of the team whose main

26 Adrian Cadbury, *Corporate Governance and Chairmanship: A Personal View* (OUP 2002) 79.

27 In our IFI peer group, only NIB has a board chairman that is non-executive and is a different person than the CEO/president of the organization.

28 Nestor and Andersson (n 3) 6.

purpose is to challenge the executive leadership and hold it accountable cannot be a member of management. In Europe, this is now a regulatory requirement for banks.[29]

Another important difference is that the IFI President, unlike the CEO or the Chairman in private FIs, is usually appointed by the shareholders. As per Table 1.3, in eight out of 11 IFI the head of the organization is appointed by the board of governors (usually the ministers of finance of the member countries). This is not necessarily a negative factor, given the level of power that is concentrated in the hands of the executive head in most IFIs in terms of running the organization—but not in terms of transactional decision making, as discussed above.

But even in IFIs where the board of directors is responsible for the appointment of the organization's head (such as the World Bank or the IMF), the appointment is rarely characterized by the relatively orderly and (internally) transparent process that prevails among best practice private FIs, run by the nomination committee of the board. Moreover, if when they are appointed by the board, there seems to be little accountability of the President to the board as such. For example, there is little evidence of a robust performance evaluation framework for the President in most of the IFIs surveyed and what exists seems to be of a rather "soft" nature. In short, one can reasonably conclude that the board is not a "sovereign" decision maker when it comes to appointing and monitoring the performance of its leader, and that its role is only a "front" for behind the scenes shareholder wrangling.

The tenure of an organization's leader is another important element of leadership effectiveness. An entrenched leader will tend to be less effective and more set in their ways. In this respect, our two peer groups seem to be on the same wavelength. Private FI peers have an average CEO tenure of 3.8 years, which is not very dissimilar to the IFI average President average tenure of 5.1 years.

When the Chairman is also the CEO, private companies will appoint a leader among the non-executive population that can step in when the Chairman/CEO is conflicted. The title varies in different jurisdictions—senior or lead independent director, independent vice chairmen—but the function is roughly the same. The way that the IFIs have sought to address the same potential conflicts is though the position of the "dean,"[30] the senior member among the

29 Capital Requirements Directive 2013 (n 5) art 88.1.e.

30 For example, both the IBRD and the EBRD boards have deans. Senior non-management directors are given specific functions even in IFIs that do not have the specific practice of appointing a dean (e.g., the EIB).

TABLE 1.3

	IFI	Board Role	Executive Role	Appointment by:	Tenure in Years of current President
1	IBRD	Chairman	President	BoD	6
2	IMF	Chairman	Managing Director	BoD	6.5
3	EIB	Chairman	President	BoG	6 (re-appointed for another six-year term, starting on the first of January 2018)
4	EBRD	Chairman	President	BoG	6 (re-elected for a second four-year term in 2016)
5	IFAD	Chairman	CEO	BoG	1
6	BSTDB	Chairman	CEO	BoG	3.5
7	ADB	Chairman	President	BoG	5
8	AIIB	Chairman	President	BoG	2
9	AfDB	Chairman	CEO / President	BoG	2.5
10	IADB	Chairman	CEO / President	BoG	12.5
11	NIB	–	CEO / President	BoD	5.5

non-management directors. The dean often assumes responsibilities related to the board's effectiveness and is the point of reference among non-management directors on issues that might be awkward for the President to address. In addition, it is a way to invest some authority in one among few directors that embody some institutional memory.[31]

3.3 *Knowledge, Skills and Experience (KSE) of Board Members*

It is an obvious point—the most obvious among the "people" drivers—that the effectiveness of a board is related to the knowledge, skills and experience of its members. And yet, lack of KSE was one of the key corporate governance

31 See discussion in subsection (e).

failings in the run up to the 2007–2008 financial crisis.[32] In the Lehman Brothers board, we had a NED population that included actresses, theater producers, but no bankers until early 2008! That is why post crisis regulation not only put the KSE of directors at the heart of supervisory expectations and controls;[33] as discussed, it also made it the explicit job of the board to ensure that there is adequate KSE on the board—some would say in direct contradiction to the "spirit" of company law in many (mostly European) jurisdictions which reserve decisions related to the composition of the board to the shareholders. Significant institutions are expected to have nomination committees that ensure that NEDs are not only "independent," but also have the demanding KSE that is required for the governance of such complex organizations.[34] While the appointment (usually informal) of some directors by certain shareholders was and still is not completely uncommon, significant FIs are expected to have "independent instances" in which such appointments are vetted—and sometimes refused. FIs ignore such best practice at their peril—for example, during the last few years it has not been uncommon among ECB-supervised banks to have the Single Supervisory Mechanism rigorously challenge director appointments.

While some IFI charters provide that board members should "be persons of high competence in economic and financial matters" (EBRD), getting the right level of KSE is quite problematic in constituency boards, and much more so in IFIs. Because of the representative nature of directorships, IFI boards have rarely the tools to "raise the bar" when it comes to the quality of individual directors. In most cases, the latter are not, in practice "elected" as in private organizations but appointed by individual shareholders.[35] It is therefore not a

32 Catherine Lawton and Stilpon Nestor, "Bank Board after the Flood: The Changing Governance of the 25 Largest European Banks" (Nestor Advisors Ltd 2010) 62, 63.

33 For example, the PRA/FCA in the UK establishes clear responsibility in vetting the competences and specific expertise of officers at various positions. Supervisory Statement of the Prudential Regulation Authority on Strengthening Individual Accountability in Banking (2017) SS28/15 28.

34 For example, in Europe the European Banking Authority requires banks to ensure that such tests are performed by the nomination committee of the board. When performing suitability evaluations, institutions shall examine skills like authenticity, language, decisiveness, communication, judgement, customer and quality-oriented, leadership, loyalty, external awareness, negotiating, persuasive, teamwork, strategic acumen, stress resistance, sense of responsibility, chairing meetings. European Securities and Markets Authorities and European Banking Authority, "Final Report on Guidelines on the Assessment of the Suitability of Members of the Management Body and Key Function Holders Under Directive 2013/36/EU and Directive 2014/65/EU" (2017) EBA/GL/2017/12.

35 In at least one IFI Board (IFAD) the KSE issue may be compounded by the fact that it is the member State, not an individual, who is elected as Board member. This gives member

surprise to find that directors with banking experience constitute only around 25 percent of the board population in our IFI peer group, on average. In comparison, in the boards of our private FI (European) peer group 44 percent of members have recent FI experience. Nevertheless, the IFI average number is not too far from that for the US top 25 banks at 26 percent.[36] Moreover, some IFI boards pack an impressive FI expertise: more than 50 percent of IMF board members have recent financial sector expertise. This might be an important underlying factor in the quality of IMF board discussions—something many knowledgeable observers have signaled to us during various engagements.

One obvious way to address the issue of suboptimal KSE is to create a board committee with responsibilities and mandate that resemble that of nomination committees in private FI boards.[37] But calls for such a vetting process have not attracted much support among IFI shareholders as they take too much power away from them—the sovereign deciders who appoint individual members in most IFIs. IFI boards have tried to address this KSE gap by providing ad hoc training or "technical briefings" for board members. The problem is that the training is limited in time and scope and often focuses on a specific issue that arises in the context of a problematical transaction that is before the board for approval. As such, the training cannot adequately raise the overall KSE level of individual members.

A "hard wired" nomination committee and policy in IFIs might fit the bill but unless a wholesale reform of board appointment processes could magically materialize there seems to be limited space for this. However, there might be space for a less constrictive, "soft" approach in which a committee of the board with governance responsibilities would maintain a profile matrix of competencies required to make board composition optimal. This body would regularly report on gaps between actual and desired board composition to the governors as they engage in director selection. A similar approach has recently been adopted by EIB in the appointment of its Management Committee, its full time executive directors appointed by the shareholders of the Bank. This body does not have power to nominate but as advisory body it can point to the needs of the board in terms of KSE or diversity.[38]

Another, less intrusive way to address the lack of levers to promote KSE (and diversity), and to also introduce some out-of-the-box, challenging thinking is

States latitude to designate multiple representatives, with mostly negative effects in board cohesiveness and dynamics.

36 Nestor and Andersson (n 3) 9.

37 The Zedillo Committee on WBG reform proposed something similar to this. Committee on the Financial Aspects of Corporate Governance (n 2) 42.

38 European Investment Bank (n 6) 9.

TABLE 1.4

	IFI	Resident Board	Non-Resident Board
1	IBRD	✓	
2	IMF	✓	
3	EIB		✓
4	EBRD	✓	
5	IFAD		✓
6	BSTDB		✓
7	ADB	✓	
8	AIIB		✓
9	AfDB	✓	
10	IADB	✓	
11	NIB		✓

to appoint members that are not shareholder representatives. There are only a few IFIs that allow non-shareholder representatives to be full participants at board meetings, albeit in an advisory, non-voting capacity.[39] The experience is that these advisory directors are an important, positive factor in board deliberations in that they help the interests and voices of various shareholders around the table to converge and to emerge as the view of the institution. This approach is highly recommended for boards that are non-resident (see Table 1.1). But it would be hard to transpose it as such to resident boards given their workload—few independent experts could accommodate bi-weekly meetings. For the latter, other mechanisms for injecting non-partisan objectivity that is independent from management might need to be identified, such as advisory panels that meet with the board from time to time.

Finally, when it comes to skills in the risk and internal control area, mention should be made of partly or wholly independent audit committees which are composed not of members of the board but of experts who report to the

39 For example, at EIB the Board of Directors can co-opt up to six experts, so as to expand the Directors' professional expertise in specific areas. These experts, who are three Directors and three Alternate Directors, have an advisory role during the Board meetings, without any voting right. European Investment Bank, "Board of Directors" <http://www.eib.org/about/governance-and-structure/statutorybodies/board_of_directors/index.htm> accessed 29 December 2017.

governors.[40] In a nutshell, these arrangements might yield positive results if the work of the committee is closely coordinated with and adequately informs the work of the board.

3.4 *Diversity*

Diversity is now recognized as a key driver of effectiveness.[41] It allows multiple perspectives on specific matters at hand and enhances the capacity of an organization to serve multiple stakeholders. Arguably, it is even more important in IFIs than in private FIs, precisely because the stakeholder universe is broader and more diverse than in private FIs.

When it comes to IFIs one needs not of course look at national (and, to a degree, ethnic) diversity. These are, by definition, present, given IFIs' intrinsically international character and representative boards.

But when it comes to gender diversity the picture is gloomy, especially when compared to private FIs. In our IFI peer group, the median of female participation in our 11-member peer group is approximately 18 percent—the outlier is the NIB with 50 percent women. In contrast, the average for our private FI peer group is approximately 35 percent in 2016, a significant difference.[42]

TABLE 1.5

IFI	Women on Board
IBRD	24%
IMF	8.7%
EIB	28.5%
EBRD	13%
IFAD	N/D
BSTDB	36.3%
ADB	8.3%
AIIB	0%
AfDB	22.2%
IADB	21.4%
NIB	50%
Average	**21.24%**

40 For example, the EIB, the IMF and the AIIB have such independent Audit Committees.

41 Hisham Farag and Chris Mallin, "Board diversity and financial fragility: Evidence from European banks" (2017) 49 IRFA 98.

42 Nestor and Andersson (n 3) 3.

The reason for this suboptimal performance is the same as in the KSE case: the lack of a mechanism to control the profile of appointees. And the solutions are the same: injection of "outside," non-constituency objectivity and independence in the board composition; and broadening of the board's profile.

3.5 *Tenure*

In complex organizations, tenure—the number of years directors spend on board—is an important factor of effectiveness: if directors stay on the board too long their capacity to challenge diminishes and boards become "stale." The Lehman board offers again a good negative benchmark: 60 percent of directors were on the board for over 12 years in 2008. In contrast, in 2016 top 25 European FI boards had an average tenure of 5.3 years while in the top five US boards tenure reached 7.7 years.[43]

In contrast to private FIs, the problem in IFIs is not that boards are "stale" but that they never ripen to full maturity: tenure is not too long, it is too short. These are complex organizations, often much more complex than "plain vanilla" commercial banks that require sophisticated credit risk management, often at maturities far longer than the private sector. Individual directors need time to understand the institution before they reach, so to speak, "peak" value as board members, in terms of their capacity to contribute to strategy, to control and challenge management and to understand the substance of the myriad decisions they are making. Also, boards need to maintain an adequate level of institutional memory[44] to properly direct the culture of the institution.

In view of these considerations, IFI tenure levels seem to be problematic. As evidenced in Table 1.6, among our 11 peers the average tenure barely reaches 2.5 years, less than half than that of private FIs.

Clearly, the "dual role" of directors discussed above is at the core of the tenure problem. As member country representatives, directors usually are civil servants and their appointments are at the mercy of political changes or simple mobility imperatives—the importance of their contribution as IFI board members takes a back seat.

3.6 *Personal Commitment of Board Members*

A common ailment among IFI boards is the personal engagement of board members in the functioning of the board. In some boards, it is not uncommon

---

43 Ibid 5.

44 Stilpon Nestor, "Avoiding Pitfalls in the New Bank Governance Framework" *The Banker* (London, 28 July 2010).

TABLE 1.6

	IFI	Average Tenure of current executive directors (in years)
1	IBRD	1.98
2	IMF	2.8
3	EIB	2.9
4	EBRD	2.2
5	IFAD	N/D
6	BSTDB	4.1
7	ADB	1.22
8	AIIB	–
9	AfDB	2.28
10	IADB	1.6
11	NIB	4.3
	Average	**2.59**

for directors to be absent from meetings and for "alternates" or counsellors to take their place. Even when the member of the board is a regular attendee, they are often more the head of an official delegation than an engaged individual board member. But well-functioning boards require engaged individuals much more than constituency spokesmen. As already noted in discussing tenure, the frequent change of faces at the table and the multiple voices behind one chair have a negative effect on board dynamics. Team cohesion suffers and "live" institutional memory is low. There is little personal responsibility invested and the discharge of director duties looks less like leadership and more like just a civil service job. In this respect, it might be useful if IFIs insisted more on personal attendance in boards and committees and limited the possibilities for substitution of the directors by alternates or other participants.

3.7 *Director Workload and Board Committees*

This is an area where comparisons between IFIs and private FIs are rather meaningless given the vastly broader mandate of IFIs in deciding operational matters. It is especially so for those IFIs those that have a resident board of executive directors, i.e., five out of 11 peers as per Table 1.1. Table 1.1 also suggests that resident boards often meet more than once a week, a far cry for the average of nine meetings/year one encounters in G-SIBs.

The issue of effectiveness is even more acute with non-resident boards that retain significant authority over lending, such as the EIB board. It is virtually impossible for any part-time individual to approve a significant number of credit transactions. They will either not exercise enough diligence, or they will rely on a team of people, usually a team at the relevant ministry that oversees the institution and appoints its director. The latter approach, while probably sound from a control perspective, creates problems of personal engagement as discussed in the previous section. It results in directors becoming spokespersons of government teams rather than taking personal responsibility and fully engaging.

One effectiveness issue that is shared with private FIs is the use of committees to lighten the board's workload and allow it to focus more on strategic issue.[45] Both private and international FIs sometimes struggle in making committees efficient and in using them as instruments of better time management rather than as additional workload. As Sir Adrian Cadbury noted "the purpose of committees is to make the board's work more manageable."[46] The representative nature of IFI boards might, again, be a drag on effectiveness: member country representatives want (or are instructed) to be present in all committees, which in turn constitutes a double effectiveness "whammy" in some IFIs: committees are overcrowded, and the Board ends up duplicating committee discussions.

Having the right skills, knowledge, and experience is arguably even more critical on committees, which are usually tasked with hammering out difficult, complex issues and finding consensus before presenting recommendations to the whole board. But here again, committee membership is determined more by constituency representation than by expertise.

3.8 *Support*

The penultimate driver rests on a simple premise: a hard-working board needs good support by an effective team led by a senior member of management. It is now a well-accepted premise that effective boards need focused, senior support. The UK Corporate Governance Code clearly frames the issue:

> Under the direction of the chairman, the company secretary's responsibilities include ensuring good information flows within the board and

45 There is a lot to be discussed on IFI Committee structure and its differences and similarities with private FIs, but it lies outside the scope of this brief paper.

46 Cadbury (n 25) 93.

> its committees and between senior management and non-executive directors, as well as facilitating induction and assisting with professional development as required.[47]

This is often an issue in private FIs where sometimes company secretaries are either too junior to convey the board's expectations to management or are too busy because they also have other important functions. From my experience these are not significant issues in IFIs which usually have dedicated functions led by senior members of management who have a high degree of institutional knowledge and expertise.[48]

Independence might however be an issue in IFIs—as is in those FIs that assign the secretariat function to senior managers such as the general counsel (a common occurrence in the US) or the CFO. The "classic" duty of company secretaries is to first and foremost serve the board. This is sometimes not easy to reconcile with the positioning of IFI company secretaries as senior management reporting to the President of the organization. Occasions might arise whereby the company secretary's "boss," i.e., the President, is challenged or "judged" by the board in which cases the company secretary might find themselves "in the middle."

3.9 *Maintenance*

Last but not least, boards need to regularly assess their effectiveness and ensure timely measures are taken to address any deficiencies. Board evaluations, either self-assessments or externally facilitated assessments, are a standard practice in private FIs. The evaluations contribute to maintaining an optimum level of effectiveness, particularly if there is a mechanism to follow up and implement recommendations targeted at improving effectiveness. All peers in the FI peer group had undertaken a board evaluation in 2015.[49] Approximately 45 percent of these evaluations were facilitated by an outside consultant.[50] Externally facilitated evaluations every few years are considered best practice

47 The UK Corporate Governance Code 2016, s B.5.

48 Another significant source of Board support in IFIs is the Evaluation Department, which, in most cases, is independent from Management, reports directly to the Board and has its own budget.

49 In Europe the annual evaluation of board effectiveness including the effectiveness of individual directors is a regulatory requirement. European Parliament and Council Directive 2013/36/EU art 97.4.

50 Nestor and Andersson (n 3) 21.

and have been enshrined in several governance codes, including the UK Corporate Governance Code.[51]

In contrast, board evaluation has been a thorny issue for many IFI boards in the past. A 2015 IMF review of evaluation processes at the organization noted that, "Directors expressed skepticism about formal Board self-assessments [...] Some questioned the need for self-evaluation by the Board—and whether it is appropriate—given that Directors are accountable to country authorities."[52]

One of the outcomes of the 2009 Zedillo report is that the World Bank established an informal board of director self-evaluation mechanism in 2010 and is currently in the process of reviewing it, informing the review with current best practice in private FIs.

Two other IFI boards, AfDB and EIB appear to have conducted formal, board evaluations in recent years. At the AfDB, the executive board has conducted annual effectiveness reviews, which have been discussed at board meetings and board retreats; the outcome of these reviews seems to be an agenda/plan for improving board effectiveness.[53] In 2014, the EIB undertook an externally facilitated board effectiveness assessment which looked critically at issues such as the time allocated by the board to discussing operational versus strategic matters, the need for adequate KSE, the performance of its Chairman, as well as the structure of committees, among other areas. Significantly, the externally facilitated assessment resulted in recommendations, some of which have been implemented but all of which were fully discussed by the board and implementation of the agreed recommendations is now part of the annual self-assessment of the board.

Other IFIs do not have proper board evaluation processes but have developed mechanisms to address board effectiveness. The EBRD seems to have gone once through an informal process involving a short questionnaire for board members. At the NIB, there is a board retreat on strategy every couple of years in which board effectiveness issues are also discussed. Another interesting practice at NIB is the development of a mechanism for each board member to self-reflect on areas on which they would benefit from training in the form of seminars or workshops. In this context, board members are asked to respond to a list of questions to probe to what extent board members feel comfortable

51 UK Corporate Governance Code 2016 (n 45) s B.6.2.

52 Independent Evaluation Office of the International Monetary, *Fund Self-Evaluation at the IMF: An IEO Assessment* (IMF 2015) 21.

53 African Development Bank Group, *African Development Bank Group Annual Report 2016* (AFDB Group 2017) <https://www.afdb.org/fileadmin/uploads/afdb/Documents/GenericDocuments/AfDB_Annual_Report_2016_EN.pdf> accessed 17 January 2018.

with certain issues and allows them to identify areas in which they may seek further training.[54]

4 Conclusions

Although this paper has called attention to some of the ways in which IFIs have sought to increase board effectiveness, it cannot offer detailed recommendations that would be fit for purpose for all IFIs. These can only be specific to each institution, its particular governance as "hard-wired" in its statutes and regulations, and its strategic objectives. It is however possible to identify four reform areas that, in the opinion of this author, appear to be "low-hanging fruits." The following are areas in which reforms can be implemented without challenging the fiendishly complex, politically sensitive packages of weighted voting, constituency design and board representation that often underpin IFI governance.

a. Allow board input in KSE and diversity—possibly by allowing the board to have an advisory voice on the matter.
b. Lengthen director tenure. In some cases, this will be difficult to do without challenging the hard-wiring of the particular IFI. There are however ways to throw institutional "sand" to slow rapid turnover momentum. For example, IFI governors could receive annual reports on board tenure and be encouraged to make statements of their intent to avoid replacing members before the end of their official tenure. Moreover, a reasoned decision/explanation could be required for all premature departures and a governor discussion scheduled for each such departure. Purely political motives could be discouraged. Also, the leadership of the IFI could initiate a discussion with constituencies on the merits and costs of short rotation spans for administrative purposes.
c. Find ways to allow for the participation of outsiders in board instances with no voting rights. This might be a way to address several issues ranging from institutional memory in short tenure boards to "missing" KSE in director populations to the "depoliticization" of certain sensitive topics.
d. Institutionalize a regular process of board self-evaluation and report key findings in annual reports.

I am quite confident that these changes would lead to effectiveness improvement. Nevertheless, one cannot not help but be a little cynical here. From one

54 Information in this area is mostly based on Nestor Advisors own experience and unofficial discussions with the management of some of the institutions.

perspective, these changes are simple tinkering at the fringes of much bigger issues. There are two real "elephants in the room," and they are intimately related: the "dual" role of IFI directors—fiduciary and representative—and the way it ties into and feeds from the weighted voting structure, the constituency structure and the weak accountability of management; and the extensive retained authority of IFI boards which often perpetuates the institution of resident boards.

These elephants roam outside the perimeter of this paper but one can but marvel at their capacity to survive for so long, in some cases since the closing days of the Second World War, more than 70 years ago!

CHAPTER 2

Gender Diversity on Boards: A Cause for Multilateral Organizations

*Marie-Anne Birken and Gian Piero Cigna**

Abstract

Good corporate decision-making requires the ability to consider and analyze issues from different perspectives. In the past, corporate governance literature has focused on ensuring that boards can draw on the diversity of their members' expertise and professional experience. Over the past few years, attention has increasingly shifted to the impact that gender diversity can bring to the decision-making process. There is now evidence to support the idea that gender-balanced boards boost the performance of companies and that companies with greater female representation on their boards are less likely to be affected by governance scandals involving bribery, fraud and other negative factors likely to depress business confidence.

In Europe, the discussion about gender diversity on boards is well advanced and a number of countries are aiming for ambitious targets. In the United States (US) the trend seems to have stalled, while in Asia it has not yet taken off, with only a few countries actively promoting gender diversity on boards.

This chapter considers the legislation and data on gender diversity on the boards of companies in Europe, the US and Asia. It critically reviews some of the measures introduced by companies, governments and institutional investors to address the gender diversity gap. It concludes by proposing concrete measures that governments, companies and investors may consider adopting to address the gender gap on boards. These measures may be appropriate for international financial institutions to pursue.

---

* Marie-Anne Birken (birkenm@ebrd.com) is General Counsel at the European Bank for Reconstruction and Development (EBRD) and Gian Piero Cigna (cignag@ebrd.com) is Senior Counsel in the EBRD's Office of the General Counsel. The contents of this publication reflect the opinions of individual authors and do not necessarily reflect the views of the EBRD. Terms and names used in this article to refer to geographical or other territories, political and economic groupings and units, do not constitute and should not be construed as constituting an express or implied position, endorsement, acceptance or expression of opinion by the EBRD or its members concerning the status of any country, territory, grouping and unit, or delimitation of its borders, or sovereignty.

 | DOI:10.1163/9789004408326_003

> *If Lehman Brothers had been a bit more Lehman Sisters ... we would not have had the degree of tragedy that we had as a result of what happened.*
>
> —CHRISTINE LAGARDE

Gender diversity is closely linked with a number of important social issues, ranging from inclusion to equality. Recent studies have highlighted that gender diversity is not just a matter of discrimination but is also closely related to good corporate governance and to growth.

In a nutshell, corporate governance is the system by which companies are directed and controls are implemented. The key benchmark for good corporate governance are the OECD Principles of Corporate Governance (the Principles)—one of the 12 Key Standards for Sound Financial Systems.[1] The Principles were first adopted in 1999 and later revised in 2004 and 2015.

Since the 1999 edition, the Principles have been emphasizing the need for independent and qualified boards, but considerations of gender diversity were only introduced in the 2015 revision. The 2015 G20/OECD Principles of Corporate Governance now provide a timid but important non-binding reference to the importance of gender equality for policy-makers in building effective corporate governance processes.

The Principles recommend considering "voluntary targets, disclosure requirements, boardroom quotas, and private initiatives" to improve gender balance on boards and in senior roles. Furthermore, the OECD Guidelines on Corporate Governance of State-Owned Enterprises[2] (SOEs) encourage "the ownership entity [to] consider the *OECD Recommendation on Gender Equality*

1 The Key Standards for Sound Financial Systems were highlighted in 1999 by the Financial Stability Forum (now known as the Financial Stability Board, an international body that monitors and makes recommendations about the global financial system) as vital for sound financial systems and deserving of priority implementation, depending on country circumstances. The Key Standards are broadly accepted as representing minimum requirements for good practice. See: <http://www.ebrd.com/what-we-do/sectors/legal-reform/corporate-governance/international-standards.html> last accessed 15 January 2018.

2 The 2015 version of the OECD Guidelines on Corporate Governance of State-Owned Enterprises is available at: <http://www.oecd.org/corporate/guidelines-corporate-governance-SOEs.htm> last accessed 15 January 2018.

in Education, Employment and Entrepreneurship."[3,4] This Recommendation promotes a series of actions to improve gender diversity, including

> encouraging measures such as voluntary targets, disclosure requirements and private initiatives that enhance gender diversity on boards and in senior management of listed companies; complementing such efforts with other measures to support effective board participation by women and expand the pool of qualified candidates; continuing to monitor and analyses the costs and benefits of different approaches—including voluntary targets, disclosure requirements or boardroom quotas—to promote gender diversity in leadership positions in private companies.

1 The Financial Crises Triggered a Different Vision of Board Diversity

In the aftermath of the 2008–2009 financial crisis, scholars[5] started looking in depth at the board composition of various firms that had been negatively affected by the crisis. The growing awareness of both the under-representation of women in leadership and the evidence of their key contributions to business has led to increased efforts to improve gender balance in senior management, including in boards.

Governments, shareholders, investors and companies have started establishing measures to attempt to close the gender gap through boardroom quotas, regulatory reforms, disclosure, targets and other tools. In some cases, they have been successful, and in others, less so. According to a 10-year survey of Fortune Global 200 companies, published in 2015, the US has seen the number

3 The "Ownership Entity" is defined as the part of the state responsible for the ownership function, or the exercise of ownership rights in SOEs.

4 The 2013 OECD Recommendation of the Council on Gender Equality in Education, Employment and Entrepreneurship is available at: <http://www.oecd.org/els/2013-oecd-recommendation-of-the-council-on-gender-equality-in-education-employment-and-entrepreneurship-9789264279391-en.htm> last accessed 15 January 2018.

5 See among others: Joseph A McCahery and Erik PM Vermeulen, "Understanding the Board of Directors after the Financial Crisis," ECGI—Law Working Paper No. 229, Lex Research Topics in Corporate Law & Economics Working Paper No. 2013–5, available at: <https://papers.ssrn.com/sol3/papers.cfm?abstract_id=%202336614> last accessed 28 March 2018; and PJ Engelen, A van den Berg, G van der Laan, "Board Diversity as a Shield During the Financial Crisis," in: S Boubaker, B Nguyen, D Nguyen (eds), *Corporate Governance* (2012), Springer, Berlin, Heidelberg.

of women on boards increase by less than one percent per year since 2004.[6] However, Europe seems to be the region where the discussion of diversity has had the greatest impact, with an increase exceeding 12 percent in the period 2011–15.[7]

The debate in Europe began officially in 2011, when the European Commission published a working paper on "The Gender Balance in Business Leadership."[8] The paper points out that:

> across Europe a typical board of ten has just one female member. In 97 percent of cases the board is chaired by a man. In 2010, women accounted for just below 12 per cent of board members in the largest publicly listed companies in the EU and for only just over 3 percent of board chairs.

The same paper also reflects on the situation in the US, where "women hold around 15 per cent of board seats in the Fortune 500 companies and chair 2 per cent of boards."

In November 2012, the European Commission proposed legislation that aimed to see women attain a 40 percent of the non-executive board-member roles in publicly listed companies, with the exception of small and medium-sized enterprises.[9] The directive remains under discussion today and although there is a broad consensus in favor of measures to improve the gender balance on boards, some European Union countries believe that binding measures at the EU level are not the best way to pursue the objective.[10]

---

6 Source: "2015 CWDI Report: Women Board Directors in APEC Economies," by Corporate Women Directors International (2015), page 5, available at: <http://globewomen.org/CWDInet/wp-content/uploads/2015/09/2015-CWDI-APEC-Women-Board-Directors-Report.pdf> last accessed 15 January 2018.

7 Source: "Gender Diversity on European Boards, Realizing Europe's Potential: Progress and Challenges," European Women on Boards (April 2016), available at: <http://european.ewob-network.eu/wp-content/uploads/2016/04/EWoB-quant-report-WEB-spreads.pdf> last accessed 15 January 2018.

8 The European Commission Working Paper is available at: <http://ec.europa.eu/justice/gender-equality/files/gender_balance_decision_making/110301_gender_balance_business_leadership_en.pdf> last accessed 15 January 2018.

9 The press release on the new EU legislative proposal is available at: <http://europa.eu/rapid/press-release_IP-12-1205_en.htm> last accessed 15 January 2018. The text of the Proposal for a Directive of the European Parliament and of the Council on improving the gender balance among non-executive directors of companies listed on stock exchanges and related measures is available at: <http://eur-lex.europa.eu/legal-content/EN/TXT/?qid=1441109473231&uri=CELEX:52012PC0614> last accessed 15 January 2018.

10 The national parliaments of Denmark, the Netherlands, Poland, Sweden, the United Kingdom and one of the two chambers of the parliament of the Czech Republic (the Chamber

However, the discussion did not stall and in June 2013 another important piece of legislation was approved. The revised Capital Requirements Directive introduced a number of requirements to improve corporate governance of financial institutions in Europe. The Directive emphasizes that

> the lack of monitoring by management bodies of management decisions is partly due to the phenomenon of 'groupthink.' This phenomenon is, inter alia, caused by a lack of diversity in the composition of management bodies. To facilitate independent opinions and critical challenge, management bodies of institutions should therefore be sufficiently diverse as regards age, gender, geographical provenance and educational and professional background to present a variety of views and experiences. Gender balance is of particular importance to ensure adequate representation of population. In particular, institutions not meeting a threshold for representation of the underrepresented gender should take appropriate action as a matter of priority.

2 Why Gender Diversity on Boards Matter

Good corporate governance standards require company boards to be diverse. This diversity ensures that a board is able to perform its oversight function effectively, and in particular to avoid "groupthink," which arises where directors all have similar backgrounds and experience and results in a lack of robust challenge in the decision-making process.

Diversity has been historically interpreted as an appropriate balance of skills, experience, independence and knowledge of the company's business. Since 2007, research has been showing the impact of gender diversity on corporate boards. For example, there is now evidence to support the hypothesis that greater female representation on boards improves companies' performance and has a positive impact on governance, reducing the likelihood of bribery, fraud and other governance scandals that may depress business confidence.

Among the many published studies, it is worth mentioning a 2013 research study by Professor Michel Ferrary at SKEMA Business School in France, who

of Deputies) submitted reasoned opinions within eight weeks of the submission of the Commission's proposal, alleging that it did not comply with the principle of subsidiarity. For further details, see: <http://www.europarl.europa.eu/legislative-train/theme-area-of-justice-and-fundamental-rights/file-gender-balance-on-boards> last accessed 28 March 2018.

concluded that companies with strong female representation on the management team perform better.[11] In 2015, MSCI—an index provider—found that companies with more women on their boards had delivered a 36 percent better return on equity since 2010 than those groups lacking gender diversity.[12] In another study, MSCI found that companies with a higher percentage of women on boards tended to have fewer instances of governance-related scandals such as bribery, corruption, fraud, and shareholder battles. Furthermore, companies with higher percentages of women on boards had higher environmental, social and governance (ESG) risk-management ratings and strategies across virtually all risk issues.[13] In 2016, the Peterson Institute for International Economics—a think-tank—published an analysis of nearly 22,000 firms from 91 countries suggesting that the presence of women in corporate leadership may improve firm performance, with the largest gains depending on the proportion of female executives.[14]

The most recent studies confirm that the relationship between diversity and business performance persists in the longer term. In January 2018, McKinsey—a global management consulting firm—published new research[15] continuing

11 In particular, Professor Michel Ferrary's study suggests that companies where at least 35 percent of the management team are women performed better during financial crises. The study analyzes the stock performance of companies in the CAC40—the Parisian stock index—and created a separate index of 10 companies whose management teams consisted of 35 percent women (the so-called "Femina Index"). By comparing the CAC40 and the Femina Index from 2007 to 2012, Ferrary found that the CAC40 lost 34.70 percent of its value during the six years period, whereas companies in the Femina Index lost only 5.28 percent.

12 This conclusion is based on a 2015 MSCI study, available at: <https://www.msci.com/documents/10199/04b6f646-d638-4878-9c61-4eb91748a82b> last accessed 15 January 2018, which looks at companies with a "strong female leadership." The study designates a company as having "strong female leadership" if the company's board has three or more women or if its percentage of women on the board is above the average for its country. A company is also considered to have "strong female leadership" if it has a female CEO and at least one woman on the board.

13 See: "2014 Survey of Women on Boards, Executive Summary," MSCI (November 2014). Available at: <https://www.msci.com/documents/10199/b08aa5c0-5304-4f6c-975f-83a0a6414838> last accessed 15 January 2018.

14 See: Marcus Noland, Tyler Moran and Barbara Kotschwar, "Is Gender Diversity Profitable? Evidence from a Global Survey," Peterson Institute for International Economics (February 2016), available at: <https://piie.com/publications/wp/wp16-3.pdf> last accessed 15 January 2018.

15 See: Vivian Hunt, Sara Prince, Sundiatu Dixon-Fyle and Lareina Yee, "Delivering Through Diversity," McKinsey & Company (January 2018). Available at: <https://www.mckinsey.com/business-functions/organization/our-insights/delivering-through-diversity> last accessed 25 January 2018.

the work initiated in 2015[16] but on a larger scale. The new research clearly shows that the statistically significant correlation between a more diverse leadership team and financial outperformance continues to hold true in an updated, enlarged and global dataset. In addition, the research highlights that there is a "penalty for opting out," as companies in the dataset showing the least gender and ethnic or cultural diversity were 29 percent less likely to achieve above-average profitability than were all other companies.

3 Gender-diverse Boards: Trends and Current Status

Based on such supporting evidence on the correlation between gender diversity and company performance, one would expect that companies would have promptly started looking to increase the presence of women on their boards and in key management positions. Recent surveys show that the trend is moving in this direction, although not always at the expected pace. Some positive results have been achieved in Europe, but to a lesser degree in the US, where "Fewer large companies are run by women than by men named John,"[17] and in Asia.

The average percentage of women on company boards in the 28 countries of the EU (see Chart 2.1) increased from 11.9 percent in 2010 to 25.3 percent in 2017,[18] while in the US women's representation on corporate boards improved only from 12.7 percent in 2010[19] to 14.2 percent in 2017.[20]

16 See: Vivian Hunt, Dennis Layton and Sara Prince, "Diversity Matters," McKinsey & Company, (2 February 2015), available at: <https://www.mckinsey.com/~/media/mckinsey/business%20functions/organization/our%20insights/why%20diversity%20matters/diversity%20matters.ashx> last accessed 25 January 2018.

17 See the *New York Times* article reporting that "Fewer large companies are run by women than by men named John, a sure indicator that the glass ceiling remains firmly in place in corporate America." The article is available at <https://www.nytimes.com/2015/03/03/upshot/fewer-women-run-big-companies-than-men-named-john.html?partner=rss&emc=rss&abt=0002&abg=1&_r=0> last accessed 15 January 2018.

18 Source: European Institute for Gender Equality <http://eige.europa.eu/gender-statistics/dgs/about> accessed 26 January 2018. The same dataset shows that the EU 28 average of female executives moved from 10.4 percent in 2012 to 15.8 percent in 2017 (while the average for CEOs was 2.5 percent in 2012 and 5.5 percent in 2017).

19 Data from "The CS Gender 3000: The Reward for Change," Credit Suisse Research Institute, September 2016.

20 Data from "Women in the Boardroom: A Global Perspective," Fifth Edition, Deloitte (June 2017), available at: <https://www2.deloitte.com/uk/en/pages/risk/articles/women-in-the-boardroom5th-edition.html > last accessed 15 January 2018.

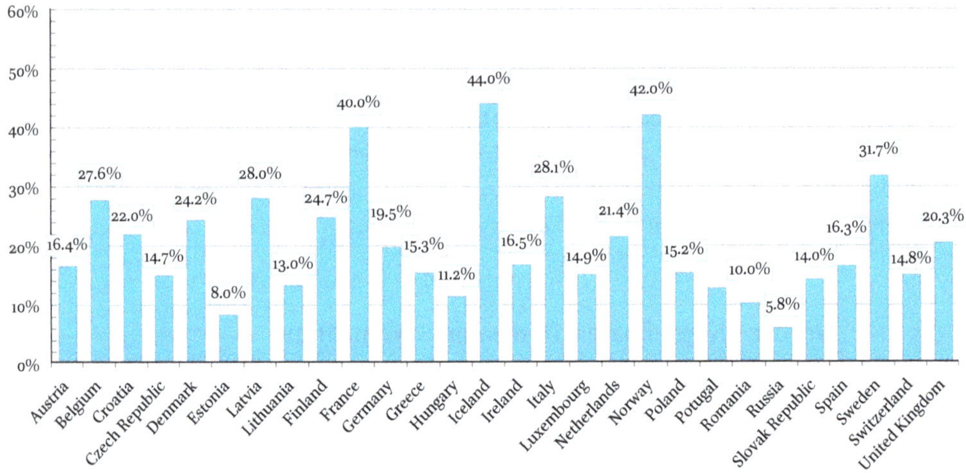

CHART 2.1 Percentage of board seats held by women in Europe, 2017
SOURCE: DATA FROM "WOMEN IN THE BOARDROOM: A GLOBAL PERSPECTIVE," FIFTH EDITION, DELOITTE (2017).

With regards to Asian economies, the situation is quite uneven (see Chart 2.2). In Japan and South Korea, the representation of women on boards barely reaches the 4 percent threshold.[21] Meanwhile, in Indonesia, the level is below 10 percent.[22] China, the largest economy in the region, has a relatively high female labor participation rate—74 percent of Chinese women work—but when it comes to their representation on boards, the average drops to less than 10 percent.[23] Women's representation on boards in India, Malaysia, the Philippines, Singapore and Thailand is slightly over the 10 percent threshold. A study by the European Bank for Reconstruction and Development (EBRD), looking at the boards of the 10 largest companies in each of the economies where the Bank operates,[24] shows that in Kazakhstan, the Kyrgyz Republic, Mongolia and Tajikistan, women's representation on boards is well below 10 percent.[25]

---

21 Ibid.

22 Ibid.

23 Source: "Women in Leadership in Asia Pacific," *The Economist* (19 September 2016), <https://www.willistowerswatson.com/en/insights/2016/09/Women-in-leadership-in-Asia-Pacific> last accessed 15 January 2018.

24 The EBRD is an international financial institution that operates in 38 economies across three continents. See <http://www.ebrd.com/where-we-are.html>. The 2016 EBRD Corporate Governance Sector Assessment is available at <http://www.ebrd.com/what-we-do/sectors/legal-reform/corporate-governance/sector-assessment.html>

25 Source: EBRD research.

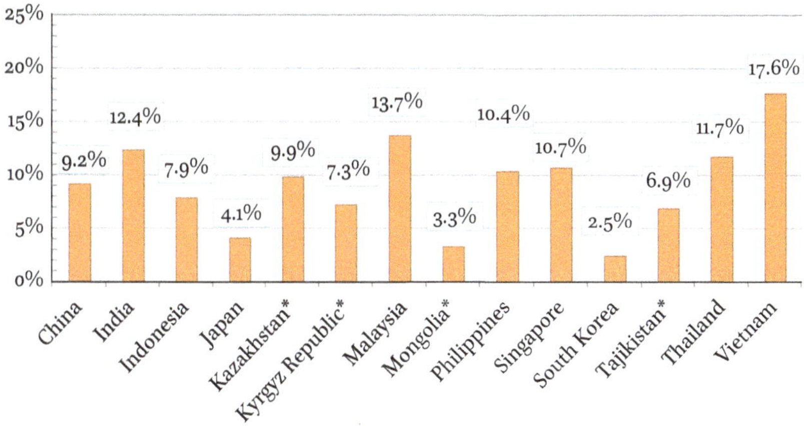

CHART 2.2 Percentage of board seats held by women in Asia, 2017
SOURCE: DATA FROM "WOMEN IN THE BOARDROOM: A GLOBAL PERSPECTIVE", FIFTH EDITION, DELOITTE (2017). * DENOTES DATA FROM EBRD RESEARCH.

4 Regulatory Requirements for Gender Diversity on Boards

In recent years, a number of regulatory requirements have been introduced (from quotas to voluntary requirements in corporate governance codes) to improve gender diversity on boards.

Out of the 12 largest markets in Europe, five now have mandatory gender quotas for boards[26] and the other seven either have an optional quota or a "comply-or-explain" recommendation in their corporate governance codes.[27]

In Norway, a gender quota of 40 percent of women on publicly listed company boards was introduced in 2003.[28] It included a severe penalty of delisting for companies that did not comply within two years from July 2005, the date when the law entered into force. France, Iceland and Spain followed suit with targets of 40 percent—although with less severe penalties—and other countries also introduced quotas, albeit with lower thresholds. In Italy, a new

26 The five European countries that have mandatory quotas are Belgium, France, Germany, Italy and Norway.

27 The seven European countries that have either an optional quota or a comply-or-explain recommendation in the corporate governance codes are Denmark, Finland, the Netherlands, Spain, Sweden, Switzerland and the UK.

28 See: Lizette Alvarez, "Norway is Set to Compel Boardrooms to Let More Women In," *New York Times* (14 July 2003) <http://www.nytimes.com/2003/07/14/world/norway-is-set-to-compel-boardrooms-to-let-more-women-in.html> last accessed 15 January 2018.

law requiring listed companies to ensure that there is a balance between genders on a board and that at least a third of the board is reserved for the under-represented gender—which is unlikely to be male—became effective in August 2011.[29] In cases of non-compliance, CONSOB—the Italian securities regulator—can issue severe fines of up to EUR1 million. So far, no companies have received sanctions. Nevertheless, the percentage of women on the boards of listed companies in Italy saw an increase of nearly 12 percent between 2012 and 2016.[30] In 2015, Germany also imposed a quota, mandating that 30 percent of supervisory board seats be filled by women.[31]

A recent study[32] has shown that the countries that have introduced mandatory quotas show higher growth of gender diversity on boards,[33] compared with those that have only voluntary recommendations. In Europe, nowadays, there is a 32 percent difference between the average percentage of women on boards in Norway and the corresponding percentage in Romania, which has only a voluntary recommendation in the national corporate governance code. There are, however, exceptions—notably, the United Kingdom (UK), which is discussed below.

5 Gender Quotas Incite Heated Debates

In France, the introduction of the gender quota was a source of much debate, and even some women were against the idea. "No one wants to be a second-class citizen," said one, explaining that she would not want to be on a board that was required by law to have a female member.[34] A common misconception is

29 Law 120/2011 "Gender Balance on the Board of Listed Companies." The law amended the text of the Legislative Decree no. 58 dated 24 February 1998, related to financial intermediation.

30 See: "Women in the Boardroom: A Global Perspective," Fifth Edition, Deloitte (June 2017).

31 Ibid.

32 See: K De Pril and M Roberts, "Gender Diversity on European Boards, Realizing Europe's Potential: Progress and Challenges," European Women on Boards (April 2016), <http://european.ewob-network.eu/wp-content/uploads/2016/04/EWoB-quant-report-WEB-spreads.pdf> last accessed 15 January 2018.

33 The countries that showed higher growth in gender diversity on boards are Italy (which had the lowest starting point, with an average of 4.2 percent female board membership in 2011), Belgium and France. In Germany, the trend is not yet apparent because the quota was only recently introduced. Source: "Women in the Boardroom: A Global Perspective," Fifth Edition, Deloitte (June 2017).

34 The citation is taken from Margaretha Wiersema and Marie Louise Mors, "What Board Directors Really Think of Gender Quotas," *Harvard Business Review* (14 November 2016),

that gender quotas lead to the selection of unqualified women or to selection based purely on gender, rather than qualifications.

Recent research, however, seems to demonstrate otherwise.

A study by Harvard University[35] found that the imposition of quotas has resulted not only in greater gender diversity, but also in a more professional and formal approach to the selection of board members. In Norway, for instance, after the introduction of gender quotas, the entire process of recruiting board directors became more rigorous and professional. The nomination requirements were clarified, the responsibility of the board nomination committee was acknowledged and the focus on the composition of boards was improved.[36]

"I am not a great supporter of quotas but in this case it's making difference," the CEO of one of Europe's largest executive search firms said in an interview on gender quotas in Norway. "It has changed the conversation. It clearly has been put on the agenda of companies."[37]

Not all countries have reached a political consensus on mandatory quotas. The US is among the few developed Western economies that have neither voluntary nor mandatory targets. Some US states, such as California, Massachusetts, Illinois and Pennsylvania, have started passing non-binding measures, but given the latest data on the gender diversity in US boards—showing that the representation of women on the boards of S&P 500 companies has not increased significantly over the past decade—there is increasing recognition that without a more formal effort the situation is unlikely to change.

In Asia, only India and Malaysia have introduced mandatory gender quotas. In India, the 2013 Companies Act requires all listed companies to have at least one woman on their board. As a result, the number of women on boards has increased by 4.7 percent over the past two years, from 7.7 percent to 12.4 percent.[38] In Malaysia, in 2011, the government approved a policy requiring companies with more than 250 employees to have 30 percent of senior management positions filled by women by 2016.[39] The target was missed and the

<https://hbr.org/2016/11/what-board-directors-really-think-of-gender-quotas> last accessed 15 January 2018.

35 Ibid.

36 Ibid.

37 See: Oliver Staley, "You know those quotas for female board members in Europe? They're working," Quartz (3 May 2016), <https://qz.com/674276/you-know-those-quotas-for-female-board-members-in-europe-theyre-working/> last accessed 15 January 2018.

38 See: "Women in the Boardroom: A Global Perspective," Fifth Edition, Deloitte (June 2017).

39 Source: Meijun Qian, "Women's Leadership and Corporate Performance," ADB Economics Working Paper Series, No. 472 (January 2016), <https://www.adb.org/sites/default/files/publication/179587/ewp-472.pdf> last accessed 15 January 2018.

deadline extended to 2020, with the Prime Minister threatening to "name and shame" companies with no women on their boards by 2018.[40]

Other countries have established gender diversity targets, but so far tangible results have been limited. For instance, in Japan, the government set a target in 2003 of 30 percent of women in corporate management positions by 2020, with the Prime Minister encouraging companies to take voluntary steps towards appointing at least one female board member by 2013. In the same year, the Tokyo Stock Exchange required companies to disclose their female board representation. Furthermore, the 2015 Corporate Governance Code included a specific clause on gender diversity. As a result, the percentage of all-male boards decreased from 79 percent in 2012 to 65 percent in 2016, but—as Chart 2.2 illustrates—women's representation on boards remains very limited.

6 Are Voluntary Recommendations in National Corporate Governance Codes the Solution?

The effectiveness of corporate governance codes depends on a robust and supportive institutional environment, where companies, investors and regulators all play a role. Codes are a starting point and not an end in themselves. A simple introduction of a specific provision in the code is not, in and of itself, capable of producing tangible results. In particular, corporate governance codes—especially those that are to be implemented under the so-called "comply-or-explain" mechanism[41]—are intended to make companies disclose the practices they have in place and to provide explanations in cases where these are not aligned with the code's recommendations. It is then up to the market—in particular, investors—to consider if these practices are sound enough or should trigger some reactions.

The problem is that in many countries markets are shallow, liquidity and corporate governance culture are limited, and trading does not seem to be driven by corporate governance considerations, such as the issuers' compliance—or

40 Source: Hwok-Aun Lee, "Malaysia's push for gender equality holds lessons for Asia," *Nikkei Asian Review*, (22 August 2017), <https://asia.nikkei.com/Politics/Malaysia-s-push-for-gender-equality-holds-lessons-for-Asia> last accessed 15 January 2018.

41 The "comply-or-explain" approach means that companies should comply with the code, but they can get away with not doing so if they are able to explain their actions convincingly to shareholders. This approach was first conceived in the UK in 1992. In 2006, it was institutionalized in the European Union with the adoption of Directive 2006/46/EC and then reconfirmed by Directive 2013/34/EU, which requires companies "whose transferable securities are admitted to trading on a regulated market" in the EU to "include a corporate governance statement in their management report."

lack of compliance—with the recommendations of the national corporate governance code. In 2010, the European Commission issued a Green Paper on Corporate Governance in Financial Institutions[42] noting that the "shareholders' lack of interest in corporate governance raises questions in general about the effectiveness of corporate governance rules based on the presumption of effective control by shareholders for all listed companies."

Recently, the EBRD completed an assessment of corporate governance in 34 economies in its region.[43] In all economies assessed, a corporate governance code is in place, but in most cases there is no clear evidence of their implementation in practice. In addition, only in four countries[44] do the codes recommend that companies take gender into consideration when appointing board directors. There are no specific requirements to have a certain level of gender representation on a board. In fact, none of the countries that have a specific gender reference in their code outmatches its peers in female representation on boards.

This situation is not limited to the economies where the EBRD operates and only in a few countries are codes making a difference.

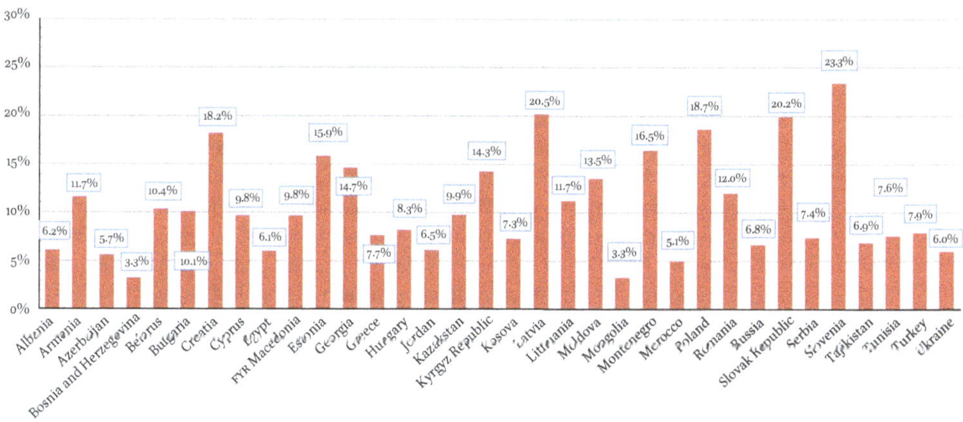

CHART 2.3 Average female presence on boards of the 10 largest (listed) companies in the EBRD region
SOURCE: EBRD RESEARCH, BASED ON INFORMATION PUBLISHED ON THE WEBSITES AND ANNUAL REPORTS OF THE 10 LARGEST (LISTED) COMPANIES IN 2015.

42 Green Paper: "Corporate governance in financial institutions and remuneration policies" {COM(2010) 285 final} {COM(2010) 286 final} {SEC(2010) 669}, <http://eur-lex.europa.eu/legal-content/EN/TXT/?uri=celex:52010DC0284> last accessed 15 January 2018.

43 See footnote 24.

44 These countries are Albania, FYR Macedonia (limited to the requirement to disclose—among others—the gender of members of management and supervisory boards), Greece, Poland and Romania.

In the UK, for instance, the code implementation is carefully assessed by investors and monitored by the Financial Reporting Council—the "owner of the code"—which produces annual monitoring reports[45] and places great emphasis on the enhancement of a corporate culture that can deliver sustainable good performance.[46] Furthermore, in addition to the code recommendations, the UK government—backing the Davies Review[47]—set a non-binding target of 25 percent women on the boards of the FTSE 100 companies by the end of 2015, which was achieved and then raised to 33 percent by 2020. In the UK there is no mandatory quota by law. However, the positive change was the result of a combined effort by many parties, including the government, specific recommendations in the code, the media, a change in the culture of companies,[48] and, last but not least, investors.

The attitude of investors and their engagement with companies for better corporate governance has grown over time, based on the understanding that good corporate governance adds value. The process has also been promoted by the active role of the UK regulator, which has recently moved to name and shame those investors that, albeit having endorsed the UK Stewardship Code,[49]

45 In the UK, the Financial Reporting Council has also established an active dialogue with investors, through the Stewardship Code, requiring it—among others—to engage with listed companies for a better implementation of the UK Corporate Governance Code.

46 See: <https://www.frc.org.uk/directors/the-culture-project> last accessed 15 January 2018.

47 The Davies Review is a government-backed commission chaired by Lord Davies, which was first introduced in 2010 to examine the under-representation of women on boards of UK listed companies. In 2011, Lord Davies released a "Women on Boards" report which aimed to raise the profile of gender equality and promote the cause among UK companies. In the report, Lord Davies set the voluntary target of 25 percent representation by women on the boards of FTSE 100 companies by the end of 2015. The target of 25 percent was met and in October 2015 Lord Davies released his five-year summary of the report, raising the target to 33 percent by 2020 on FTSE 350 boards. The Lord Davies Review, "Women on Boards" (February 2011) is available at: <https://www.gov.uk/government/uploads/system/uploads/attachment_data/file/31480/11-745-women-on-boards.pdf> last accessed 15 January 2018. The Review undertaken in 2015 is available at: <https://www.gov.uk/government/uploads/system/uploads/attachment_data/file/482059/BIS-15-585-women-on-boards-davies-review-5-year-summary-october-2015.pdf> last accessed 15 January 2018.

48 In this regard, it is worth noting the "30% Club," a global campaign that signs up board chairs and CEOs to prioritize action to create a better balance of men and women at all levels of their organizations rather than treating the matter as a "women's issue." See more at: <https://30percentclub.org/> last accessed 15 January 2018.

49 The UK Stewardship Code aims to enhance the quality of engagement between investors and companies. The Stewardship Code consists of seven Principles. Principle 3 is about "monitoring their investee companies" with a clear focus on corporate governance. About 300 asset managers, asset owners and service providers have signed up to the Stewardship Code. Signatories are encouraged to publish a statement on their website showing the extent to which they have complied with the Code ("comply or explain"), to notify the

do not dedicate enough effort to "engaging"[50] with companies for better compliance with the corporate governance code.[51]

As a result, investors are now playing a key role in triggering the change. For example, Legal & General Investment Management (LGIM), the London-based fund company that oversees USD1 trillion of assets, recently toughened its voting stance after deciding that simply urging companies to take action on board diversity has not delivered results. LGIM began pushing for better board diversity in the US eight years ago and has committed to voting against nomination committee chairs at any company in the S&P 500 index that still has an all-male board from 2017 onwards. LGIM decided to vote against all-male boards at Britain's largest companies in 2015, and extended that policy to include FTSE 250 companies in 2016.[52] Aviva Investors, the London-headquartered asset manager, also decided to vote against all-male boardrooms in the UK in 2014.[53]

Financial Reporting Council (FRC) when they have done so and whenever the statement is updated. The UK Stewardship Code is available at: <https://www.frc.org.uk/investors/uk-stewardship-code> last accessed 15 January 2018.

50 The UK Stewardship Code makes clear that "For investors, stewardship is more than just voting. Activities may include monitoring and engaging with companies on matters such as strategy, performance, risk, capital structure, and corporate governance, including culture and remuneration. Engagement is purposeful dialogue with companies on these matters as well as on issues that are the immediate subject of votes at general meetings." (Guidance to Principle 1).

51 In the UK, the FRC is the "owner" of the UK Corporate Governance Code and the UK Stewardship Code. The FRC publishes an annual monitoring report on the level of company compliance with the code. The Council realized that in some cases, the signing of the Stewardship Code was merely a declaration, with no material action undertaken. Hence, the FRC started reviewing the quality of compliance statements and began to "name and shame" or "name and shine" asset managers, asset owners and service providers, by grouping them into tiers based on the quality of their Code statements. See: <https://www.frc.org.uk/investors/uk-stewardship-code/uk-stewardship-code-statements> last accessed 15 January 2018.

52 "Corporate Governance and Responsible Investment Policy—UK 2016" LGIM states at page 6: "Voting on structure and operation of boards. LGIM will usually support the board's recommendations and nominees for election to the board. However, if the company does not provide a satisfactory explanation then LGIM will oppose (...) the chairman of the board and/or the chairman of the nominations committee, of a FTSE100 company where there is not a minimum of 25% women at board level; the chairman of FTSE 250 companies, where there is not a minimum of 20% women at board level. We will use our discretion when considering voting against the chairman of the board, also taking into account the percentage of female representation below board level and the disclosures relating to diversity; the (re)election of the chairman or the chairman of the nomination committee if the board has failed to address the issue of diversity through the disclosure of policies, the implementation of measurable targets, or actual board change consistent with company strategy."

53 "UK Corporate Governance and Corporate Responsibility Voting Policy," Aviva Investors (2016), states at page 3: "3.2. Gender diversity. (...) We are unlikely to support the

Several of the world's largest fund companies, including BlackRock, Vanguard, Fidelity and Aberdeen, are also pressing for greater gender diversity on boards, but have not yet committed to voting against directors at companies with all-male boards.[54]

These initiatives are not limited to the UK or the private sector: Rhode Island Pension Fund—the pension fund administered by the US state of Rhode Island—has now committed to voting against any slate of directors nominated by the company that would result in women (or racial minorities) accounting for less than 30 percent of board seats.[55]

Outside major developed markets, the development finance institutions are among the largest investors. Since 1991, the EBRD has invested over EUR119 billion in more than 5,000 projects across private and public sectors in the economies where it invests.[56] The EBRD is one of the signatories to the development finance institutions' (DFI's) Corporate Governance Initiative,[57] which focuses on the improvement of corporate governance at investee companies of the respective DFIs. This Initiative, which has gathered more than 30 development finance institutions worldwide—representing a total of almost USD1 trillion in assets—has however not yet resulted in clear and concrete efforts to promote gender diversity on the boards of investee companies.

Most of the major DFIs, including the EBRD, have gender diversity policies governing their operations. The EBRD *Strategy for the Promotion of Gender Equality 2016–2020*[58] was adopted in 2016 and commits to supporting

---

resolution to adopt the Report & Accounts and/or the re-election of the Chairman of the Nomination Committee if we consider that the Board has not sufficiently addressed gender diversity and the reasons have not been adequately explained in the Report & Accounts."

54 See: Madison Marriage, "All-male boards in the US face investor backlash," *Financial Times* (16 April 2017), <https://www.ft.com/content/2b915d48-1f81-11e7-a454-ab04428977f9> last accessed 15 January 2018.

55 See: "Women in the Boardroom: A Global Perspective," Fifth Edition, Deloitte (June 2017). The 2016 Annual Report of the Rhode Island Pension Fund is available at: <https://d1ok7k7mywg42z.cloudfront.net/assets/58b967d6d4c96156fd020df1/2016_Annual_Report_RI_Treasury.pdf> last accessed 25 January 2018. It states on page 15 that "Rhode Island Treasury voted against more than 220 corporate board candidates at companies including Amazon, Delta Air Lines, and Intel, because their boards were severely lacking in gender or racial/ethnic diversity."

56 Source: EBRD, unaudited data as of 31 December 2017.

57 In September 2011, 30 development financial institutions signed a corporate governance statement, which is available at: <http://cgdevelopmentframework.com/> last accessed 15 January 2018.

58 The EBRD Strategy for the Promotion of Gender Equality 2016–2020 is available at: <http://www.ebrd.com/documents/gender/ebrd-strategy-for-the-promotion-of-gender-equality.pdf> last accessed 15 January 2018.

companies that express an interest in addressing gender equality by increasing the presence of women among non-executive directors on boards and in senior management.[59] IFC—a member of the World Bank Group and the largest development financial institution focusing exclusively on the private sector in developing countries—has set a target of 30 percent female representation for IFC-nominated director positions.[60]

However, even if most DFIs have adopted a gender policy, the board composition of the institutions themselves suggests that they are not necessarily leading by example.

Among the 12 major treaty-based international financial institutions, only the Nordic Investment Bank shows a 50:50 gender-balanced board, while currently the Asian Infrastructure Investment Bank and the Eurasian Development Bank have no women serving on their boards. The EBRD is not faring well, either: less than 10 percent of its directors are women.

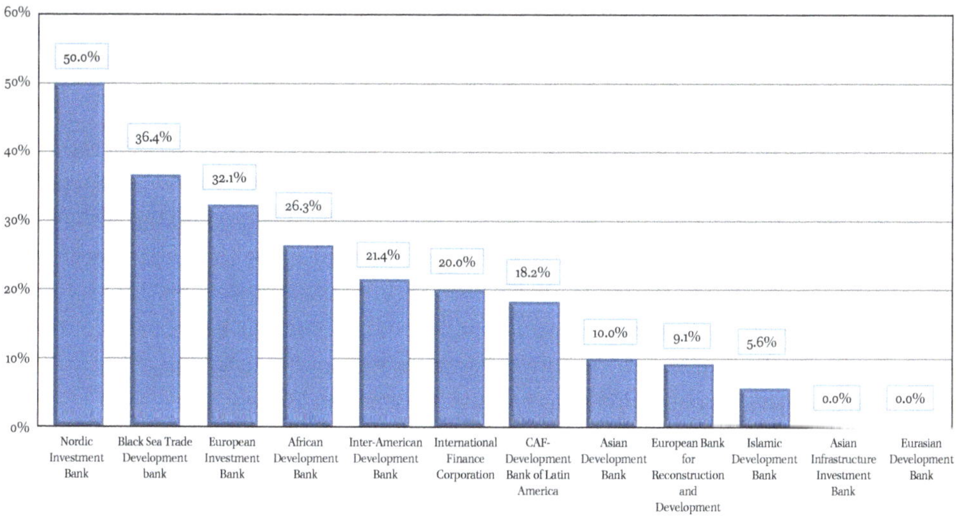

CHART 2.4 Percentage of women on the boards of 12 major international financial institutions

NOTE: BASED ON THE BOARD COMPOSITION (DIRECTORS ONLY—ALTERNATE DIRECTORS WERE NOT CONSIDERED) PUBLISHED ON THE WEBSITES OF THESE INSTITUTIONS. DATA ACCESSED ON 25 JANUARY 2018.

59 "Women in the Boardroom: A Global Perspective," Fifth Edition, Deloitte (June 2017).

60 See the IFC Corporate Governance, Women on Board webpage at: <http://www.ifc.org/wps/wcm/connect/topics_ext_content/ifc_external_corporate_site/ifc+cg/topics/women+on+boards> last accessed 15 January 2018.

Moreover, none of these institutions seems to have gone the extra mile yet—as LGIM, Aviva or the Rhode Island Pension Fund have done—and taken a strong stance against all-male boards in its investee companies. This might be the next important step, but it needs to be implemented in a coordinated fashion, as changes cannot be achieved by one action or one player alone.

7 A Lot Has Been Done, But Efforts Should Continue

When discussing the importance of gender diversity on the boards of companies in developing markets, it seems there is still a lot of misunderstanding and a lack of knowledge about this important issue. In particular, it appears that the issue is still largely understood to be a social matter, not an issue of governance or one that affects economic growth.

Priorities for reform should include the continuation of work with governments to make a stronger business case for gender diversity on boards. This should entail capacity-building and corporate governance training, with targeted media communication explaining the value of board diversity as a governance issue and a driver of company performance.

The media, in particular, are a powerful means of creating the necessary culture that can trigger changes. The role of the media in improving corporate governance culture and behaviour has been largely demonstrated[61] and we believe that the results achieved in the UK are also due to media exposure highlighting the importance of the issue and the need for reform. The media are important in shaping corporate policy and should not be ignored in any analysis of a country's corporate governance system. "People who actively resist diversity probably don't have all the information."[62]

Companies should also be encouraged to disclose their board compositions on their websites and in their annual reports, thus allowing investors and other stakeholders to assess the situation and trigger further action. Examples in the

61 See among others: Baixiao Liu and John J. McConnell, "The role of the media in corporate governance: Do the media influence managers' capital allocation decisions?," *Journal of Financial Economics*, Volume 110, Issue 1, (October 2013), pages 1–17; and Alexander Dyck and Luigi Zingales, "The Corporate Governance Role of the Media," NBER Working Paper No. 9309 (November 2002).

62 Quote from Julie McKay, PwC Chief Diversity and Inclusion Officer. In *The Guardian*, 10 October 2016 <https://www.theguardian.com/sustainable-business/2016/oct/10/gender-diversity-at-work-using-education-to-tackle-the-backlash> last accessed 25 January 2018.

UK and France, where companies that do not adhere to the code are named and shamed by the regulators[63] and the media have been largely successful as catalysts for change.

Most importantly, there is a need to start creating a culture among investors that promotes gender diversity and a common approach to exerting more pressure on their investees. DFIs—especially those that have endorsed the mission to improve corporate governance in their investee companies—have an important role to play in this regard by imposing higher governance standards on their investee companies, including requiring them to improve their board nomination processes and ensuring that nomination is based on qualifications and diversity requirements. There should be more robust challenge at general shareholders' meetings, in particular with regard to the appointment of board and board committee members. There should also be stronger efforts to convince boards and controlling shareholders to cast a wider net in their search for talented directors, beyond their usual comfort zone, while also promoting mechanisms[64] that allow minority representation at the board. The Italian "*voto di lista*" mechanism[65] might be a good example to follow, if supported by the necessary engagement from investors. These measures should be supported by training and education, particularly for women, to ensure that there is an increased pool of qualified women who can take up director roles.

63 The most recent report by the French Autorité des Marchés Financiers on corporate governance, executive compensation, internal control and risk management was published on 22 November 2017 and is available in French at: <http://www.amf-france.org/Publications/Rapports-etudes-et-analyses/Gouvernement-d-entreprise?docId=workspace%3A%2F%2FSpacesStore%2F03140cfe-4026-49f8-a66e-131b0b8e0daf&langSwitch=true> last accessed 25 January 2018. The most recent full report available in English is the 2015 Report by the AMF on Corporate Governance and Executive Remuneration, available at: <http://www.amf-france.org/en_US/Publications/Rapports-etudes-et-analyses/Societes-cotees-et-operations-financieres.html?docId=workspace%3A%2F%2FSpacesStore%2Fca40eea2-a001-4733-8829-251472fff252> last accessed 25 January 2018. On the UK approach, please see footnotes 45 and onward, above.

64 For instance, cumulative voting, which is the procedure of voting for company directors whereby each shareholder is entitled to one vote per share, multiplied by the number of directors that are to be elected. This is advantageous for minority shareholders, because they can apply all of their votes to one candidate, thus making the appointment of that person more likely.

65 The "*voto di lista*" mechanism is compulsory for Italian listed companies. It calls for shareholders to vote on slates of nominees, submitted by controlling shareholders and minorities alike. A mechanism of this kind aims to ensure minority representation on corporate boards, providing that at least one director is elected from the slate submitted by minority shareholders.

CHAPTER 3

International Financial Institution Governance: The Role of Shareholders

*Whitney Debevoise**

Abstract

This chapter addresses the integral role of shareholders in the good governance of international financial institutions. It is divided into five parts, beginning firstly with consideration of the generally held concerns of all shareholders, notably, veto rights, the powers of governors, the role of executive directors, and the essential leadership responsibilities of an institution's president. Second, the relationship between shareholders, good governance and the mobilizing of resources, in particular funding the institution effectively and developing a sustainable financial model is examined. Third, the chapter looks at the indispensable role of shareholders in maintaining a domestic legal environment conducive to the success of an international financial institution. Fourth, it highlights the role that shareholders may play in inter-institutional relationships. Fifth, and by way conclusion, this chapter argues that good shareholder governance is crucial to the success of all international financial institutions, both old and new.

The inaugural Asian Infrastructure Investment Bank (AIIB) legal conference held in Beijing in October 2017 had Good Governance and Modern International Financial Institutions as its theme, thereby transmitting an important message about AIIB's ethos and aspirations as a multilateral development bank. Against that background, this chapter addresses the role of shareholders in good governance at an international financial institution (IFI). Shareholders come in several sizes—large, medium and small—and types (borrowers and non-borrowers).[1] Regardless of size or type, IFI shareholders share certain

* Partner, Arnold & Porter, Washington, D.C.; US Executive Director, The World Bank, 2007–2010.

1 At the World Bank, not all countries borrow; when their GDP per capita reaches a threshold, they "graduate." AIIB all members are currently eligible to borrow regardless of their per capita income.

common interests. But not all shareholders are equal, so this chapter addresses both shareholder concerns generally as well as more specific interests, particularly those of the largest shareholder of an IFI, including shareholders with veto rights.

There can be several types of shareholder representatives, usually known as governors and directors, or as they are frequently called—executive directors. Their respective functions are set out in an IFI's Articles of Agreement, but their overall perspective on governance can be rooted in the same concerns.[2] Some of the key concerns include effective leadership for the organization, the financial health and sustainability of the institution, mobilizing resources when needed, fiduciary concerns for taxpayer money, providing a conducive domestic legal environment for the IFI, promoting the bank domestically, respecting the international character of the bank, and attention to the bank's relationship with other organizations, domestic and international. Some shareholders are also driven by a desire to maximize resources for a particular constituency, but that factor does not change many of the basics. Among those basics are recurring themes such as reputation risk, transparency and the proper balance between politics and economics.

1 General Shareholder Concerns

One lens for understanding shareholder concerns at an IFI is the Articles of Agreement of the institution in question. What responsibilities are considered so significant that shareholders reserve the power to act for their most senior representatives—usually called governors and usually cabinet ministers or central bank governors? Similarly, what are the responsibilities delegated by governors to executive directors and what are the responsibilities further delegated to bank management? Finally, what are the decisions considered so significant that one single shareholder or small group of shareholders can block or veto action?

1.1 *Veto Rights*

Interestingly, at the International Bank for Reconstruction and Development (World Bank), unlike the International Monetary Fund, veto rights are

2 There can be some differences, however. Governors may be somewhat more inclined to think largely in representational terms, whereas directors who represent multiple countries may give slightly more weight to fiduciary concerns.

extremely limited, and the veto is not a factor in the daily life of the Bank. The US, the largest shareholder of the International Bank for Reconstruction and Development, can veto amendments to the Articles of Agreement. This provision makes sense when viewed from the perspective of the Bank's financial model which is built on a small amount of paid-in capital, callable capital and a sizeable amount of borrowing in the capital markets. At the time of the Bank's founding, of course, the target financial market was Wall Street, because the world's other major markets had yet to recover from World War II. In order to win the confidence of Wall Street, it was important for investors to understand that the financial model would not change. This model was anchored in the Articles of Agreement, and investors wanted assurance that the Articles would not change. Accordingly, the threshold for amendment of the Articles of Agreement was set at 85 percent, giving the US a veto.[3] The AIIB has adopted this approach in its Articles of Agreement, giving its current, largest shareholder a veto over amendment of the Articles.[4]

Increases in the number of directors at the World Bank require a four-fifths majority of the total voting power, so the United States, which currently holds less than 17 percent, cannot veto any such increase. Indeed, when the World Bank increased the number of its directors from 24 to 25 in 2010, the possibility of a US veto was not a factor.

Increases in World Bank capital require a three-fourths majority of the total voting power, so the US cannot veto capital increases. All shareholders are given preemption rights but no shareholder is "obligated to subscribe any part of the increased capital."[5] Furthermore, a simple majority determines the terms of subscription, so the US has no veto on that subject.

Loans and guaranties are approved by a simple majority of the voting power. Once again, the US has no veto. If the US opposes a loan or guaranty it must either convince Bank management not to bring the loan forward to the Board or build a majority coalition to stop the loan. The need to build coalitions at an IFI, particularly when it is for a positive purpose, is a key element in IFI governance and may explain why so many decisions are taken by consensus with no formal polling. On the other hand, most IFIs have weighted voting and are therefore able to move forward after a healthy debate.

3 Articles of Agreement of the International Bank for Reconstruction and Development (dated 27 December 1945, as amended through 2012) (World Bank Articles of Agreement), art VIII(a).

4 Articles of Agreement of the Asian Infrastructure Investment Bank (dated 29 June 2015, entered into force 25 December 2015) (AIIB Articles of Agreement), arts 28 and 53(1).

5 See n 4, World Bank Articles of Agreement, art II, s 3(c).

1.2 *Powers of Governors*

The powers reserved to the Governors at the World Bank comprise a short list:

1. Admission of new members and the conditions for their admission.
2. Increases or decreases in capital stock.
3. Suspension of a member.
4. Deciding appeals of interpretations of the Articles given by the Executive Directors.
5. Arrangements to cooperate with other international organizations (other than informal arrangements of a temporary and administrative character).
6. A decision to suspend permanently the operations of the Bank and to distribute its assets.
7. Determining the distribution of the net income of the Bank.[6]

In practice, this list is even shorter, as for example, the distribution of net income is essentially decided by the Executive Directors, albeit with input from capitals, prior to the submission to the Governors for formal approval. Further, although the Articles provide that the Governors shall determine the salary and terms of the contract of service of the President, in practice, this task is undertaken by the Executive Directors.

The reserved powers of the AIIB Board of Governors are similar, although they do differ in one important respect. Selection of the President of the World Bank is formally in the hands of the Executive Directors, whereas at the AIIB, the Governors hold this power. Since Executive Directors at the World Bank cast a single vote on behalf of a constituency,[7] a member could "vote for" a candidate it in fact opposes, whereas at the AIIB, a member could always oppose a candidate it did not want.

1.3 *Executive Directors*

The powers of the Executive Directors of the World Bank include responsibility for the conduct of the general operations of the Bank and for that purpose, they exercise all the powers delegated to them by the Board of Governors. These delegated powers are extensive since the Governors have essentially retained only the powers provided in the Articles. This is appropriate since Governors are high-ranking officials in national governments or central banks and already have full agendas.

6 See n 4, World Bank Articles of Agreement, art V, s 2(b).

7 Ibid, World Bank Articles of Agreement, art V, s 4(g).

1.4 *Effective Leadership—The President*

The allocation of power between the Executive Directors and the President of the World Bank has evolved since the formation of the Bank. Formally, the President is the "chief of the operating staff of the Bank"[8] and conducts, "under the direction of the Executive Directors, the ordinary business of the Bank."[9] "Subject to the general control of the Executive Directors," the President is "responsible for the organization, appointment and dismissal of the officers and staff."[10]

The division of responsibility between the President and the Executive Directors was largely defined in negotiations between John Jay McCloy and the Executive Directors as he was recruited to serve as President. The allocation was formalized with the Board's Committee on Organization in June 1947. Essentially, the Executive Directors are responsible for policy decisions; however, all policy proposals must originate with management. This arrangement permits the President and staff to execute on policies and guidance provided by the shareholder representatives. It also lends stability to the institution since policies once adopted should be consistently applied and not be constantly reevaluated. It also helps to reduce to a certain extent the political component of decision-making because management can justify its actions as the even-handed application of approved policy.

The most important task of shareholder representatives is the selection of the president or head of the organization. Regardless of prevailing conventions with respect to nationality or leadership eligibility or rotation, the power to select the head of the organization must be exercised responsibly. A failure to do so can lead to paralysis of the institution and undermine its core mission.

Once the shareholders make their choice, they need to allow the head to lead. Shareholders can make suggestions and advocate. That is why they have representatives, be they governors or directors, but they must not micromanage. In this regard, IFIs should be no different than any other organization with a board of directors and management.

The Trustee's Handbook of the American Association of Independent Schools, for example, states that the most important function of a trustee is the selection and annual review of the head of the organization. So, from the smallest non-profit to the largest IFI, selection of the head of the organization is a key governance responsibility.

The recent evolution on this subject is reflected in AIIB's Articles of Agreement which specifies that election shall be through an "open, transparent and

8 See n 4, World Bank Articles of Agreement, art V, s 5(b).
9 Ibid.
10 Ibid.

merits-based process."[11] That said, the process is an election with weighted voting and not free from politics. For example, one relevant criterion may appropriately be the ability of the president to secure crucial support from the largest shareholder(s). The key is for the shareholders with the most power to exercise that power responsibly by reaching out to other shareholders in an open, transparent way and promoting the best candidate available. Interestingly, the AIIB Articles of Agreement extend the notion of an open, transparent and merits-based process to the selection of Vice-Presidents.[12]

Other aspects of good governance that are present in the private and non-profit sectors, such as the annual review of the head of the organization and succession planning, deserve more thought when considering an IFI. There may be sound political reasons why these concepts and tools cannot be deployed at IFIs, but more thought should be given to how to use annual meetings, development committee meetings and strategic planning exercises to achieve some of the same results as an annual goal setting and head-review process.

The other key dimension in the intersection between Executive Directors and the President and senior management is the degree of delegated authority, particularly for financings. Normally delegation is handled by establishing numerical thresholds for operations, with the Directors reserving the right to withdraw delegated authority for a specific transaction and pull it for board discussion. The theory is that policy issues can lurk even in smaller operations. On the other hand, the power to pull projects for full board discussion may have the perverse effect of lowering management's own internal controls because some may assume that the directors are, in fact, examining every transaction closely, even those proposed under delegated authority. In practice, the sheer volume of the documentation for such operations may militate against such careful scrutiny. Ultimately, the Directors and management must earn each other's trust in order to achieve the appropriate and most efficient level of delegation for the institution.

2 Mobilizing Resources

2.1 *Funding*

Shareholders also have a duty to foster an institution that can fulfill its stated purposes. This essentially involves resources. Resource mobilization starts

11 See n 5, AIIB Articles of Agreement, art 29(i).
12 Ibid, AIIB Articles of Agreement, art 30(i).

with capital or grants but does not end there.[13] Shareholders can make an important contribution by making sure that the institution can access domestic capital markets and do so efficiently. This may involve accommodations in domestic securities laws and regulations. For example, in the US, the IBRD arm of the World Bank benefits from a statutory exemption from the registration requirements of the Securities Act of 1933 and the reporting requirements of the Securities Exchange Act of 1934.[14] The same applies for the International Finance Corporation[15] and other multilateral development banks in which the US is a shareholder, the Asian Development Bank, the Inter-American Development Bank, the African Development Bank and the European Bank for Reconstruction and Development. Interestingly, when the International Development Association (IDA) arm of the World Bank Group, went to market for the first time in March 2018, it accessed the Rule 144A/Regulation S market. Rather than registering securities with the SEC on Schedule B, which is what the European Investment Bank[16] and a number of other multilateral development banks do, IDA decided to use the institutional investor market until an explicit exemption can be arranged.

Another important source of financial support is grants. IDA, for example, depends on a triennial pledging process. For many years, the US led by example, making the largest donations to IDA. In recent IDA rounds, other donors have surpassed the US, although since inception, the US has contributed more than any other nation to IDA. The United Kingdom's leading donor position in IDA-16 reflected, in part, a national commitment to spend 0.7 percent of GDP on Official Development Assistance in keeping with its Millennium Summit and other commitments. Since IDA provides leverage of nearly 10:1 for the UK, a strong IDA contribution also leveraged the resources of the UK. With the decision in IDA-18 to permit IDA to access the market, leverage should increase for all IDA donors.

As important as the pledging process for IDA and other soft-loan windows of MDBs may be, following through on pledges is equally important. In the US,

---

13 Shareholders can also induce donors to create trust funds, although sound administration of trust funds and their incorporation into an IFI work program have their own governance issues.

14 Bretton Woods Agreements Act, 22 U.S.C.§286k-1.

15 22 U.S.C.§282k. See e.g., New Zealand, Securities Act (International Finance Corporation), Exemption Notice 2009, <http://www.legislation.govt.nz/regulation/public/2009/0297/12.0/whole.html> accessed 14 May 2018.

16 See e.g., European Investment Bank Registration Statement under Schedule B of the Securities Act of 1933, <https://www.sec.gov/Archive/edgar/data/33745/000095015718000325/forms-b.htm> accessed 21 March 2018.

this requires legislative approval of the grant. Theoretically, legislation authorizing the US contribution to IDA (or any other grant to the soft-loan window of an international financial institution) is required. Once authorized, the current year's contribution must also be included in appropriation legislation on an annual basis throughout the three-year IDA funding period. At times, the Congress combines the authorization and the current-year appropriation. At times, it dispenses with the authorization altogether.[17] Each is important, however, because each originates in a different committee of the House and of the Senate which can give the Executive Branch several levers to pull in obtaining legislative approval.

At times, the US Congress attaches conditions to IDA authorizations, and some of the conditions or mandates extend beyond IDA to IBRD and IFC. Some involve voting instructions to US shareholder representatives. For example, the Congress has directed the US Executive Director at the World Bank to oppose Cuban membership and the US Treasury to withhold US payments if an IFI should approve assistance to Cuba.[18] Others involve policy directives instructing the US Executive Director to advocate certain positions. For example, at times, the Congress has instructed the US Executive Director of the World Bank to use the voice of the US to advocate for the adoption of particular procurement policies and internal justice reforms. The Congress also directs the US Executive Director how to vote on certain matters.[19] For example, the Congress has instructed the US Executive Director at the World Bank to use the vote of the US to oppose loans to countries designated as major producers of illicit drugs,[20] supporters of international terrorism,[21] nuclear proliferators,[22] human traffickers[23] and production of palm oil, sugar or citrus crops for export if the financial assistance would cause harm to US producers.[24] A well-known example of a voting directive is the Pelosi Amendment, which prohibits the U.S Executive Director from voting for any category A environmental project

17 See also Louis Fisher, "The Authorization-Appropriation Process in Congress: Formal Rules and Informal Practices" (1979) 29 Cath. U.L. Rev. 51 (surveying Congressional use of authorization and appropriation legislation).

18 Public Law No. 104–114 (1996).

19 Although such directives may be unconstitutional on separation-of-powers grounds, no Executive Director or Administration has ever challenged such a directive, beyond a reservation of rights in a Presidential signing statement.

20 22 U.S.C. § 2291j(a)(2).

21 22 U.S.C. § 262p-4q.

22 22 U.S.C. § 6302.

23 22 U.S.C. § 7107.

24 22 U.S.C. § 262g.

for which the environmental impact statement has not been posted on the World Bank's website at least 120 days prior to the date of the vote.[25]

Some such policy directives have resulted in substantive changes in policies at the multilateral development banks.[26] For example, most multilateral financial institutions in which the US is a member now have an accountability mechanism such as the Inspection Panel at the World Bank.[27] Such units investigate claims by parties adversely affected by Bank projects, for example by a forced resettlement, that the Bank has not followed its own policies for addressing such situations. In the case of the World Bank, the Inspection Panel resulted from US advocacy following Congressional directives in IDA appropriations legislation.

The governance aspect of such shareholder action may be seen as problematic for a multilateral. What if every shareholder conditioned its grants or capital contributions to the adoption of particular policies? Also, are such legislative directives not in violation of provisions such as Article III, Section 2 of the World Bank Articles of Agreement, which provides that "each member shall deal with the Bank only through its Treasury, central bank, stabilization fund or other similar fiscal agency," namely through its Governor and the respective Executive Director for its constituency? On the other hand, each country may establish its own internal procedures for establishing policy priorities and instructing its shareholder representatives. One might question whether voting instructions are helpful because they might interfere with the shareholder representative's ability to negotiate acceptable solutions. On the other hand, since multilateral development bank grants and loans involve public money, some political organs may want to be in a position to say that its representatives opposed the use of taxpayer funds for project X or initiative Y. At times, though, particularly when it comes to major institutional initiatives, it may be useful for all shareholder representatives to know that when the shareholder representatives from the executive branch of a large shareholder speak, they are speaking not only on behalf of the executive branch of that member but also on behalf of the legislative branch which controls the member's grants and capital contribution to the institution. For some this will be seen as leadership; for others, interference. For the good of the institution and of the shareholder in question, such techniques should be used responsibly and not overused.

25 International Development and Finance Act of 1989, Public Law No. 101–240, 103 Stat. 2492, 2511 (codified as amended at 22 U.S.C. 262m-7 (1990)).

26 See Bowles and Karmos, "Environmental Reform at the World Bank: The Role of the US Congress" (1995) 35 Va. J. Int'l L. 777.

27 Resolution No. IBRD 93–10 and Resolution No. IDA 93–96.

2.2 *A Sustainable Model*

Resource mobilization also involves the development and maintenance of a strong, sustainable financial model. After all, the institution must earn the trust of the financial community. Rating agencies and lenders are looking for strong shareholder commitment in the form of both paid-in and callable capital but also sound lending and risk management policies. Similarly, shareholders need to promote policies that will induce donors to make grants, for example to IDA or other trust funds. Strong fiduciary policies and controls also figure in the equation. Together all of these produce a strong, sustainable financial model that inspires confidence, produces a high rating—triple-A in the cases of the World Bank and AIIB—and access to markets in the required amounts and at the lowest rates possible.

A strong, sustainable financial model starts with a solid balance sheet with solid assets. This requires prudent investment decisions. As with all banks, good loans result from a complex of credit policies for both sovereign lending and corporate debt and equity, as the case may be. Credit allocation is key, as are single borrower, country and sectoral limits. The institution must have a skilled treasury function to invest the funds not immediately needed in operations, including policies on permitted investments and the use of derivatives. There should also be a well-run pension system for employees, likely a defined contribution plan and not a defined benefit plan. Appropriate policies are needed for the establishment and use of reserves and for provisioning. Pricing policies for loans, guarantees, derivatives and equity investments are important.

The liability and capital sections of the balance sheet also figure in the equation. The institution needs a borrowing plan and attention to debt management, including attention to the debt profile and to currency and asset-liability matches. Capital ratios also require attention and constant review. All of these policies should be of concern to shareholders, particularly to the largest shareholders with the largest callable capital. At the same time borrowing countries have an interest in the extent to which the balance sheet can be stretched without increasing the cost of IFI loans.

Another important component of a sustainable financial model involves the budget. Here shareholders need to keep an eye on budget policies and the budget process. This involves administrative expenses, including particularly salary structures and benefits, including training, pension, and medical benefits, as well as travel and home-leave policies and procurement for the institution itself. The information technology spend needs to be understood and monitored. Adequate resources for fiduciary controls, internal and external audit, accountability and institutional integrity mechanisms are all important, as are functions inherent in a development bank such as economic and operational research, project monitoring and results measurement. Finally, external relations and the management of the institution's real estate needs cannot be neglected.

Some development institutions have been known to place some expenses which most would consider ordinary business expenses below the line. Nevertheless, responsible shareholders have an interest in having the income statement look as normal as possible to the market and to taxpayers.

A key tool for shareholders lies in the budget process. This starts with discussions about medium-term strategy, which can be part of a mechanism for deciding priorities and allocating resources accordingly. There can be a tendency at multilateral institutions to resolve difficult discussions about resource allocation by attempting to please all constituencies by spreading resources thinly across many uses with the result that some are underfunded. Here large shareholders need to support focus and act responsibly when advancing their own policy initiatives.

3 Conducive Legal Environment

Another aspect of good governance and shareholder responsibility concerns providing a conducive domestic legal environment for the institution. As mentioned above, if the IFI desires to access the capital markets of a shareholder, measures can be adopted to facilitate access to markets and to make access as efficient as possible, while protecting investors. The same applies to measures to facilitate the IFI's lending function, a key activity that should not be impeded by domestic registration or regulatory requirements. Modern IFIs may have sizeable treasuries that need to be invested and managed, including with the use of derivatives. They should be permitted to do so without being subjected to domestic registration, central clearing and margin requirements.[28]

Shareholders can also assist IFIs through the extension to the institutions and their personnel of privileges and immunities. The Articles of Agreement of the World Bank and AIIB call for no less.[29] The Articles of Agreement and

28 The US Commodity Futures Trading Commission and the federal banking agencies have accorded the World Bank, the other IFIs in which the US is a shareholder and certain other IFIs recognized in Europe suitable exemptions from these requirements. See CFTC definition of major swap participant, CFTC rule on central clearing and Federal Reserve Board regulation on margin.

29 See World Bank Articles of Agreement, art VII, s 10 (n 4), AIIB Articles of Agreement, Article 44(2) (n 5). See also Jamaica, The International Finance Corporation Agreement Act 3 of 1964 (5 March 1964).

headquarters agreement of an IFI may provide for tax and customs duty exemptions, currency transfer, special immigration status, labor law regimes and other accommodations for the organization, its shareholder representatives, employees, families and members of their households. The archives of the organization and its bank accounts should be protected from interference by governments and third parties. This can be accomplished through the incorporation of the Articles into domestic law, either expressly or as a self-executing treaty or by adoption of domestic legislation and regulations providing the necessary privileges and immunities.

Another important area of shareholder support concerns security and local law enforcement. Cybersecurity is crucial for IFIs given the extensive data about members and projects in their possession and combat against cybersecurity often requires healthy interaction with domestic agencies. Support from shareholders in this area can be invaluable.

4 Domestic Promotion of the IFI

Domestic promotion of the IFI involves outreach to the Executive and Legislative Branches as well as the general population. Key subjects for communications with these domestic constituencies include IFI results, procurement benefits and oversight and accountability. In this regard, a shareholder's task will be greatly facilitated by a robust IFI disclosure policy. In particular, a disclosure policy with a presumption of disclosure and exceptions to disclosure contributes more than a policy that operates under the proposition that documents are presumptively restricted and only disclosable if specifically authorized. The World Bank had the latter for many years but wisely changed to the former in 2010.[30] The AIIB has left the door open to this approach in Article 34(4) of the Articles of Agreement.

As shareholder representatives promote IFIs domestically, however, they need to make clear to their authorities, and in particular to the Legislative Branch, that the shareholder representatives in the Executive Branch are the sole channel for engaging with the IFI. This point is explicit in Article III(2) of the World Bank's Articles of Agreement and in Article 30(1) of the AIIB Articles of Agreement. The tendency of some legislatures may be to think of an IFI as another domestic agency, particularly when appropriating grant funds. A properly sensitized shareholder representative needs to convey the point, however, that there is no direct jurisdiction.

30 See World Bank, "The World Bank Policy on Access to Information" (1 July 2010).

A similar sensitivity needs to be observed between shareholder representatives, usually governors, and IFI presidents. Astute IFI presidents and governors can develop a prudent sense of when to use the direct channel and when to use the director-level channel.

The Articles of Agreement of the World Bank also contain a provision designed to protect the international character of the Bank. Article IV, Section 10 prohibits interference in the political affairs of any member and enjoins the Bank not to be influenced in its decisions by the political character of a member. Shareholders, particularly large shareholders need to recall that, "Only economic considerations shall be relevant to … decisions."[31] There have been examples when a large shareholder has sought a particular outcome for political reasons, but the arguments in favor or in opposition must be economic in nature. The AIIB Articles contain the same principles.[32] This does not mean that shareholder representatives cannot forcefully advocate with management to bring forward or to oppose key projects or initiatives, but Board members may not do so on purely political grounds.

5 Relations with International Organizations

International development today is a highly networked business. This is a matter of necessity because there is not enough public money available to meet all the needs. Today, the development assistance architecture requires cooperation with other IFIs. Cooperation begins with other IFIs, frequently through the Development Committee, but also through informal networks of MDB Presidents, general counsels, chief financial officers and anti-corruption units. Cooperation with the United Nations is also important. Although the World Bank secured a "declaration of independence" from the United Nations in 1947, the Bank still cooperates closely with the United Nations at many levels and on many subjects, from disaster relief and recovery to countries in conflict, to global health crises to climate change. Cooperation in economic sanctions is also addressed with the World Bank giving "due regard" to UN sanctions. Cooperation in-country with UN organizations as well as with peacekeeping missions is frequently extensive, particularly in conflict-affected states. These many points of intersection with the international community underscore the need for cultivating good relations with other international organizations as a development bank seeks to fulfill its mission.

31 See n 4, World Bank Articles of Agreement, art IV, s 10.

32 See n 5, AIIB Articles of Agreement, art 31.

6 Conclusion

The role of shareholders in IFI governance has many dimensions and lies at the heart of the Articles of Agreement of an IFI. Although shareholders can have diverging interests over specific policies or operations, there actually is a remarkable degree of convergence on a series of broad themes integral to good IFI governance. This starts with a proper structuring of the relationships and distribution of power and authority among the Governors, the Executive Directors and the President and management. It extends to mobilizing resources, both capital and grants, but also includes many shared views about ensuring that the institution pursues a sustainable financial model. Shareholders have responsibility for ensuring a conducive domestic legal environment for the IFI and for promoting the IFI domestically and with other international organizations. Whether an IFI of longstanding or a new IFI like AIIB, good shareholder governance is crucial for success.

PART 2

The Governance Basis of International Financial Institutions

CHAPTER 4

The Rule of Law in the International Monetary Fund: Past, Present and Future

*Yan Liu**

Abstract

The International Monetary Fund (the "Fund") has evolved considerably since 1945 to respond to the changes in the global economy with its constant mandate to maintain and safeguard a stable international monetary system. Throughout its evolution, the Fund continues to adhere to the rule of law, which is key to the legitimacy, credibility and effectiveness of the Fund as an institution. The Legal Department of the Fund plays a critical role in ensuring that the Fund effectively responds to the changing developments in the international monetary and financial systems while maintaining the rule of law. The responsibilities of legal counsels at the Fund have been expanding over the years to keep up with the Fund's evolution, ranging from traditional in-house counselors, trusted advisors to membership to active public policy contributors. In discharging these responsibilities, legal counsels must maintain independence, objectivity and consistency to ensure credibility and effectiveness of their legal advice, which is pertinent to upholding the rule of law at the Fund.

1 Introduction

The International Monetary Fund (the "Fund") has evolved since 1945 with developments in the global economy. While its overall objective remains the promotion of international monetary and financial stability, the Fund has adapted its role and policies to respond to the changing developments in the

* Assistant General Counsel of the Legal Department, International Monetary Fund. Email: YLiu@IMF.org. The views expressed in this paper are those of the author and do not necessarily represent the views of the IMF, its Executive Board, or IMF management. The author would like to thank Kyung Kwak for her valuable inputs and comments on this article.

international monetary and financial systems over the years.[1] These changes have taken place gradually, but more recently, they were accelerated by several regional and global financial crises where the Fund provided a large amount of financing to members facing acute balance of payments difficulties, and reformed its policies to better prevent and resolve crises. The role of legal counsels at the Fund has also been changing and expanding over the past 70 years to keep up with the Fund's evolution. They not only provide advice on the law of the Fund but also assist member countries in designing and building effective and accountable institutions to support economic stability and growth.

Throughout its evolution, one thing remains unchanged at the Fund, that is, the institution continues to adhere to the rule of law. The rule of law is key to the legitimacy, credibility and effectiveness of the Fund as an institution, and plays a key role in promoting sustainable and equitable growth and financial stability. The Fund is an international organization established by an international treaty, the Articles of Agreement. While the Articles of Agreement are sufficiently flexible to respond to changes in the global economy, they have been amended seven times to implement major policy reforms. This reflects the recognition by the Fund and its membership that there are limitations to the adoption of reforms through interpretation of the Articles and is an important indicator of the acceptance of the rule of law at the Fund.

---

1 The purposes of the Fund are listed in the Articles of Agreement, Article I:

The purposes of the International Monetary Fund are:

(i) To promote international monetary cooperation through a permanent institution which provides the machinery for consultation and collaboration on international monetary problems.

(ii) To facilitate the expansion and balanced growth of international trade, and to contribute thereby to the promotion and maintenance of high levels of employment and real income and to the development of the productive resources of all members as primary objectives of economic policy.

(iii) To promote exchange stability, to maintain orderly exchange arrangements among members, and to avoid competitive exchange depreciation.

(iv) To assist in the establishment of a multilateral system of payments in respect of current transactions between members and in the elimination of foreign exchange restrictions which hamper the growth of world trade.

(v) To give confidence to members by making the general resources of the Fund temporarily available to them under adequate safeguards, thus providing them with opportunity to correct maladjustments in their balance of payments without resorting to measures destructive of national or international prosperity.

(vi) In accordance with the above, to shorten the duration and lessen the degree of disequilibrium in the international balances of payments of members.

The Fund shall be guided in all its policies and decisions by the purposes set forth in this Article.

The Legal Department of the Fund plays a critical role in ensuring the Fund's adherence to the rule of law. Its independence, consistency and continuity are particularly pertinent to upholding the rule of law at the Fund. Since there is no mandatory form of judicial review of the Fund's decisions, legal counsels play an important role in advising the Fund's decision-making organs on the consistency of their decisions with the Articles of Agreement and other applicable rules and regulations, and on the consistency of Fund members' actions with their obligations under the Articles. This chapter will focus on three important roles of legal counsels at the Fund: in house counselors, trusted advisors to membership and public policy contributors. It first provides an overview of the Fund's governance structure and key functions which have been shaping those roles. It then turns to the roles of the legal counsels, illustrating their expanded roles in response to the evolution of the Fund over the years. The chapter then discusses the key ingredients for making legal counsels and the Legal Department effective in maintaining the rule of law at the Fund.

2 Fund's Governance Structure

The Fund's governance structure consists of the Board of Governors, the Executive Board, and the Managing Director. The Board of Governors is the highest decision-making organ of the Fund. It consists of one governor (and one alternate governor) for each member country who is usually the member's Central Bank Governor or Finance Minister appointed in accordance with national procedures. All powers of the Fund are vested in the Board of Governors,[2] but it can delegate to the Executive Board all except certain reserved powers.[3] These reserved powers include admission of new members, approval of revisions to quota (a member's share of financial resources and voting power within the Fund), requiring a member to withdraw from membership, approval of allocation of Special Drawing Rights (SDRS), which is the IMF's unit of account, decision to liquidate the Fund and deciding appeals on interpretation of the Articles of Agreement. The Board of Governors made the delegation to

2 Articles of Agreement, Article XII, Section 2(a) provides that "[A]ll powers under this Agreement not conferred directly on the Board of Governors, the Executive Board, or the Managing Director shall be vested in the Board of Governors."

3 Articles of Agreement, Article XII, Section 2(b) authorizes the Board of Governors to "delegate to the Executive Board authority to exercise any powers of the Board of Governors, except the powers conferred directly by this Agreement on the Board of Governors."

the Executive Board in the broadest possible terms in 1946 (amended in 1978).[4] As a result, the bulk of decisions to be taken was shifted from the Board of Governors to the Executive Board.

The Executive Board is responsible for conducting the business of the Fund,[5] and functions in continuous session.[6] Its powers consist of those directly conferred upon it by the Articles of Agreement and also those that have been delegated by the Board of Governors. Accordingly, the Executive Board is responsible for taking almost all of the Fund's key decisions. It comprises 24 members who used to be elected or appointed by the Fund's members before the 2010 Fund governance reform. In 2010, the Fund embarked on a far-reaching reform of its governance structure by, among other things, creating an all-elected Executive Board. As a result of this reform which became effective in January 2016, all members of the Executive Board are now elected by the Fund's members every two years, strengthening the democracy of the Executive Board governance structure. Executive Directors are officials of the Fund and legally accountable to the Fund for the discharge of their duties.

Decisions taken by the Board of Governors and the Executive Board are based on a weighted voting system.[7] When a country joins the Fund, it is assigned an initial quota in the same range as the quotas of existing members[8] of broadly comparable economic size and characteristics. The quota, which is based on the relative size of the member's economy in the world economy, largely determines a member's voting power in Fund decisions. The 2010 reform delivers an unprecedented 100 percent increase in total quotas and a major realignment of quota shares to reflect the changing relative weights of the Fund member countries in the global economy. In particular, it shifted more than six percent of quota shares from over-represented to under-represented member countries and more than six percent of quota shares to dynamic emerging market and developing countries. The reform represents a major step towards better reflecting the increasing role of dynamic emerging market and developing countries in the Fund's governance structure. All decisions of

4 This delegation which is formulated in Section 15 of the Fund's By-Laws reads as follows: "The Executive Board is authorized by the Board of Governors to exercise all the powers of the Board of Governors except those conferred directly by the Articles of Agreement on the Board of Governors."

5 Articles of Agreement, Article XII, Section 3(a).

6 Articles of Agreement, Article XII, Section 3(g).

7 The votes cast by members consists of basic votes and quota based votes (one additional vote for each SDR100,000 of quota).

8 http://www.imf.org/external/np/sec/memdir/members.htm.

the Board of Governors or the Executive Board are made by a majority of the votes cast except as otherwise specifically provided.[9]

Finally, the Managing Director is selected by the Executive Board and performs the powers conferred on him or her by the Articles of Agreement. While there is no delegation of authority as such by the Executive Board to the Managing Director, the Managing Director performs his or her functions under the direction and general control of the Executive Board. The Managing Director conducts the ordinary business of the Fund under the direction of the Executive Board.[10] He or she is the chief of the staff and is responsible for the organization, appointment and dismissal of the staff of the Fund subject to the general control of the Executive Board.[11] The Managing Director and staff, in the discharge of their functions, owe their duty entirely to the Fund and each member of the Fund is required to respect the international character of such duty and refrain from all attempts to influence any of the staff in the discharge of their functions.[12] In addition, the Managing Director is the Chairman of the Executive Board, where he or she has no vote except to break a deadlock in case of an equal division of votes.[13]

Accordingly, responding to the Fund's governance structure, there are four principal sources of Fund laws. The first source is the Articles of Agreement, the founding charter of the Fund. The Articles of Agreement are an international agreement whose interpretation is governed by the rules on international treaty interpretation. The Charter defines the purposes of the Fund, its core mandate and certain functions that the Fund needs to perform in furtherance of these purposes. The Articles of Agreement also establish certain obligations that members are required to observe. The second source is the Fund's Bylaws and resolutions adopted by the Board of Governors. The third source is rules and regulations, and decisions adopted by the Executive Board. The final source refers to General Administrative Orders and staff guidance notes issued by the Managing Director.

Notwithstanding the above, several powers of the Fund are not conferred specifically to any of the three organs, but rather are conferred upon "the

9 Articles of Agreement, Article XII, Section 5(c). There are two types of special majorities; 70% (e.g., a change in the rate of charge under Article V, Section 8(d)) and 85% (e.g., adoption of a new repurchase period under Article V, Section 7(c) and (d)).

10 Articles of Agreement, Article XII, Section 4(b).

11 Ibid.

12 Articles of Agreement, Article XII, Section 4(c).

13 Articles of Agreement. Article XII, Section 4(a).

Fund." In general terms, the Fund typically refers to the Executive Board but, given that the Articles do not expressly define "the Fund" or the issue of who can speak for the Fund, a reference to the Fund in a Fund document or communication can have different meanings in different contexts. It would depend on which organ has the power to decide on that particular matter mentioned in the document or communication. For instance, if the statement relates to admission of a new member, the Fund refers to the Board of Governors since admission to Fund membership is a power directly conferred upon the Board of Governors. Similarly, a statement on the appointment of a new Department Director would imply a reference to the Managing Director who is directly conferred with the power to appoint Fund staff.

3 Fund's Powers

The Fund's mandate originate in its Articles of Agreement. The overall objective of the Fund to promote international monetary and financial stability remains unchanged since its establishment in 1945. The Articles of Agreement generally confer three types of powers upon the Fund in furtherance of this objective: (i) oversight powers to monitor and promote the observance of members' obligations under the Articles of Agreement; (ii) financing powers to provide financial assistance to members to help them address balance of payments problems; and (iii) advisory powers to provide financial and technical services to members upon request.

3.1 *Oversight Powers*

The oversight powers refer to the Fund's responsibility to promote international financial stability and monetary cooperation, and to exercise oversight over members' compliance with their obligations under the Articles of Agreement. Article IV, Section 3 requires the Fund to conduct both bilateral and multilateral surveillance, which are mutually supportive and reinforcing and provide effective integrated surveillance in a highly-integrated world economy. In conducting such surveillance, the Fund pays due regard to country circumstances, recognizes the importance of continuous dialogue, candor and evenhandedness, and emphasizes the collaborative nature of the exercise.

Article IV of the Articles of Agreement sets forth certain obligations that members are required to observe concerning their exchange rate policies as well as domestic economic and financial sector policies. Under Article IV, members undertake to collaborate with the Fund and other members to assure orderly exchange arrangements and to promote a stable system of exchange rates.[14] Article IV, Section 3 requires the Fund to conduct both bilateral and multilateral surveillance. Recognizing the increasingly important international dimensions of surveillance and of cross-country spillovers, the Fund adopted in 2012 an integrated surveillance decision under Article IV, making consultations a vehicle for both bilateral and multilateral surveillance, to achieve better operational integration of these responsibilities.[15] This decision helps ensure that these responsibilities are mutually supportive and reinforcing, allowing the Fund to discuss the full range of spillovers from a member's policies that affect global stability.

In its bilateral surveillance with individual member countries, the Fund exercises firm surveillance over members' exchange rate policies under Article IV, Section 3(b) where the Fund assesses whether a member's exchange rate policies are promoting balance of payments stability.[16] Members are required to avoid manipulating exchange rates or the international monetary system in order to prevent effective balance of payments adjustment or to gain an unfair competitive advantage over other members. The Fund also exercises general oversight over members' domestic and financial policies under Article IV, Section 3(a) where the Fund assesses whether these policies are promoting domestic stability, and advises the member on policy adjustments necessary for these purposes. In this regard, members are required to (i) endeavor to direct their policies toward the objective of fostering orderly economic growth with reasonable price stability, with due regard to their circumstances and (ii) seek to promote stability by fostering orderly underlying economic and financial conditions and a monetary system that does not tend to produce erratic disruptions.

Article IV assumes that if each member adopts policies that promote its own balance of payments stability and domestic stability, it will contribute to an orderly and stable system of exchange rates. In order for the Fund to exercise this oversight power, members are required to provide the information necessary to enable the Fund to conduct surveillance,[17] and to consult with the Fund regarding these policies when requested by the Fund.[18] While

14 Articles of Agreement, Article IV, Section 1. The Fund recognizes that members have legitimate policy objectives including domestic social and political policy objectives that are beyond the scope of Article IV.

15 International Monetary Fund, "Factsheet—Integrated Surveillance Decision" (2013), <http://www.imf.org/external/np/exr/facts/isd.htm> accessed 30 September 2013.

16 Ibid.

17 Article of Agreement, Article IV, Section 3(b).

18 Articles of Agreement, Article IV Section 3(b) with respect to exchange rate policies and Section 1 with respect to domestic policies.

bilateral surveillance normally takes place annually, the Fund engages in continuous and frank dialogue with its members over their policies. In the context of bilateral surveillance, the Fund's assessment and advice take into account the impact of a member's policies on other members to the extent that the member's policies undermine the promotion of its own balance of payments or domestic stability.

At the multilateral level, Article IV, Section 3(a) requires the Fund to oversee the international monetary system to ensure its effective operation. In the context of multilateral surveillance, the Fund focuses on issues that may affect the effective operation of the international monetary system, including global economic and financial stability, and the spillovers arising from policies of individual members that may significantly influence the effective operation of the international monetary system. While the Fund may not require a member to change its policies in the interest of the effective operation of the international monetary system, members are encouraged to implement their policies that are conducive to achieving this objective. Multilateral surveillance can take several forms. For instance, the Fund has conducted multilateral exercises through analyses and assessments in the *World Economic Outlook*, the *Global Financial Stability Report* and the *Early Warning Exercise*.

3.2 *Financing Powers*

The financing powers refer to the Fund's ability to provide financial assistance to members to help them address balance of payments problems.[19] The Articles of Agreement require the Fund's financing assistance to meet two requirements. First, it is used to resolve, rather than delay the resolution of, the member's balance of payments problem, and cannot be provided for any other purposes. A member may use the Fund's general resources only to the extent it has a balance of payments need, i.e., a need arising from its balance of payments or its reserve position or developments in its reserves.[20] The definition of balance of payments need has been sufficiently flexible to enable the Fund to provide financing in a variety of circumstances. Second, the member will be in a position to repay the Fund in accordance with the relevant maturity schedule.[21] These conditions, while distinct, are related since the resolution of

19 As set out in Articles of Agreement, Article I(v), the purpose of IMF financing is to "[T]o give confidence to members by making the general resources of the Fund temporarily available to them under adequate safeguards, thus providing them with opportunity to correct maladjustments in their balance of payments without resorting to measures destructive of national or international prosperity."

20 Articles of Agreement, Article V, Section 3(b)(ii).

21 Articles of Agreement, Article V, Section 3(a) provides that "[T]he Fund shall adopt policies on the use of its general resources, including policies on stand-by or similar

a member's balance of payments problem will enhance its capacity to repay the Fund.

To operationalize these requirements, the Fund extends financing to a member only if the member is prepared to implement a program of economic, financial and structural reform designed to address the underlying balance of payments problem. The member has the primary responsibility for designing the program. If the program is successfully implemented, the member will restore or maintain balance of payments viability and macroeconomic stability, while setting the stage for sustained growth. This will in turn enable the member to repay the Fund. To achieve these objectives, the Fund's financing is disbursed in installments that are linked to conditions. The Fund's Executive Board reviews a member's performance under the member's financing arrangement where the member must show that it has met an economic target or implemented a structural reform in order to receive a disbursement. In respect of program-related structural conditions, a failure to meet such a structural condition would not in itself result in the non-completion of a program review by the Fund's Executive Board. Rather, completion of a program review would require a judgment by the Executive Board that there are compensating factors giving confidence that program objectives are being achieved. This aims to ensure progress in program implementation and to reduce risks to the Fund resources. These conditions are drawn from the member's reform program and vary case by case depending on the member's specific circumstances.

The Fund's policies on conditionality have evolved over the years in response to changing economic circumstances. In the early 1980s, with the Fund's growing involvement in low income and transition countries, the Fund's conditionality expanded from its traditional focus on macroeconomic policies to include structural measures. This reflects the Fund's recognition that severe structural problems ranging from lack of robust legal and institutional frameworks for bank resolution and corporate insolvency to prevalent corruption hindered economic stability and growth in those countries. In recent years, conditionality in the Fund supported programs has become nimbler and better tailored to the specific challenges faced by the member.[22]

arrangements, and may adopt special policies for special balance of payments problems, that will assist members to solve their balance of payments programs in a manner that is consistent with the provisions of this Agreement and that will establish adequate safeguards for the temporary use of the general resources of the Fund."

22 Conditionality has become more focused on critical structural reforms that are within the Fund's core areas and its design has reflected countries' specific circumstances. For example, for Fund supported programs for fragile states, such countries' vulnerabilities and capacity constraints are taken into consideration in program design.

3.3 *Advisory Powers*

Article IV, Section 2(b) allows the Fund to perform, upon request, financial and technical services, which are consistent with the Fund's purposes. Technical services generally take the form of the Fund providing technical assistance and training to help member governments put in place or enhance effective institutions, legal frameworks, and policies to promote economic stability and growth. It is open to any Fund member to request these services, and these services are voluntary for both the Fund and the member country, that is, the services are only provided to the member if requested, and the Fund is under no obligation to honor the request. The Fund's technical assistance and training cover a wide array of areas of importance to the Fund, including macroeconomic policy framework and management; balance of payment issues; monetary policy and exchange rate policy; financial stability frameworks; debt and asset liability management; fiscal policy and institutional frameworks; data dissemination standards; and legislative frameworks. Over the years, technical services have been integrated with and informed the policy dialogue between the Fund and its members under surveillance as well as Fund-supported programs. The Fund cooperates closely with other providers of capacity development. Given its focus on core areas of expertise and limited resources, the Fund seeks to avoid duplication in coverage and to enhance complementarity with other capacity development providers.

4 Roles of Legal Counsels

Legal counsels play a range of different roles at the Fund in assisting the institution in discharging its three powers noted above. Generally speaking, their roles fall into three categories.

First, legal counsels take on a traditional role as the Fund's in-house counselor. They advise the Fund's organs on the "legality" of their decisions. In doing so, they need to ensure that three principles must be observed. First, all decisions are consistent with the Articles of Agreement. Second, all decisions of a subordinate organ must be consistent with higher norms. For instance, the Executive Board must, in the exercise of its delegated authority, comply with the decisions of the Board of Governors. Third, all individual decisions of a Fund organ must be consistent with the general decisions of that organ. The Executive Board adopts both general and individual decisions. It adopts the general decisions to establish, for instance, the general parameters for providing the Fund's financial assistance including the maximum amount of the assistance and program length. It also takes individual decisions to grant financial assistance to a member. The Legal Department has advised that such individual decisions must be consistent with the terms and principles of the general decisions given their subordinate nature. Finally, exercise of any discretionary powers by any Fund organ cannot be discriminatory. In this regard, the principle of uniform treatment of all members implied from the Articles of Agreement is regarded as a general principle of the law of the Fund. However, the principle of uniformity of treatment does not require equal treatment of all members, but rather similar treatment of similarly situated members. Adherence to these principles is pertinent to the integrity of the rule of law and central to the credibility and legitimacy of the Fund's decision-making organs.

Legal counsels also advise on whether Fund members' actions are consistent with their obligations under the Articles of Agreement. For instance, when a member introduces a measure, which impacts the operation of its foreign exchange system such as limitations on the allocation of foreign exchange for current payments and transfers or taxes on foreign exchange transactions, legal counsel needs to determine whether such measure imposes restrictions on the making of payments and payments for current international transactions without the approval of the Fund. Finally, legal counsels advise the Fund's organs and membership on interpretation of the Articles of Agreement and the decisions adopted by the Fund's organs and also on the correct application of the rules and policies.

Second, legal counsels act as trusted advisors to member authorities. An increasing number of legal counsels at the Fund are engaged in assisting members in reforming their legal and institutional frameworks. Traditionally, legal technical assistance of the Fund's Legal Department focused on central banking, bank insolvency, and tax and budget legislation. However, events over the past 20 years and in particular the Asian crisis and the global financial crisis have underscored the important role that the law plays in contributing to financial stability and integrity at the global, regional and national levels. The Fund's Legal Department has expanded its legal technical assistance into new areas and is actively involved in strengthening financial sector legal frameworks.

For instance, large bank failures during the global financial crisis brought home the lack of adequate tools to resolve "too-big-to-fail" institutions, and misaligned incentives and lack of robust mechanisms for cross-border bank resolution and cooperation. This left some country authorities with little choice but to take unilateral actions, which contributed to the high fiscal costs of the crisis and resulted in disorderly resolution in some cases. Developing an effective framework for cross-border resolution is a key priority in the global regulatory reform. The Fund's Legal Department contributed to the establishment of an international standard for the resolution of systemically important banks, the Key Attributes of Effective Resolution Regimes for Financial Institutions ("Key Attributes"),[23] in close collaboration with the Financial Stability Board. These Key Attributes call for countries to put in place resolution regimes that give the authorities comprehensive resolution powers while establishing effective mechanisms for cross-border cooperation and for the allocation of losses to private stakeholders. Legal counsels have been assisting members in strengthening their resolution and crisis management frameworks in line with the best practices envisaged in the Key Attributes.

Many countries are paying increasing attention to the magnitude and macroeconomic implications of corporate debt overhang.[24] High repayment burdens reduce the ability of enterprises to invest, while also reducing banks' willingness to lend. High levels of corporate over-indebtedness can quickly translate into high levels of non-performing loans. As a result, bank capital that could be used to support fresh lending is locked up, and thus credit supply by financial institutions is limited. Banks often try to "evergreen" their loans to over-indebted businesses hoping that the situation will improve, which can contribute to the misallocation of financing and maintaining "zombie" companies. The lack of credit exacerbates the distress of corporates and this reinforces the negative loop by increasing loan defaults. Rising nonperforming loans, falling collateral values, and higher borrowing costs can quickly erode banks' capital buffers and have systemic consequences for the banking sector, and threaten financial stability. Building on its experience during the Asian crisis, the Legal Department has been assisting member countries including Italy, India and Mongolia in developing a comprehensive strategy to tackle corporate over-indebtedness and in designing and implementing reform measures including enhancing debt enforcement regimes, strengthening corporate insolvency systems, developing an out of court restructuring mechanism, removing tax disincentives to support debt restructuring, improving prudential regulation and supervision, and strengthening the capacity and integrity of the institutional framework.

A final example relates to anti-money laundering and combating the financing of terrorism (AML/CFT) which now accounts for a lion's share of technical assistance of the Fund's Legal Department. The Fund's involvement in AML/CFT dates back to the early 2000s in response to calls from the

23 <http://www.fsb.org/what-we-do/policy-development/effective-resolution-regimes-and-policies/key-attributes-of-effective-resolution-regimes-for-financial-institutions>

24 For instance, debt overhangs are holding back economic recovery in several euro area countries as the financial crisis and ensuing recessions have left many European countries with large debt overhangs and with high levels of non-performing loans.

international community due to concerns that money laundering and terrorist financing can threaten the stability of a country's financial sector or its external stability more generally. A robust AML/CFT regime helps enhance the integrity and stability of financial sectors, which in turn helps countries become integrated into the global financial system and strengthen governance and tax administration. Over the past 17 years, the Fund has helped shape international and national AML/CFT policies and supported member countries in building defenses against money laundering and terrorist financing. The Legal Department which now undertakes all Fund's work in this area has been involved in more than 120 assessments of members' compliance with the international AML/CFT standard and established an extensive capacity building program to help member countries strengthen their AML/CFT frameworks. In 2009, the Fund launched a donor supported trust fund to finance AML/CFT capacity development in its member countries.[25] The Legal Department has provided technical assistance on AML/CFT to more than 120 countries.

Finally, legal counsels at the Fund are public policy contributors. They are often called upon to provide policy advice, in addition to legal advice, and are directly involved in the development of Fund policies. There are several reasons for this role. First, given their involvement in assessing legality of all policies in the Fund, they are uniquely placed to bring an institutional perspective and memory to bear on these policy discussions and debates. Second, legal counsels need to help management think through the potential impact and implications of the proposal and ensure that all possible impacts and consequences of the policy have been anticipated. This would help legal counsels to formulate the policy clearly and correctly in a legally binding decision. Moreover, legal counsels seek to find practical solutions which are consistent with the Articles of Agreement, rules and regulations, decisions by the Executive Board while at the same time achieving the intended policy objectives. The Fund has developed the practice of having legal counsels on board in the early stages of policy development. Three examples illustrate the broad array of areas where legal counsels are contributing to policy development.

The Legal Department plays a lead role in the Fund's work on withdrawal of correspondent banking relationships (CBRs). Correspondent banking relationship involves a correspondent bank providing a deposit account or other liability account and a range of services to a respondent bank and its customers and requires an exchange of messages between banks to settle transactions by crediting or debiting accounts. This work stream is in response to the membership's

25 IMF, *Topical Trust Funds Aim to Expand IMF's Capacity Building*, <http://www.imf.org/external/np/exr/key/ttf.htm>

concerns over pullback by global banks from correspondent banking in certain pockets of the world. In today's highly interconnected economic world, correspondent banking plays an important role in supporting economic growth and promoting financial inclusion. Withdrawal of CBRs could accentuate financial fragilities in some countries, and undermine their growth, development and financial inclusion prospects by increasing costs of financial services. The Fund has been focusing on identifying drivers leading to CBR withdrawals, analyzing and monitoring risks, and providing advice on how to tackle CBR challenges.[26] Legal counsels are deeply involved in examining the factors behind this phenomenon which go beyond legal issues. In this regard, their work recognizes that CBR withdrawals reflect individual banks' business decisions based on an assessment of the profitability and risks of CBRs, and indicates that these decisions have been shaped by the recent changes in the regulatory, supervisory and enforcement landscape, notably with respect to more rigorous prudential requirements, and enhanced implementation and enforcement of the AML/CFT standards (in particular "know your customer" requirements), and economic and trade sanctions. Given the multitude of drivers, there is no one-size-fits-all solution, and responses need to be tailored to the country circumstances. The Fund has been facilitating candid and constructive dialogue among public and private sector stakeholders to identify concrete solutions to help countries address CBR pressures. In this regard, the Legal Department played a key role in the design and implementation of the Caribbean Initiative launched in February 2017, a regional approach that brings global and respondent banks together to develop actionable and practical measures to tackle CBRs problems in the Caribbean.[27] Similar regional initiatives will be launched in the Pacific and Africa in 2018.

Recent years witness the quick evolution of digital technology which is transforming the financial services industry, creating both opportunities and challenges for consumers, service providers and regulators. So-called FinTech that leverages technology enabled innovation such as big data, artificial intelligence, and cryptography offer the promise of providing financial services more quickly and at a lower cost. The widespread adoption of technologies bodes well for financial inclusion but presents challenges for regulation and

26 International Monetary Fund, "The Withdrawal of Correspondent Banking Relationships: A Case for Policy Action" (2016) SDN/16/06, <https://www.imf.org/external/pubs/ft/sdn/2016/sdn1606.pdf> accessed 30 June 2016. International Monetary Fund, "Recent Trends in Correspondent Banking Relationships—Further Considerations" (2017) <https://www.imf.org/~/media/Files/Publications/PP/031617.ashx> accessed 21 April 2017.

27 Id.

supervision. Developments in FinTech raise important questions that are not only national but also global in scale. Given its mandate to promote a stable international monetary system, the Fund has been closely monitoring the development of FinTech with a focus on the impact of this new wave of innovative technologies on cross border payments.[28] The Legal Department has been actively involved in examining how the law can contribute to the efforts to strike the right balance between addressing the risks associated with the development of the new FinTech industry, while avoiding overregulation that could stifle innovation. Its work points to the need for regulatory authorities to ensure that trust is maintained in an evolving financial system. In particular, regulators may need to complement their focus on entities with increasing attention to activities. Since financial services are increasingly provided by a diverse group of firms and market platforms, governance needs to be strengthened to ensure the integrity of data, algorithms and platforms. Finally, legal principles need to be modernized to clarify rights and obligations under the new global financial landscape.

5 Independence, Consistency and Continuity

Across these roles, legal counsels at the Fund provide legal advice to multiple parties at the Fund: the Board of Governors, the Executive Board, Fund management and other Fund departments. With such diverse recipients, it is paramount for legal counsels to maintain credibility and effectiveness of their legal advice, which helps ensure the rule of law at the Fund. To achieve this, they are guided by four key principles.

The first and foremost principle relates to independence and objectivity of legal counsels. Their responsibility is to provide objective, impartial and consistent advice based on a thorough and well-founded legal analysis of the Articles of Agreement, rules and regulations, and decisions by the Fund decision making organs. They are not advocates of any Fund organ or member, and their relationship is with the law, not the institution. This is particularly important given that there is no provision in the Fund's Articles of Agreement for judicial review of a decision of a Fund organ. The Fund does not have an independent

28 International Monetary Fund, "Virtual Currencies and Beyond: Initial Considerations" (2016) <https://www.imf.org/external/pubs/ft/sdn/2016/sdn1603.pdf> accessed 20 January 2016. International Monetary Fund, "Fintech and Financial Services: Initial Considerations" (2017) SDN/17/05, <https://www.imf.org/~/media/Files/Publications/SDN/2017/sdn1705.ashx> accessed 16June 2017.

dispute resolution process, except in the administrative law area.[29] However, a member may request a formal interpretation of the Articles of Agreement.[30] Such request will be put to the Executive Board, with an appeal to the Board of Governors whose decision is final.[31] Therefore, the Fund is the sole judge of whether a decision taken by one of its organs is consistent with the Articles of Agreement. This power is strengthened by its immunity from judicial process.[32] This procedure was only used 10 times in the early days of the Fund, and it has not been used since then.

Experience has shown that the Fund can operate properly without any mandatory form of judicial review of the Fund's decisions. The absence of judicial review has not been viewed by the Fund as an exemption from the rule of law. Instead, the Fund has always recognized the importance of abiding by its charter, rules and regulations. In this regard, legal counsels are regularly called upon to provide advice on the legality of a decision by a Fund organ. The Fund organs have been sufficiently sensitive to legal concerns and receptive to legal advice. In practice, they normally involve legal counsels in the early stages of policy development to ensure the legality of the decision and rely on their advice for the resolution of legal issues. To the extent that a reform proposal, while making sense from a policy perspective, could not be introduced through interpretation of the Articles of Agreement, legal counsels have been advising on the need to amend the Articles. Amendments of the Articles requires a proposal of the Board of Governors and approval by three fifths of the

29 The Fund has in place two levels of review for the formal channels of resolution of employment disputes between the Fund and its staff. The first level of review is conducted by the Grievance Committee, a three-person committee established in 1980 which is headed by a professional arbitrator or lawyers appointed by the Managing Director, and composed of one staff appointee from the Staff Association, and another appointed by Fund management. The committee makes recommendations to the Managing Director on challenges brought by staff to a decision of the Fund. The second level of review is conducted by the IMF Administrative Tribunal established by the Board of Governors in 1994 and composed of five members. The tribunal is an independent judicial body and its decisions are final and binding on the Fund and the staff member.

30 Articles of Agreement, Article XXIX(a) reads as follows: "Any question of interpretation of the provisions of this Agreement arising between any member and the Fund or between any members of the Fund shall be submitted to the Executive for its decision."

31 Articles of Agreement, Article XXIX (b). Any question referred to the Board of Governors shall be considered by a Committee on Interpretation of the Board of Governors. The Board of Governors shall establish the membership, procedures and voting majorities of the Committee. A decision of the Committee shall be the decision of the Board of Governors unless the Board of Governors, by 85% majority of the total voting power, decision otherwise.

32 Articles of Agreement, Article IX, Section 3.

member countries having 85 percent of the total voting power.[33] The Articles of Agreement have been amended seven times, evidencing the Fund's acceptance that there are limitations to the adoption of reforms through interpretation of the charter. Independence and objectivity of legal counsels at the Fund is pivotal to the legitimacy of the Fund's decisions. If legal counsels are perceived to be an advocate of a Fund organ or a member, it would undermine the credibility of their role. Finally, legal counsels strive to maintain consistency of legal advice to provide predictability, contributing to credibility and ensuring uniform treatment of its members.

The second principle is that legal counsels are to perform the functions of not only compliance officers but also problem solvers. Legal counsels need to ensure consistency of the decisions of the Fund's organs with the Articles of Agreement, rules and regulations as well as correct application of those policies. If a policy proposal is found to be inconsistent, their responsibility does not end with such an assessment. Rather they need to find ways to modify the proposal so that it can be accommodated under the existing legal framework, while still achieving the intended objectives. Providing legal advice in a balanced and accurate manner requires legal counsels to understand the policy rationale behind the decision, the objectives it is intended to achieve, and how it has been applied since its adoption. Legal counsels also need to appreciate the nuances of the decision-making process, while being proactive and innovative.

The third principle concerns the need to distinguish legal advice from policy advice. As noted above, legal counsels are often called upon to provide both legal and policy advice. It is critical that they understand where the line is between these two, since mixing legal and policy issues could undermine the clarity and credibility of their legal advice. On legal issues, legal counsels must take full and exclusive responsibility. However, on policy issues, their views are just one of the voices in the policy debate. The line between these two is not always clear, and whether an issue is a legal or policy one must be determined by legal counsels. It is also important that they clearly communicate such determination to the Fund's organs and departments so that there is a shared understanding of the line between legal and policy advice.

The final principle concerns communication. It is critical that legal counsels can explain their advice clearly and effectively to the Board of Governors, the Executive Board, management, colleagues in other departments, and member countries. They need to walk them through the legal analysis that provides the

33 Articles of Agreement, Article XXVIII.

basis for their advice in a clear way, and not using legal jargons. This would help them understand and accept legal advice.

In addition to these principles, continuity is crucial to the effectiveness of the Legal Department as a whole. Experience shows that continuity enables the department to maintain an institutional memory and perspective which in turn allows legal counsels to advise on policy consistency and coherence. The Legal Department at the Fund has benefited from considerable continuity. First, legal counsels at the Fund tend to stay in the Legal Department. Second, there have only been six General Counsels over the past 70 years.

6 Conclusion

While the Fund's mandate to maintain a stable international monetary system has remained constant since 1945, the Fund has evolved considerably to adapt to changes in the global economy. The role of the Fund's Legal Department has changed and grown significantly along with the Fund's evolution. Over the past 20 years, legal counsels' responsibilities have diversified ranging from traditional in-house counselors, trusted advisors to members to active public policy contributors. They have been playing an important role in ensuring that the Fund effectively responds to the changing developments in the international monetary and financial systems while maintaining the rule of law. In this regard, independence, consistency and continuity of the Legal Department is critical to the effectiveness of Fund as an institution. As the Fund will continue to change to meet new challenges in the international monetary system, the rule of law will remain the cornerstone in ensuring the legitimacy and credibility of the Fund to safeguard the international financial architecture.

CHAPTER 5

Governance of the Asian Infrastructure Investment Bank in Comparative Context

*Natalie Lichtenstein**

Abstract

The Asian Infrastructure Investment Bank (AIIB) was launched in 2016 with governance arrangements that build on the foundations of its progenitors, with adaptations and updates reflecting AIIB's own focus and founders. AIIB follows multilateral development banks (MDBs) such as the World Bank, Asian Development Bank, European Bank for Reconstruction and Development and Inter-American Development Bank in its governance structure (Board of Governors, Board of Directors and President). AIIB includes expanded powers for the Board of Governors to add flexibility in areas such as new types of financing and assistance to non-members. AIIB's Board of Directors serve on a part-time non-resident basis, with detailed powers for policy, oversight and delegation. AIIB's President is limited to two terms. AIIB's voting structure is tied to shareholding but less so than in many other MDBs, as basic votes for all members and Founding Member Votes for founders reduce the impact of shareholding to less than 90 percent of total voting power. The underlying comparisons with other MDBs are spelled out in detail in this chapter, summarizing AIIB's heritage and innovation in governance.

Governance in public international financial institutions began at least as far back as the July 1944 discussions at Bretton Woods, New Hampshire on the formation of the International Bank for Reconstruction and Development (IBRD) and the International Monetary Fund (IMF). Seventy years later, discussions were launched to create the Asian Infrastructure Investment Bank (AIIB), currently the newest multilateral development bank (MDB) to follow in

* Ms. Lichtenstein is an Adjunct Professor, Johns Hopkins School of Advanced International Studies, Washington, DC. She was formerly the Inaugural General Counsel for the Asian Infrastructure Investment Bank, and Assistant General Counsel at the World Bank. This article draws in part upon her book, see Natalie Lichtenstein, *A Comparative Guide to the Asian Infrastructure Investment Bank* (OUP 2018). Email: lichtenstein@jhu.edu.

 | DOI:10.1163/9789004408326_006

IBRD's pioneering footsteps. In the intervening decades, a score of other MDBs has been established, each one adapting the MDB model and its governance characteristics to different goals in a different context, all with the objective of pooling financial contributions and commitments of countries into a new development finance institution.

This article traces the influence of MDB governance structures on the governance arrangements for AIIB, comparing relevant legal frameworks. After a brief introduction to AIIB (Section 1) and MDB Origins (Section 2), Section 3 describes AIIB's governing bodies (Board of Governors, Board of Directors, President) and Section 4 describes AIIB's decision-making rules (voting and majorities). Section 5 offers concluding observations.

1 AIIB

AIIB was formally established in January 2016 as a USD100 billion MDB—financing infrastructure for the development of Asia, from the Pacific to the Mediterranean. Its 57 founders, mostly countries from Asia and Europe, decided to address this goal by setting up a new MDB, drawing from both successes and dissatisfactions at existing MDBs. This decision reflected the priority they placed on the urgency of mobilizing finance for infrastructure, rather than a focus on a new institution for its own sake. They expected a quicker startup by adapting an existing structure, instead directing the energy of the negotiators (and the AIIB board and management), to find innovative ways to improve upon the perceived shortcomings in the framework and operation of existing MDBs.

Indeed, each MDB in turn has been built upon the foundations of its predecessors. For AIIB, as for others, credibility for a brand new financial institution could be enhanced by reliance on arrangements that were known, workable and respected. Investors and rating agencies could more easily assess AIIB through common MDB frameworks. Both public and private sector clients could more easily compare recognizable financial products and operational policies. Moreover, familiar yet improved operating processes could be less burdensome, while harmonization with other MDB practices would be in line with current MDB coordination efforts. The vast and varied MDB experiences could be utilized for operations, administration and legal interpretations, while aiming at greater effectiveness.

At the two-year milestone (January 2018), these benefits of adapting the MDB model appear to have been borne out in reality. As an international organization, AIIB counts among its first 84 approved members countries in East

Asia, South Asia, Central Asia, Western Asia and Oceania as well as non-Asian countries in Europe, Africa, Latin America and North America. AIIB's investments in infrastructure in its first two years totaled over USD4 billion.[1] As an international financial institution, AIIB enjoys a triple-A rating in international capital markets.[2] AIIB's multinational management and staff have taken up residence at its headquarters in Beijing, home of its initiator and largest shareholder, the People's Republic of China.

2 MDB Origins

Before turning to a comparison of AIIB's governance with governance provisions at other MDBs, a short introduction to these institutions is in order. This Section summarizes the progression of MDBs. Sections 3 and 4 will then discuss the similarities and differences found in the AIIB Charter and the Charters of those MDBs that serve as the principal comparators for the design of AIIB governance.[3]

2.1 *World Bank (IBRD) 1945*

The IBRD Charter was negotiated by 44 country delegations at the same 1944 conference as the IMF charter, and had been the subject of several years of preceding discussions, principally between the US and the UK.[4] IBRD took second place in urgency and interest to the IMF, in the economic, financial

1 See the list of projects and approval dates on the AIIB website, www.aiib.org. Table 4.1 in Lichtenstein (n *) summarizes the AIIB investment operations approved in 2016–2017.

2 See for example the Standard and Poor's rating assignment in n 59 below.

3 The Articles of Agreement of the Asian Infrastructure Investment Bank (dated 29 June 2015, entered into force 25 December 2015) are referred to here as the AIIB Charter.

The constituent documents for other MDBs are referred to as their Charters, as follows:

- IBRD Charter (Articles of Agreement of the International Bank for Reconstruction and Development, dated 27 December 27 1945, as amended through 2012).
- EIB Charter (Statute of the European Investment Bank, version dated 1 July 2013).
- IADB Charter (Agreement Establishing the Inter-American Development Bank, dated 8 April 1959, as amended through 1995).
- AfDB Charter (Agreement Establishing the African Development Bank, dated 4 August 1963, as amended through 2001).
- ADB Charter (Agreement Establishing the Asian Development Bank, dated 4 December 1965).
- EBRD Charter (Agreement Establishing the European Bank for Reconstruction and Development, dated 29 May 1990, as amended through 2012).

4 For a general history of the negotiations that led to the establishment of the IMF and IBRD, see Ed Conway, *The Summit: Bretton Woods, 1944* (Pegasus Books 2014). For a succinct legal

and political disruptions of the ongoing World War. IBRD's dual purposes of reconstruction and development were a response to the perceived needs for a post-war world, and were unique at the time, as was its structure. Several key IBRD financial and governance provisions can be seen in an earlier unsuccessful effort to create an Inter-American Bank, including the all-important capital structure and voting patterns.[5] IBRD's original emphasis on providing guarantees of private sector loans derived from pre-war financial situations, but changed quickly to an emphasis on government guaranteed loans, always for productive purposes.

To illustrate how much the international arena was in flux at that moment, note that the IMF and IBRD negotiations predated the finalization of the charter of the United Nations in 1945.[6] As of 2017, both the IMF and IBRD have 189 members, nearly every current UN member.[7] In 1947, US shareholding gave it a controlling voting power in IBRD of 35 percent; today, US voting power hovers just above the 15 percent minimum necessary to keep a veto on Charter amendments that require an 85 percent majority.[8]

history of the IBRD Charter, see Henry J Bitterman, "Negotiation of the Articles of Agreement of the International Bank for Reconstruction and Development" (1971) 5 Intl Lawyer 59.

5 The Inter-American Bank (IAB) was a proposed intergovernmental institution, under a convention signed in 1940 by the United States and eight Latin American countries (Bolivia, Brazil, Colombia, Dominican Republic, Ecuador, Mexico, Nicaragua and Paraguay). Domestic approvals for US participation proved elusive and the IAB did not come into existence. See Eugenio Diaz-Bonilla and Maria Victoria del Campo, *A Long and Winding Road: The Creation of the Inter-American Development Bank* (no publishing information 2010) 32–41. The IAB would have had a corporate structure, with paid-up capital at 50 percent and the remainder subject to call with three months' notice. Voting power would have been based on shareholding, with a type of basic votes for all. The IAB would have been authorized to make loans, take deposits and issue bonds, among its other purposes and powers. US Department of State Bulletin (1940), 516 (listing Inter-American Bank By-Laws, s 2A and 5A). IAB's corporate and capital structure may have been derived from the Bank for International Settlements, the first such international financial institution, established in 1930 with a structure based on a Swiss company limited by shares. For more discussion of the impact of IAB on the IBRD setup, and through it, to the other MDBs, see Eric Helleiner, *Forgotten Foundations of Bretton Woods: International Development and the Making of the Postwar Order* (Cornell UP 2014), especially ch 2, and Bitterman (n 4) 61–62.

6 The Charter of the United Nations (done in San Francisco in June 1945, entered into force on 24 October 1945) 1 UNTS XVI.

7 IMF membership is a prerequisite for IBRD membership. IBRD Charter, art II, s 1. Andorra, Cuba, Democratic People's Republic of Korea, Liechtenstein and Monaco are UN members but not IMF and IBRD members.

8 The IBRD Charter, art VIII (a), requires approval by three-fifths of members having 85% of total voting power for its amendment. The original IBRD threshold was 80 percent; the IBRD Charter was amended in 1989 to change to 85%, in connection with an agreement for the

An important facet of IBRD's history has been the creation of affiliated institutions to take on development-related functions that were beyond its Charter-based remit—rather than taking the route of Charter amendment. IBRD was joined by a separate yet affiliated institution established in 1960 to provide concessional finance to the less developed areas of the world, the International Development Association (IDA). Together, IBRD and IDA are often referred to as the World Bank. In addition, the World Bank Group refers to IBRD, IDA, the International Finance Corporation (IFC, a private investment-oriented affiliate, established in 1956 to provide finance without government guarantee and, later, equity investment), the Multilateral Investment Guarantee Agency (MIGA, a political risk insurance affiliate, established in 1988) and the International Centre for the Settlement of Investment Disputes (ICSID, an affiliate for investor-State dispute settlement, established in 1965). MDB Charters that came after the IBRD Charter have often included some of these additional functions from the start, such as non-government lending, equity investment and concessional funding for less developed countries.

2.2 *European Investment Bank (EIB) 1957*

EIB grew out of years of discussions within Europe on its post-war development that included, inter alia, concerns over potential competition with the recently-established IBRD and its new private sector arm, IFC.[9] EIB was established to contribute to the balanced and steady development of the European internal market, through loans and guarantees.[10] EIB's overall governance framework was built upon the IBRD Charter, such as its Board of Governors and Board of Directors, while many other governance aspects were entirely new, such as the Management Committee and the non-resident status of the Board of Directors.[11] EIB was the first of the MDBs described here to adapt the IBRD model, though EIB's structure and function as an institution of the European Union (EU) differentiate it from the others. In that sense, it had a more general influence on the governance design at AIIB.

US voting power to drop below 20 percent (and, among others, Japan to increase its voting power, becoming the second largest shareholder).

9 Regarding the comparison and competition with IBRD and IFC, see European Investment Bank (EIB), *The Bank of the European Union: The EIB, 1958–2008* (European Investment Bank 2008) 32–34.

10 EIB Charter art 2, referring to the Treaty on the Functioning of the European Union, art 309 (ex art 267, Treaty establishing the European Community). The EIB Charter was amended to allow for equity investments by EIB itself in 2009. EIB art 18-2.

11 EIB (n 9) 44–45.

2.3 *Inter-American Development Bank (IADB) 1959.*

IADB was founded in 1959, yet its story can be traced through the preceding century of the economic and political history of Latin America as a region with its northern neighbor, the US. An "International American Bank" had been proposed in 1890 as a private regional banking institution, and later, an intergovernmental financial institution, the Inter-American Bank, nearly came to life in 1940, as noted earlier.[12] Latin American countries renewed the push for a similar institution in the 1950s, when they did not find that IBRD fully met regional needs in its early years.[13] Early on, the proposal for this new regional institution was not initially supported by the US, likely concerned about competition with IBRD for support. Then, the winds of US foreign policy changed with tensions in the region and brought the US to the negotiating table, becoming IADB's key funder and largest shareholder.[14]

IADB's purpose is to contribute to the economic and social development of its regional member countries, through loans and guarantees; filling a gap in the IBRD Charter, technical assistance is also expressly authorized.[15] While IADB's initial governance framework mirrored that of IBRD, later innovations came from IADB's regional character. Originally, IADB members were all regional countries and only members of the Organization of American States (OAS). Following a decline in US financial support in the late 1960s, the IADB Charter was amended in the 1970s to allow Canada and other non-OAS regional countries to join, and then to bring in non-regional members and their capital (Europe and Japan, initially). IADB thus led the way with Charter clauses specifying the shareholding for regional developing members (now 50.005 percent), the US (now 30 percent) and Canada (4 percent). IADB also pioneered

12 See Diaz-Bonilla and del Campo (n 5) 4–11 (International American Bank) and 32–41 (Inter-American Bank).

13 Ibid 58–59 (dissatisfaction with existing international financial institutions).

14 In earlier times, the United States reportedly was cool to the IADB proposal until US bilateral activities in Latin America met with public outcry. See Diane Tussie, *The Multilateral Development Banks, Volume 4: The Inter-American Development Bank* (Lynne Rienner Publishers 1995) 18–19, citing as a motivating factor for US participation in IADB negotiations the hostility encountered by US Vice President Richard Nixon in his 1958 trip to Latin America. It has also been suggested that final US agreement to join the IADB negotiations was timed days before a public proposal by US President Eisenhower to establish an Arab development institution in the wake of US problems in Lebanon and elsewhere in the Middle East in 1958. See Diaz-Bonilla and del Campo (n 5) 68–69. The US share of IADB capital at its inception was 42% and it was the largest funder of the Fund for Special Operations, the soft-loan window.

15 IADB Charter, art I, s 1 (purpose), art III, s 4 (operations) and art VI (technical assistance).

the introduction of specific regional majority requirements for key decisions.[16] Interestingly, IADB members also established a separate entity for private sector and equity investment, the Inter-American Investment Corporation, as EIB had with its European Investment Fund, both parallels to IBRD's addition of the IFC.

2.4 *African Development Bank (AfDB) 1963*

Regional economic history also lay behind the formation of AfDB as an African financial institution in the post-colonial era. The UN Economic Commission for Africa played a seminal role in AfDB's establishment (as its Asian equivalent did for Asian Development Bank). Nonetheless, it was the economic and political relations among different groups of African countries that determined the timing and contours of the bank that emerged. Relations with developed countries had an impact regarding decisions to join the bank and on forms of concessional financing (e.g., relations with France and the US).[17] However, non-regionals were not part of the AfDB membership discussions until much later.

AfDB's purpose is to contribute to the sustainable economic development and social progress of its regional members, through loans, guarantees and equity investment.[18] AfDB's overall governance arrangements were also based on the IBRD model, with adjustments over time in response to its own institutional experience; for instance, the President was originally selected by the Board of Directors, as at IBRD, and later this was changed to election by the Board of Governors, as at IADB and ADB.[19] The need for concessional finance led to the innovative African Development Fund, a separate entity jointly owned by AfDB and non-regional donors.[20] Then, in the 1980s, AfDB followed the IADB

16 For IADB regional shareholding requirements, see IADB art VIII, s 4 (b) and the detailed listing in n 102.

17 Robert KA Gardiner and James Pickett, *The African Development Bank 1964–1984* (The African Development Bank 1984) 8–13.

18 AfDB Charter, art 1 (purpose) and art 14-1 (methods of operation). Technical assistance is also among AfDB's functions. AfDB Charter, art 2-1 (e). The word "sustainable" was added in 2001. AfDB Board of Governors' Resolution No. B/BG/2001/08, Amendments to the Agreement Establishing the African Development Bank, adopted 29 May 2001, entered into force 5 July 2002.

19 AfDB Charter, art 36 (as amended in 1979, see note 79 for details). The appointment process for Vice-Presidents was also changed in response to AfDB's experience. See note 83 for details.

20 The African Development Fund (AfDF) was originally set up as an AfDB special fund with AfDB funding, as the response of potential donors was not encouraging. By 1972, the AfDF was established as a separate international institution, by AfDB and non-regional donors.

experiment and opened up AfDB itself to non-regional members and their capital contributions, limiting their share (now 40 percent non-regional and 60 percent regional).[21]

2.5 *Asian Development Bank (ADB) 1965*

A proposal for a regional development bank in Asia had been floated by Japan in the early 1960s, without gaining traction. Around the same time, a similar idea was under discussion among other Asian countries through the UN Economic Commission for Asia and the Far East. Like the Latin America countries proposing IADB a decade earlier, they had found the extent of IBRD support for their development less than expected.[22] Similarly, the US was an important player and potential funder in Asia as well, and yet was also initially cool to the ADB proposal, not perceiving the depth of the unmet needs, and concerned about competition with IBRD. Again, the winds of US foreign policy shifted (in connection with the US war in Southeast Asia), buoying the ADB proposal to a successful conclusion with full US support.[23] Japan and the US have continued since as the two largest shareholders and supporters of ADB.

ADB was established to foster economic growth and co-operation in Asia and to contribute to the economic development of developing member countries.[24] ADB's governance provisions are closely modelled on the IBRD provisions and have not been amended. The ADB Charter was the first to include both regional and non-regional members from the outset but does not require specific regional majorities for its qualified majority decisions; it does ensure that regional shareholding will stay at 60 percent,[25] preserving the regional character of the institution. The ADB Charter also permits all types

See Andres Rigo Sureda, "The Law Applicable to the Activities of International Development Banks" in (2004) Collected Courses of The Hague Academy of International Law 308, paras 410–420.

21 AfDB Charter, art 5-4.

22 At the time, a high proportion of World Bank Group financing for Asia was directed to larger Asian developing countries (65 percent of IBRD and 95 percent of IDA financing for Asia went to India and Pakistan). Dick Wilson, *A Bank for Half the World, The Story of the Asian Development Bank 1966–86* (Asian Development Bank 1987) 6.

23 After initial opposition, the United States warmed to the ADB proposal only after the United States sought to improve its standing in Southeast Asia after the start of the Vietnam War. See Dick Wilson (n 22) 12–13, citing US President Lyndon Johnson's change of view on ADB as part of a large commitment of US assistance to Southeast Asia in April 1965.

24 ADB Charter, art 1 (purpose) and art 11 (methods of operation).

25 The regional shareholding minimum is found in ADB Charter, art 5-1.

of operations (loans and guarantees for both public and private entities and equity investment) as well as the establishment of special funds (often a mechanism for concessional finance contributed by donors) and provision of technical assistance.[26] The drafting of the ADB Charter took into account the IBRD, IADB and AfDB Charters, and served as a foundation for the EBRD Charter and later the AIIB Charter.

2.6 *European Bank for Reconstruction and Development* (*EBRD*) *1990*

Following ADB by some 25 years, EBRD began as a regional initiative among Europeans, in response to the newly emerging need for assistance to Central and Eastern Europe. With a longstanding regional investment bank (EIB) already in operation, EBRD was set up with a specialized set of goals: "to foster the transition towards open market-oriented economies and to promote private and entrepreneurial initiative in the Central and Eastern European countries committed to and applying the principles of multiparty democracy, pluralism and market economics."[27] Politics was no less a part of EBRD's creation than for its predecessors, reflecting differing views of key European protagonists (France, Germany, UK), European institutions (the EU and EIB were original EBRD members), and the US and Japan.[28]

To serve its specific purposes, EBRD is authorized to make loans to and invest in the equity capital of private enterprises, and state-owned enterprises that meet certain conditions; guarantees in some circumstances and technical assistance are also expressly authorized.[29] Also specifically designed for EBRD is the requirement that not more than 40 percent of its committed loans, guarantees and equity investment be provided to the state sector.[30] While its operational mandate is unique, EBRD's governance arrangements are closely aligned with its predecessors. For both political and economic reasons, EBRD was established with a combination of regional and non-regional shareholders from the start. EBRD eventually found itself undertaking Charter amendments to expand its countries of operation beyond the geographical confines

26 ADB Charter, art 11 (methods of operation), art 19 (Special Funds) and art 21 (vi)(technical assistance).

27 EBRD Charter, art 1.

28 Stephen Weber, "Origins of the European Bank for Reconstruction and Development," (1994) 48 Intl Organization 1, 15–16, also pointing out that US skepticism about regional banks was long-standing and deep.

29 EBRD Charter, art 11-1.

30 EBRD Charter, art 11-3.

of Central and Eastern Europe to include Mongolia and the Southern and Eastern Mediterranean.[31]

2.7 *AIIB Establishment*

With these precedents in mind, let us turn to the details of AIIB's establishment. The specific proposal for AIIB was floated in October 2013 by Chinese President Xi Jinping during a Southeast Asian visit, focused on the infrastructure needs of Asia. Though there had been some earlier similar proposals,[32] the October 2013 proposal took shape, and by October 2014, 22 Asian countries, organized by China, had concluded a Memorandum of Understanding on Establishing the Asian Infrastructure Investment Bank. These countries, joined in the subsequent Charter negotiations by 37 others from Asia, Europe, Africa and Latin America, agreed on the AIIB Charter, signed in June 2015. AIIB's largest shareholder at inception was China with over 25 percent of the voting power, followed by India (around 8 percent) and Russia (around six percent); non-regional members hold nearly 25 percent of the shareholding. Yet the two largest shareholders in IBRD, ADB and EBRD were notably absent (the US and Japan). Twenty-seven new AIIB members were approved in 2017, bringing the total to 84 (48 regional and 36 non-regional).

AIIB was established "to foster sustainable economic development, create wealth and improve infrastructure connectivity in Asia by investing in infrastructure and other productive sectors" and to promote regional cooperation and partnership in addressing development challenges.[33] Its scope of operations reflects the experience of others, so that it includes loans, guarantees, equity investment, Special Fund operations and technical assistance.

---

31 EBRD Board of Governors' Resolution No. 90, Amendment to the Agreement Establishing the Bank in order to Admit Mongolia as a Country of Operations, adopted 30 January 2004, entered into force 15 October 2006. EBRD Board of Governors' Resolution No. 137, Amendment of the Agreement Establishing the Bank in order to Enable the Bank to Operate in Countries of the Southern and Eastern Mediterranean, adopted 30 September 2011, entered into force 12 September 2013.

32 Earlier proposals included a 2005 report from the UN Economic and Social Commission for Asia and the Pacific that suggested the establishment of an Asian Investment Bank, adapted from the EIB model, to meet the region's infrastructure needs and promote regional development. See UN Economic and Social Commission for Asia and the Pacific, *Implementing the Monterrey Consensus in the Asian and Pacific Region: Achieving Coherence and Consistency* (United Nations 2005) 154.

In 2009, a Chinese think-tank suggested the formation of a new development bank focused on infrastructure. See Mike Callaghan and Paul Hubbard, "The Asian Infrastructure Investment Bank: Multilateralism on the Silk Road," (2016) 2 China Economic J 116, singling out the 2009 proposal by the China Center for International Economic Exchanges.

33 AIIB Charter, art 1-1.

Themes. This highly selective overview reveals some themes that are echoed in the more recent AIIB story. There is considerable reluctance at every turn to start a new institution. One can see the US as an exemplar of this view (for IADB, ADB, EBRD and AIIB), but the sentiment is widely shared. There are also different perceptions of the weight of problems with existing MDBs compared to costs and uncertain dynamics in new ones. It is often the regional countries for whom the dissatisfaction with current options propels the establishment of a new entity. Consider here the Latin American countries wanting IADB to take on social projects, public investment in industry and local currency lending, or the smaller southeast Asian nations making the case for ADB, as IBRD/IDA funding was directed to larger former colonies.[34] The driving force of geopolitics proved inescapable in each case.

Resistance from existing MDBs is not surprising. For IBRD, the rise of the regional development banks has been described as "at once a tribute and a rebuke."[35] Yet, the existing institutions also helped with the design and drafting of subsequent Charters, and, once the new institutions were established, with the details of getting up and running. Another theme is the importance of the scope of membership, especially in the interaction between finance and governance, as seen in the opening to non-regional members for IADB and AfDB.

Not mentioned here are a number of other MDBs and similar international financial institutions, many subregional and some more specialized. While not discussed in any detail, they form part of the MDB family and offer variations in governance and other provisions. The Caribbean Development Bank, Islamic Development Bank, and Black Sea Trade and Development Bank operate under charters and governance structures that are largely comparable to the MDBs described above, in their specific geographic areas. Other subregional institutions include the Andean Development Bank (CAF), Nordic Investment Bank and the Council of Europe Development Bank, among others. The International Fund for Agricultural Development (IFAD) is another source of development finance, as a UN specialized agency with worldwide operations.

3 AIIB's Governing Bodies

AIIB shares its overall governance structure with many other MDBs, with a common hierarchy of three governance levels: Board of Governors, Board of

34 See n 14, n 22 and n 23.

35 Edward S Mason and Robert E Asher, *The World Bank Since Bretton Woods* (The Brookings Institution 1973) 578.

Directors and President. The Board of Governors is the Bank's highest authority, composed of one Governor appointed by each member, meeting annually. The Board of Directors is responsible for the direction of the general operations of the Bank and is composed of Directors elected by one or more Governors representing particular members, meeting at least quarterly. The President, elected by the Board of Governors, conducts the current business of the Bank, under the direction of the Board of Directors.

3.1 *Board of Governors*

The AIIB Board of Governors meets annually, as do other Boards of Governors in well-publicized Annual Meetings; other meetings can be called by the Board of Governors or Board of Directors, though this is very rare in MDB practice.[36] Most frequently, decisions of the Board of Governors are taken in a vote without a meeting, on recommendation by the Board of Directors, and for AIIB, electronic meetings may take place in special circumstances (a new provision).[37] The Board of Governors elects its Chairman and Vice-Chairman at each annual meeting, and can establish committees that report to the Board.[38]

Under the AIIB Charter, all powers of the Bank are vested in the Board of Governors, as is the case in other MDBs.[39] The Board of Governors may delegate most of its powers to the Board of Directors; certain key powers are specified in the Charter and cannot be delegated (known as reserved powers).[40] The reserved powers of the AIIB Board of Governors listed in the AIIB Charter are comparable and often identical to the reserved powers of other MDB Boards of

36 AIIB Charter, art 22-1 (composition) and 24-1 (meetings). For the comparable provisions in others, see generally AfDB Charter, arts 30 and 31; ADB Charter, arts 27 and 29; EBRD Charter, arts 23 and 25; IADB Charter, art VIII, s 2 and IBRD Charter, art V, s 2.

37 AIIB Charter, art 24-3, and AIIB Rules of Procedure of the Board of Governors, s 2 (c). Another recent example of electronic meetings, for the Board of Directors, can be found in the By-Laws of the European Stability Mechanism, s 3–8 (8 December 2014). See also the Statutes of the Bank for International Settlements, dated 20 January 1930, as amended through 7 November 2016, art 31-2.

38 AIIB Charter, art 22-2 and AIIB Rules of Procedure of the Board of Governors, ss 6 (b) and 9. In December 2017, AIIB's Board of Governors added a provision to its Rules of Procedure (Section 7) for an Advisory Group to advise the Chair on urgent procedural issues related to meetings, and other tasks; the Group is comprised of the current Chair, the previous Chair and the Vice Chairs. This new mechanism is comparable to the procedures committees set up for some other MDB annual meetings; on its face, the Group appears potentially simpler and more responsive, though less broad in its composition.

39 AIIB art 23-1. AfDB Charter, art 29-1; ADB Charter, art 28-1; EBRD Charter, art 24-1; IADB Charter, art VIII, s 2 (a); and IBRD Charter, art V, s 2 (a).

40 AIIB Charter, art 23-2.

Governors.[41] In addition, the AIIB Charter assigns a number of other powers solely to the Board of Governors, and these cannot be delegated either. Most of these specifically assigned powers are new for AIIB, and they include: variations in the classification of the Asia region; change to the non-resident status of the Board of Directors; variation in the 75 percent regional shareholding requirement; allocation of net income to other purposes; increase in the lending limit; establishment of subsidiaries; framework for trust funds; financing for non-member recipients; and new types of financing.[42]

At the start, the AIIB Board of Governors indeed delegated to the AIIB Board of Directors all of its powers that are not reserved or specifically assigned, following the practice of the others.[43] One difference in AIIB powers is that the power to approve arrangements for cooperation with other international organizations is directly assigned to the Board of Directors in the AIIB Charter; in others, it is often reserved to the Board of Governors.[44] In practice, many of these cooperation arrangements are now administrative and technical in nature, and can be more appropriately decided by the Board of Directors, or by the management under guidance from the Board of Directors.

3.2 *Board of Directors*

The overall structure and powers of the AIIB Board of Directors are very similar to its predecessors, with some notable distinguishing features. These include

41 See AfDB Charter, art 29-2; ADB Charter, art 28-2; EBRD Charter, art 24-2; IADB Charter, art VIII, s 2 (b); and IBRD Charter, art V, s 2 (b).

42 Specifically assigned powers of the AIIB Board of Governors can be found in the AIIB Charter as follows: Asia definition (art 1-2); exceptions to 75% regional shareholding, and review of capital stock (arts 5-2 and 5-3); non-par value shares (art 7-1); non-member recipient (art 11-1(b)); new types of financing (art 11-2 (vi)); increase in lending limit (art 12-1); trust fund framework (art 16-7); subsidiaries (art 16-8); allocation of net income to other purposes (art 18-1); size or composition of the Board of Directors (art 25-2); number of constituency members for second Alternate Director (art 25-3); change in non-residential status of the Board of Directors (art 27-1); and extension of the final date for Signatories to ratify (art 58-1).

43 AIIB By-Laws, s 6. This Section further provides that the Board of Directors shall not take any action pursuant to powers delegated by the Board of Governors which is inconsistent with any action taken by the Board of Governors. This delegation and proviso are also common. See AfDB General Regulations art 4-1; ADB By-Laws s 8; EBRD By-Laws s 8 (a); IADB By-Laws s 4; and IBRD By-Laws s 14.

44 AIIB Charter, art 35. The power to approve general agreements with other international organizations is a reserved power of the Board of Governors in AfDB, ADB, EBRD, IADB and IBRD, in varying terms. See AfDB Charter, art 29-2; ADB Charter, art 28-2; EBRD Charter, art 24-2; IADB Charter, art VIII, s 2 (b); and IBRD Charter, art V, s 2 (b).

the Board's non-resident status and expanded powers of delegation and oversight that go with it.

3.2.1 Size and Constituency Structure

The size of MDB Boards of Directors varies considerably, and this can have an impact on the openness of discussions, cohesiveness and consensus-building. Each Director casts the votes of one or more members in a constituency; often, members with large voting power have their own Director (single member constituency) or may dominate the Directorship in a group constituency.

The AIIB Board of Directors has 12 Directors (representing 61 members, with 23 more approved for membership, as of January 2018), with one single member constituency; nine Directors are regional and three Directors are non-regional, reflecting the 75 percent regional shareholding in AIIB.[45] The size and composition of the AIIB Board of Directors may be changed by a decision of the AIIB Board of Governors.[46] These basic provisions for the composition of the AIIB Board of Directors are comparable to other MDBs in many respects.[47] Often, the proportion of regional and non-regional Directors is specified, usually in line with the proportion of regional and non-regional shareholding; the exception is IBRD which is global and does not categorize members as regional and non-regional. The table below compares Board composition, in terms of number of Directors, members represented, regional/non-regional proportions and single member constituencies.

Composition of MDB Boards of Directors (January 2018)

Institution	Number of Directors	Number of Members	Regional Directors (Members represented)	Non-Regional Directors (Members represented)	Single Member constituencies
AfDB	20	81	13 (54)	7 (26)	United States

45 AIIB Charter, art 25-1. As of 31 December 2017, only India has a single member constituency on AIIB's Board. (AIIB's largest member, China, is joined in its constituency by Hong Kong, China.) By March 21, 2018, AIIB had 64 members.

46 AIIB Charter, art 25-2. A Super Majority vote is required: An affirmative vote of two-thirds of the total number of Governors, representing not less than three-fourths of the total voting power of the members, as per art 28-2 (ii).

47 AfDB Charter, arts 33 and 34; ADB Charter, arts 30 and 32; EBRD Charter, arts 26 and 28; IADB Charter, art VIII, s 3; and IBRD Charter, art V, s 4.

ADB[a]	12	67	8 (48)	4 (19)	China Japan United States
AIIB	12	61 (+ 23 pending)	9 (40 + 8)	3 (21 + 15)	India
EBRD[b]	23	68	19 (56 + EIB, EU)	4 (10)	France Germany Italy Japan United Kingdom United States EIB EU
IADB[c]	14	48	11 (28)	3 (20)	Appointed: United States Canada
IBRD[d]	25	189	*not applicable*		Appointed: China France Germany Japan United Kingdom United States Elected: Russia Saudi Arabia

a ADB began with a ten-member board. ADB Charter, art 30-1.

b EBRD's 23 Directors are grouped under EBRD Charter, art 26-1, in several ways. Eleven Directors represent Belgium, Denmark, France, the Federal Republic of Germany, Greece, Ireland, Italy, Luxembourg, the Netherlands, Portugal, Spain, the United Kingdom, EU and EIB. Twelve represent other members, of whom: four represent Central and Eastern European countries eligible for assistance from the Bank; four represent other European countries; and four represent non-European countries.

c At IADB, one Executive Director is appointed by the largest shareholder (US), not less than three are elected by nonregional members, and not less than ten others are elected by the remaining regional members.

d IBRD began with a 12-member board. The five largest shareholders each appoint their own Executive Director. Currently, UK and France are tied for fifth-largest shareholder and each appoint an Executive Director.

Each AIIB Director appoints an Alternate Director, as is typical in the other MDBs. In AIIB, Directors representing five or more members may also appoint a second Alternate Director.[48] This feature increases the opportunities for members in a constituency to participate directly in the work of the Board.[49] Increasing the number of Board positions facilitates the designation by AIIB Founding Members of a Director or Alternate Director on a permanent or rotating basis, a privilege enshrined in the AIIB Charter.[50] Both the second Alternate Director position and this privilege of designation aim at broadening the voice of smaller members in AIIB governance.

3.2.2 Non-resident Board

The AIIB Board of Directors is set up as a part-time board, on a non-residential basis, meeting periodically throughout the year as the business of the Bank requires.[51] Regular meetings are held quarterly; meetings are called by the Chairman (AIIB President) or if requested by three Directors.[52] The Board of Directors can also hold electronic meetings or vote without a meeting; decisions on an absence of objection basis are also permitted.[53]

At the other MDBs discussed here, the Boards of Directors are resident (AfDB, ADB, EBRD, IADB and IBRD), with the Directors, Alternates and constituency staff based at the bank's headquarters and frequent meetings

48 AIIB Charter, art 25-3. Board of Governors' Resolution No. 8, Appointment of Additional Alternate Director, adopted 16 January 2016 provided that Directors who cast the votes of five or more members, whether through election or assignment of votes, shall be entitled to appoint an additional Alternate Director. This decision has now been enshrined in the AIIB By-Laws, s 10 (b). The IMF Charter has a similar provision, added in 2008. Articles of Agreement of the International Monetary Fund, dated 27 December 1945, as amended through 2016, art XII, s 3 (e).

49 In 2017, six constituencies had two Alternate Directors; once the additional approved members finalize membership and join constituencies (more than 20 were pending as of January 2018), other constituencies would likely have more than five members and be eligible for a second Alternate Director.

50 AIIB Charter, Schedule B, paragraph 10. Founding Members are those of the 57 Charter signatories that complete membership by a deadline (currently, 31 December 2018). AIIB Charter, art 3-1 (b). In January 2018, there were 54 Founding Members.

51 AIIB Charter, art 27-1. The Board of Governors can take a decision to alter the non-residential basis, by a Super Majority vote (two-thirds of Governors representing not less than three-fourths of total voting power). There is a similar provision for the New Development Bank. Articles of Agreement of the New Development Bank (done 15 July 2014, entered into force 15 July 2015), art 12 (g).

52 AIIB By-Laws, s 10 (a) (quarterly meetings) and AIIB Charter, art 27-1 (calling meetings).

53 AIIB Charter, art 27-4 and AIIB Rules of Procedure of the Board of Directors, s 5 (d) and (e). A review of AIIB Board minutes shows several virtual meetings and many absence of objection decisions. See Board of Directors (Meetings and Minutes) <www.aiib.org> accessed 31 December 2017.

(sometimes twice a week at the World Bank Group, and usually twice a month at EBRD). Looking across the MDB world, however, the pattern is more varied. EIB has had a non-resident Board since its 1957 launch among six geographically-joined countries.[54] Other international financial institutions that have functioned for decades with non-resident Board mechanisms include the Council of Europe Development Bank, the Andean Development Bank (CAF), Caribbean Development Bank, Nordic Investment Bank, Islamic Development Bank, Black Sea Trade and Development Bank, the International Fund for Agricultural Development, and most recently, the European Stability Mechanism and the New Development Bank.[55]

The non-resident Board model for AIIB drew much attention during AIIB's establishment process, as many commentators made comparisons to the better-known resident Board structures.[56] Few noted the non-resident Boards in the international financial institutions listed above or commented upon the general practice in private companies. What is also less widely considered is the debate in MDB Charter negotiations until resident Boards were finally agreed. Famously, discussions on the IBRD and IMF Charters at Bretton Woods in 1944 featured a debate on residency, which was not settled in favor of resident boards until the inaugural meeting of the Boards of Governors in 1946. The debate included different views of Board functions, as well as cost:

> [John Maynard] Keynes reopened the argument made at Atlantic City and Bretton Woods, that the directors should be men holding positions with their own governments, that they would be needed only occasionally to decide issues since the main work would be carried on by the Managing Director [IMF] and President [IBRD] and their staffs. The US representatives again urged that the directors and alternates would have to be available at all times for quick decisions, and that they could

54 Belgium, France, Germany, Italy, Luxembourg and the Netherlands. The EIB Board of Directors continues to be non-resident, even as EIB members today are the 28 EU members.

55 In 2017, one rating agency, in assigning its AAA rating to AIIB, noted the non-resident Board and commented: "We do not see this as undermining its oversight or the decision making in any meaningful way." Standard and Poor's Research Update, "Asian Infrastructure Investment Bank Assigned 'AAA/A-1+' Rating: Outlook Stable" (18 July 2017).

56 The AIIB Charter not only provides explicitly for the Board of Directors to function "on a non-residential basis" in art 27-1, but also omits the references found in some other MDB charters to the Board functioning at the principal office of the Bank. See AfDB Charter, art 34-1; ADB Charter, art 32-1; EBRD Charter, art 28-1; IADB Charter, art VIII, s 3 (e); and IBRD Charter, art V, s 4 (e).

> develop the information and judgment needed for the business through board discussions. Keynes also argued that 48 salaries would impose an excessive burden, and that that number of men could be employed more usefully in their own countries, and since both Executive Directors and alternates were not needed all the time, they could divide work and salaries.[57]

The US prevailed, and the IMF and IBRD were established with full-time, resident boards. Decades later, the issue of Board residency featured again in the negotiations on the AfDB Charter (1963), ADB Charter (1965) and the EBRD Charter (1990), before the resident board option was agreed.[58] Governance reform discussions at the World Bank Group have also included proposals for a non-resident Board to clarify accountability and strengthen oversight, though no reforms in this area were adopted.[59]

3.2.3 Board Powers

Generally, the AIIB Board of Directors is responsible for the direction of the general operations of AIIB;[60] the Board of Directors also exercises the powers delegated by the Board of Governors, as noted above. In addition, the Board of Directors is assigned other decisions throughout the AIIB Charter, including: interpretation of the AIIB Charter; arrangements with other international organizations (noted earlier); and appointment of Vice Presidents on the

57 Bitterman (n 4) 87. John Maynard Keynes led the delegation for the United Kingdom. For the IBRD and IMF Charters, Atlantic City refers to the pre-negotiation meetings in June 1944 and Bretton Woods refers to the negotiations in July 1944.

58 The issue of Board residency had been debated in the preparation of AfDB, and the Directors did not actually become resident until 1970. Gardiner and Pickett (n 17) 23. For ADB, during the negotiations on the Charter, cost-consciousness led to at least one proposal for a part-time Board. Wilson (n 22) 27. For EBRD, a majority of the European Community countries originally favored a non-resident board in order to economize on cost, as in the EIB. Paul A Menkveld, *Origin and Role of the European Bank for Reconstruction and Development* (Graham & Trotman 1991) 78. Apparently, the United States argued in favor of a resident board at EBRD to have a powerful voice in day-to-day functions, so as to assure that the vague compromises in negotiations would be implemented. Weber (n 28) 19.

59 One proposal to transform the World Bank Board from its resident, full-time status can be seen in the Zedillo Commission Report. High-Level Commission on Modernization of World Bank Group Governance, *Repowering the World Bank for the 21st Century* (World Bank 2009) Recommendation #2 (known as the Zedillo Commission Report for its Chairman, Ernesto Zedillo).

60 AIIB Charter, art 26. The references to "operations of the Bank" in the AIIB Charter means all activities of the Bank, not just its investment operations. This terminology is common in other Charters.

recommendation of the President.[61] In addition, the AIIB Charter enumerates several specific powers of the Board of Directors—some similar to other MDBs, but several that set AIIB apart.[62]

- The AIIB Board of Directors *prepares the work of the Board of Governors*, such as preparing decisions for their approval. This function is regularly carried out by other MDB Boards of Directors.[63]
- The AIIB Board of Directors has the authority to *establish the policies of the Bank*; this is the practice elsewhere but it is not always explicit. Major operational and financial policies require Board approval by a majority representing not less than three-fourths of total voting power.[64] The Board may, under Bank policies, delegate authority to the President, and decisions on such delegation also require approval of the Board of Directors by the same majority. This higher majority for certain decisions by the Board of Directors on policy matters recalls a provision in the EBRD Charter, requiring a two-thirds majority for general policy decisions,[65] but is not found in other MDBs.
- The AIIB Board of Directors has the authority to *take decisions on the financing operations* of AIIB, and to delegate that authority to the President.[66] Delegation decisions require the same 75 percent majority as for delegation

61 Decisions of the Board of Directors specifically mentioned in the AIIB Charter include: setting policies on percentage of an entity's equity investment (art 14-3); the appointment of Vice-Presidents (art 30-1); arrangements with international organizations (art 35); and, perhaps most importantly, the power to issue interpretations of the AIIB Charter, with a final appeal to the Board of Governors (art 54).

62 Other MDB Charter provisions on the powers of the Board of Directors can be found in: AfDB Charter, art 32; ADB Charter, art 31; EBRD Charter, art 27; IADB Charter, art VIII, s 3 (a); and IBRD Charter, art V, s 4 (a). However, IADB and IBRD do not have enumerated powers in the same way.

63 AIIB Charter, art 26 (i). Only the later Charters spell this out as well. See AfDB Charter, art 32-1; ADB Charter, art 31 (i); and EBRD Charter, art 27 (i).

64 AIIB Charter, art 26 (ii).

65 EBRD Charter, art 29-3. The meaning of this provision at the time negotiations on the EBRD Charter were concluded is set out in the Chairman's Report on the Agreement Establishing the EBRD: "Delegates intended that, in the case of differing views on whether or not issues involved "general policy," decisions would be made by the Board on the basis of advice from the Legal Counsel. In general, decisions on individual operations would not involve such issues, but "general policy issues" would include, inter alia, the budget; the annual program of operations; borrowing policy, including borrowing limits; interest rate policy; exchange risk management policy; the drawing down of notes; underwriting policy and the organizational structure of the Bank."

66 AIIB Charter, art 26 (iii). AIIB operations include: making, co-financing, or participating in direct loans; equity investment; guarantees; use of Special Fund resources; technical assistance; and other types of financing determined by the Board of Governors under

under policies. Many MDBs Boards exercise this approval authority, but only later Charters make this explicit;[67] none provide for delegation. In practice, some MDB Boards of Directors decide on many operations on absence-of-objection or other streamlined procedure, without actual discussion. Delegation at AIIB offers the possibility of a clearer division of responsibilities between the Board of Directors and the President, so that the Board of Directors can hold the President accountable for approvals of operations, according to the terms of its delegation. Accountability is less clear-cut when the Board takes the final decision itself.[68] The importance of this possible delegation, however, can be seen in the higher majority required for its approval.

- The Board of Directors has the authority to *approve AIIB's strategy, annual plan, and budget*.[69] How the content of the strategy and annual plan will evolve over time is likely to be worked out between the Board and management. Other MDBs have similar planning documents without Charter-based requirements. The annual budgets are also approved by the Board of Directors and generally reported to the Board of Governors in other MDBs.[70]
- The AIIB Board of Directors is authorized to *appoint committees*, as in some other MDBs.[71] Three committees were set up in 2017: the Audit and Risk Committee, Budget and Human Resources Committee, and the Policy and Strategy Committee.

---

art 11-2. Delegation of this authority requires approval by a majority representing not less than three-fourths of total voting power.

67 See AfDB Charter, art 32-2; ADB Charter, art 31 (ii); and EBRD Charter, art 27 (ii).

68 The Zedillo Report recommended that the IBRD Board delegate responsibility for the approval of all operations to Management, in order to remove the co-managerial role and eliminate the conflict of interest, and to strengthen accountability. Moving operational approvals to the President could also enhance flexibility and efficiency, and free up Board time and staff resources. Zedillo (n 63) para 128.

69 AIIB Charter, art 26 (v).

70 ADB Charter, art 31 (iv); EBRD Charter, art 27 (iv); and IADB Charter, art VIII, s 3 (i). The requirement to submit the annual budget approved by the Board of Directors to the Board of Governors for information is found in the AIIB By-Laws, s 5 (c). The approval and reporting requirements are found in the By-Laws for IBRD (s 18 (b)) and the General Regulations for AfDB (s 8-1).

71 AIIB Charter, art 26 (vi). The Board's power to appoint committees is found in the Charters for IADB (art VIII, s 3 (i)) and IBRD (art V, s 4 (i)). It is not found in the Charters for AfDB, ADB and EBRD; rather, ADB By-Laws (s 12) and EBRD Rules of Procedure of the Board of Directors (s 11) contain a similar power. The AfDB Board of Directors does also have a committee structure similar to these others.

- Approving AIIB's balance sheet and statement of profit and loss is a reserved power of the Board of Governors. *Submitting the audited accounts* for each financial year for approval of the Board of Governors is the responsibility of the Board of Directors. This allocation of responsibilities is found in other MDBs as well, whether in the Charters as in AfDB, ADB and EBRD or in the By-Laws as in IBRD and IADB.[72]

3.2.4 Board Oversight Mechanism

In a provision unique to the AIIB Charter, the Board of Directors is expressly required to supervise the management and operation of AIIB on a regular basis.[73] This general function is understood to be part of the Board's overall responsibility in other MDB Boards of Directors, so that making it explicit for AIIB adds more definition to the Board's role in the non-residential context, where physical presence is not an element of oversight. Indeed, the AIIB Charter further requires the Board of Directors to establish an oversight mechanism for this purpose, "in line with principles of transparency, openness, independence and accountability." The AIIB Chief Negotiators' Report records what the negotiators expected in respect of the oversight mechanism:

> Representatives agreed that the oversight mechanism to be established by the Board of Directors under Article 26 (iv) would be designed in line with the principles of transparency, openness, independence and accountability, and would address such areas as audit, evaluation, fraud and corruption, project complaints and staff grievances, and reflect the Bank's character as a multilateral financial institution focused on infrastructure development.

The oversight bodies at other MDBs—such as evaluation, accountability, integrity and internal dispute resolution—have been added and refined over time, necessarily in a piecemeal fashion. Coming later, AIIB may be able to organize some of these functions in a coordinated way from the start. AIIB's oversight functions include: the anti-corruption and project complaint mechanisms under AIIB's Compliance, Effectiveness and Integrity Unit; the ethics rules for staff and Board; the internal and external audit offices and the Board's

72 AIIB Charter, art 26 (v). AfDB Charter, arts 29-2 (g) and 32-4; ADB Charter, arts 28-2 (viii) and 31 (iii); EBRD Charter, arts 24-2 (viii) and 27 (iii); IADB By-Laws s 10; and IBRD By-Laws, s 18.

73 AIIB Charter, art 26 (iv).

Audit and Risk Committee; and the staff dispute resolution process under the AIIB Staff Regulations.[74]

3.3 *President*

The AIIB President is required to be a national of a regional member country, as in AfDB and ADB.[75] The President is elected by the Board of Governors, by a Super Majority vote; some other MDBs also require a qualified majority vote for President, though a lower one.[76] The Super Majority requirement, including 75 percent of the total voting power, ensures that the person elected has very substantial support from the shareholders, while it also could allow one or a handful of shareholders to exercise a veto.

That said, there have been unbroken nationality traditions for the heads of IBRD (US), the IMF (European) and ADB (Japanese), even where there is no

74 Elements of the oversight mechanism can be seen in outline on the AIIB website <www.aiib.org> accessed 31 December 2017. For the anti-corruption function, see AIIB's Policy on Prohibited Practices (December 2016). For project complaints, a Complaints Handling Mechanism is under development. For ethics, see AIIB's Code of Conduct for Board Officials and Code of Conduct for Bank Personnel, approved by the Board of Governors at its Inaugural Meeting in January 2016. For audit, see the Audit and Risk Committee of the Board of Directors, which includes two external members. For staff dispute mechanisms, see AIIB Staff Regulations (November 2016). External inputs and scrutiny are also provided by AIIB's International Advisory Panel, a group of worldwide experts that advises the President, and by the availability of AIIB information under its Public Information Interim Policy.

75 AIIB Charter, art 29-1. AfDB Charter, art 36-1 and ADB Charter, art 34-1.

76 AIIB Charter, art 29-1. A Super Majority vote requires two-thirds of Governors with three-fourths of total voting power. This is higher than the majority votes required for election of the President at AfDB, ADB, EBRD, IADB and IBRD. AfDB Charter, art 36-1 and IADB Charter, art VIII, s 5 (a) (a majority of total voting power including a majority of total regional voting power); ADB Charter, art 34-1 and EBRD Charter, art 30-1 (a majority of Governors with a majority of total voting power).

Originally, the AfDB President was elected by the Board of Directors; this was changed to election by the Board of Governors by amendment of the AfDB Charter in 1979. AfDB Board of Governors' Resolution 05-79, *Concerning the Amendments of the Agreement Establishing the African Development Bank to Enable Non-African Countries to Become Members Thereof*, approved May 17, 1979, entered into force May 7, 1982, Annex, paragraphs 12 and 16.

In IBRD, the selection of the President is decided by the Executive Directors (the Board of Directors), not the Board of Governors, and by a simple majority. IBRD Charter, art V, s 5 (a). Until 2012, the selection was invariably announced as unanimous. In 2012, the announcement noted that the process had yielded multiple nominees, and that the final nominees received support from different member countries. "World Bank's Executive Directors Select Dr. Jim Yong Kim 12th President of the World Bank Group," World Bank Press Release, 16 April 2012.

veto at play.[77] To balance this history of nationality traditions, the AIIB Charter formally includes an open, transparent and merit-based selection process, a requirement that has been mentioned in other MDBs but not included in their Charters.[78] The AIIB Charter similarly provides for Vice-Presidents to be selected on the basis of an open, transparent and merit-based process; Vice-Presidents are appointed by the Board of Directors on the recommendation of the President,[79] as in ADB, EBRD and IADB.[80] In addition, there is a two-term

77 The role of informal political arrangements regarding nationality of senior appointments in international financial institutions is well-documented. See, eg, Jacob Katz Cogan, "Representation and Power in International Organization: The Operational Constitution and its Critics," [2009] 103 AJIL 209, 227–229.

78 AIIB Charter, art 29-1. At IBRD, this process requirement can be seen in the Report on the Selection Process of the President, adopted by the IBRD Executive Directors, in response to Development Committee communiques calling for an open, merit-based and transparent selection process. Development Committee (formally known as the Joint Ministerial Committee of the Boards of Governors of the World Bank and International Monetary Fund on the Transfer of Real Resources to Developing Countries), *Strengthening Governance and Accountability: Shareholder Stewardship and Oversight, Background Document* (DC2011-0006, 4 April 2011) Annex 2.

Similarly, the IMF process for the selection of the Managing Director has referred to an open, merit-based and transparent selection process following evolving reforms dating back to 2007. See, for example, Communiqué of the International Monetary and Financial Committee of the Board of Governors of the International Monetary Fund, 4 October 2009, para 5.

79 AIIB Charter, art 30-1. As of December 2017, AIIB has 5 Vice-Presidents (Corporate Secretary, Chief Financial Officer, Chief Investment Officer, Policy & Strategy, and Chief Administration Officer). AIIB Senior Management also includes the General Counsel and Chief Risk Officer, appointed by the President. See AIIB, *Connecting Asia for the future, Annual Report and Accounts 2016* (AIIB 2017) 11.

80 ADB Charter, 35-1 and EBRD Charter, art 31-1.

For IADB, the Executive Vice President and other Vice Presidents are also appointed by the Board of Directors on the recommendation of the President. IADB Charter, art VIII, s 5 (b) and (c).

IBRD Charter, art V, s 5 does not refer to Vice-Presidents but only to officers and staff, all appointed by the President.

AfDB Charter, art 37-2 empowers the President to appoint Vice-Presidents, "provided that he shall act in consultation with the Board of Directors in the exercise of his powers of appointment and release of Vice-Presidents." Originally, AfDB Vice-Presidents were also appointed by the Board of Directors on the recommendation of the President; the AfDB Charter was amended to the language quoted by AfDB Board of Governors' Resolution B/BG/97/05, *Concerning Measures to Enhance Governance of the African Development Bank and Amending the Agreement Establishing the Bank*, adopted 29 May 1997, entered into force 2 May 1998, para 5.

limit for the AIIB President (each term is five years).[81] AIIB's two-term limit is also found in AfDB and at IADB.[82]

The *powers of the President* under the AIIB Charter flow from the dual role as the chief executive of AIIB and as Chairman of the Board of Directors. As the Bank's chief executive, the President is "chief of the staff of the Bank" and conducts, under the direction of the Board of Directors, the current business of AIIB.[83] Additional specific powers of the President include the responsibility for the organization, appointment and dismissal of officers and staff, in accordance with regulations adopted by the Board of Directors,[84] and the preparation of the administrative budget to be presented to the Board of Directors for approval.[85] As previously noted, the Board of Directors may also delegate authority to the President, including under Bank policies and for decisions on operations.[86]

4 AIIB Decision-making

4.1 *Voting Power*

AIIB follows an MDB practice of weighted voting, rather than equal votes for each member. The total voting power of each AIIB member consists of the sum of its share votes, basic votes and, in the case of a Founding Member, its Founding Member votes.[87]

- *Share votes*. Share votes are equal to one vote for each share of stock held by a member. Larger shareholders consequently hold more share votes, and, as a result, rules for the allocation of capital subscriptions have an impact on relative voting power. Share votes are common in the MDBs, and underpin

81 AIIB Charter, art 29-2. The President's term is five years in AfDB (art 36-1), ADB (art 34-2) and IADB (art VIII, s 5 (a)) and four years at EBRD (art 30-1). The President's initial term in IBRD is also five years, and successive terms may be up to five years. IBRD By-Laws, s 13 (c).

82 AfDB Charter, art 36-1. For IADB, see Regulations for the Election of the President (s 2 (c)): "The Governors state their firm will that no President shall hold office for more than two consecutive terms of five years."

83 AIIB Charter, art 29-4. By virtue of this clause, the President is also the legal representative of AIIB.

84 AIIB Charter, art 30-2.

85 AIIB By-Laws, s 5 (c).

86 AIIB Charter, art 26.

87 AIIB Charter, art 28-1.

the weighted voting system that differentiates them from many other international organizations.[88]

- *Basic votes*. Basic votes are the same for each member, and are a common but not universal feature in MDBs. Basic votes provide an element of voting power that recognizes the equality of members, in contrast to the differentiated economic weight of members usually reflected in share votes. For AIIB, the exact number of basic votes is recalculated each time voting power is determined, to meet the requirement that the total number of basic votes allocated to all members must always equal 12 percent of total votes. The number of basic votes assigned to each member changes with changes in the number of share votes and Founding Member votes, and in the number of members. Basic votes have the effect of increasing the relative voting power of smaller shareholders (above their shareholding percentage) while reducing the relative voting power of larger shareholders (below their shareholding percentage). In AIIB (and ADB and IBRD), basic votes are set as a percentage, because setting basic votes as a fixed number of votes specified in the Charter in other cases has meant that a member's basic votes stayed the same while share votes increased with subscriptions to stock. Using a fixed number gradually reduced the weight and benefit of basic votes.[89]
- *Founding Member votes*. Founding Member votes are fixed at 600 votes per member. Founding Member votes are assigned to those Signatories who

88 See AfDB Charter, art 35 (share votes and 625 basic votes); ADB Charter, art 33 (share votes and 20 percent basic votes); EBRD Charter, art 29 (share votes only); IADB Charter, art VIII, s 4 (share votes and 135 basic votes); and IBRD Charter, art V, s 3 (share votes and 5.55 percent basic votes).

89 When the concept of basic votes was introduced in IBRD in 1945, each member had 250 votes (basic votes) plus one vote for each share of stock held (share votes). (IBRD Charter, art V, s 3 (a), prior to its amendment in 2012.) Originally, IBRD basic votes represented about 11 percent of total voting power (basic votes plus share votes). Over time, each member's basic votes remained at the fixed number, while the overall number of share votes increased with each increase in IBRD capital and shares held by members. As a result, IBRD basic votes represented only 2.86 percent of total voting power when voice reform discussions were underway in the mid-2000s. As part of those reforms, the IBRD Charter was amended to set basic votes as a percentage of total votes, equal to 5.55 percent of total votes, so that the proportion of basic votes would be maintained when share votes increase. In ADB, basic votes have been at a percentage of total votes (20 percent) since the beginning; a fixed number of basic votes was set in the original Charters for AfDB (625) and IADB (135), now less than 1 percent of total voting power in each. See n 92 for Charter references.

become Founding Members by completing membership requirements before the deadline set in the AIIB Charter.[90]
- Under the original allocations in Schedule A of the AIIB Charter, the weight of all Founding Member votes in total AIIB voting power would have been around 3 percent. Combined with the weight of total basic votes (12 percent), that would mean that votes not tied to shareholding would account for about 15 percent, and votes tied to shareholding would weigh about 85 percent. This compares with an 80 percent weight for share votes in ADB (20 percent basic votes) and a 94.5 percent weight for share votes in IBRD (5.5 percent basic votes); in AfDB and IADB, share votes account for over 99 percent of voting power, and in EBRD, share votes are 100 percent of voting power (no basic votes).

4.2 *Qualified Majorities*

In general, decisions by the AIIB Board of Governors and the Board of Directors require a majority of votes cast.[91] For the Board of Governors, there are two types of higher majority votes (qualified majorities): a *Super Majority vote* requires an affirmative vote of two-thirds of the total number of Governors, representing not less than three-fourths of the total voting power of the members; and a *Special Majority vote* requires an affirmative vote of a majority of the total number of Governors, representing not less than a majority of the total voting power.[92] Super Majority decisions are usually key institutional matters, and include: capital increases; individual members subscription increases, modifying the regional shareholding percentage; provision of assistance to non-members; increase in the lending limit; allocation of net income to "other purposes"; changes in the Board of Directors; modifying the non-resident basis for the Board of Directors; election of the President; and amendment of the Charter.[93] Other institutionally important decisions require a Special Majority

---

90 AIIB art 3-1 (b). As of January 2018, AIIB had 54 Founding Members and the deadline for completion of membership requirements by the remaining three Signatories under art 58-1 had been extended to 31 December 2018.

91 AIIB Charter, art 28-2 (i) and 28-3 (ii).

92 AIIB Charter, art 28-2 (ii) and (iii).

93 AIIB Charter, art 4-3 (increase in capital), art 5-3 (increase of a subscription of a member), art 5-2 and 5-3 (modifying the percentage of capital stock held by regional members), art 11-1 (b) (provision of assistance to non-members); art 12-1 (increase in the lending limit), art 18-1 (allocation of net income to other purposes), art 25-2 (changes in the size or composition of the Board of Directors), art 27-1 (modifying the non-resident basis for the Board of Directors), art 29-1 and 29-2 (election of the President; removal or suspension from office), art 38 (suspension or restoration of membership), art 41 (termination of operations), art 43-1 (ii)(distribution of assets), and art 53-1(amendment of the Charter).

vote, including: admission of members; approval of other types of financing; and establishment of subsidiaries.[94]

Qualified majorities for Governors' decisions have been streamlined in the AIIB Charter, into these two clearly defined categories, Super Majority and Special Majority. Other MDBs also have qualified majorities for many similar decisions, and in most cases, the percentage of total voting power required is 75 percent.[95] The most notable exceptions are at IBRD (Charter amendment requires 85 percent and changing the number of Executive Directors requires 80 percent),[96] and at EBRD (Charter amendments require an 80 percent majority and certain decisions on country access to its resources require an 85 percent majority).[97] In IADB and AfDB, some decisions require separate qualified majorities for regional and non-regional members.[98]

Amendments of the AIIB Charter require a Super Majority vote, except that unanimity is required to amend: (i) each member's right to withdraw from the Bank; (ii) the limitations on liability of members; and (iii) the pre-emptive rights pertaining to purchase of capital stock. AIIB Charter, art 53-1 and 53-2. Other MDBs have similar unanimity requirements. AfDB Charter, art 60-3; ADB Charter, art 59-2; EBRD Charter, art 56-2 (adds to the list amendments to its purpose and functions); IADB Charter, art XII (b) (slightly different); and IBRD Charter, art VIII (b).

94 AIIB Charter, art 3-2 (admission of members), art 7-1 (issuance of non-par stock), art 11-2(vi) (approval of other types of financing), art 16-8 (establishment of subsidiaries) and art 58-1 (extension of the deadline for deposit of instruments of ratification).

95 For a detailed comparison of qualified majorities, see Lichtenstein (n *), Table 7.4.

96 IBRD Charter, art V, s 4 (b) (Governors representing four-fifths majority of total voting power to increase the number of Executive Directors) and art VIII (a) (three-fifths of members having 85 percent of total voting power to amend the Charter).

97 EBRD Charter, art 56-1 for Charter amendments (three-fourths of members, including at least two Central and Eastern European countries, holding four-fifths of total voting power). The EBRD majority for access decisions is three-fourths of the Governors representing 85 percent of the total voting power. EBRD Charter, art 8-4 (iii).

98 Specific regional majorities were introduced with the advent of non-regional membership in IADB, and later in AfDB. These include:
- capital increases (not in AfDB; IADB Charter, art II, s 2(e));
- changes in composition of the Board of Directors, with a special regional majority for changes in regional rules (AfDB Charter, art 33-1; IADB Charter, art VIII, s 3(b)(ii));
- election of the President (AfDB Charter, art 36; IADB Charter, art VIII, s 5 (a));
- quorum for the Board of Governors and for the Board of Directors (AfDB Charter, arts 31-2 and 34-2, later amended to delete the regional majority and require 70 percent of total voting power; IADB Charter, art VIII, ss 2 (e) and 3 (f));
- suspension of membership (AfDB Charter, art 44, later amended to delete the regional majority and require 70% of total voting power; IADB Charter, art IX, s 2—depending on whether the member is regional or non-regional);
- termination and distribution of assets (AfDB Charter, art 47-1, later amended to delete the regional majority and require 70 percent of total voting power and art 49-1 (ii), later amended to delete any qualified majority; IADB art X, ss 2 and 4 (a)); and
- amendment (AfDB Charter, art 60-1; IADB Charter, art XII (a)).

For the AIIB Board of Directors, there are three qualified majority decisions (requiring 75 percent of total voting power), as already discussed: (i) approval of major operational and financial policies; (ii) delegation of authority to the President under Bank policies; and (iii) delegation of authority to take decisions on operations.[99] Boards of Directors in other MDBs generally operate without formal votes, although voting power plays a role in reaching agreement. In AIIB, this mechanism can be seen in the Board's Rules of Procedure, which follows other precedents in providing that the Chairman shall ordinarily ascertain the sense of the meeting without a formal vote, although a Director may require that his views be recorded or that a formal vote be taken.[100] While actual voting is rare, the voting power represented by each Director would be taken into account in ascertaining the sense of the meeting as to whether a majority of voting power would be in favor of the decision taken.

Two additional aspects of decision-making are often influential. First, voting power is heavily dependent on shareholding in AIIB as elsewhere, as noted above. Shareholding in turn depends on the rules for allocation of capital subscriptions. For AIIB, the basic principle and parameters have been established in the AIIB Chief Negotiators' Report as the relative share in the global economy.[101] Using economic strength to guide shareholding reflects the essential role of capital subscriptions in the MDB financial structure, as the capital market finance raised by the MDB relies in large part on the financial strength of the callable capital commitments of the MDB shareholders.[102] Secondly, AIIB follows other regional MDBs in maintaining a minimum regional shareholding (75 percent).[103] Both of these factors play a role when considering the possibility of veto power, which is another dimension of MDB governance.

99 AIIB Charter, art 26 (ii) and (iii). EBRD requires a two-thirds' majority for policy decisions of the Board of Directors. See n 69 for more details.

100 AIIB Rules of Procedure of the Board of Directors, s 5 (a). See AFDB Rules of Procedure of the Board of Directors, s 8-1; ADB Rules of Procedure of the Board of Directors, s 5 (a); EBRD Rules of Procedure of the Board of Directors, s 5 (a); IADB Regulations of the Board of Executive Directors, Part III, s 3 (a); and IBRD Rules of Procedure for Meeting of the Executive Directors, s 4.

101 The AIIB Chief Negotiators' Report states, as to allocation of capital: "Representatives noted that the basic parameter for allocation of capital stock to members would be the relative share of the global economy of members within the regional and non-regional groupings, respectively. Members' shares of the global economy would be measured by reference to Gross Domestic Product (GDP), with the understanding that GDP share would be indicative only for non-regional members."

102 Lichtenstein (n *), paras 6.03-6.05.

103 AIIB Charter, art 5-2 and 5-3.

5 Conclusions

From the preceding discussions, we can see that AIIB has maintained a basic MDB governance model while making its own modifications, as others have before. Among these adaptations, AIIB's Board of Governors has additional powers to allow AIIB to respond to changes over time, without forcing AIIB to fit new initiatives within unchangeable rules, provided there is sufficient consensus among the members.[104] AIIB's Board of Directors follows the practice of a few MDBs and is non-resident, with clearly provided powers to approve policy and operations, delegate authority and supervise management; its oversight powers are highlighted. AIIB's President has traditional powers with the express possibility of delegated authority, and is limited to two terms. The selection of the President and Vice-Presidents through an open, transparent and merit-based process sets a new legal standard. The desirability of a greater voice for regional and smaller members is recognized by adding a second Alternate Director for larger Board constituencies, rotation privileges for Founding Members and the 12 percent weight for basic votes.

In terms of legal structure, the interplay of the legal provisions in the AIIB Charter and the parties' agreements recorded in the Chief Negotiators' Report gives AIIB a firm basis for adjusting to changes in the future. By providing specifics on such matters as GDP as the basic parameter for capital allocation, the Chief Negotiators' Report keeps today's details clear and transparent without enshrining them in the AIIB Charter where they may someday become outdated. Should Charter amendment become necessary, the AIIB Charter follows a model that requires a high-majority Board of Governors decision without mandating an additional approval process under each member's domestic procedures.

In sum, AIIB's governance features both MDB heritage and innovation, as AIIB takes its place in the family of MDBs.

---

104 Examples of flexible provisions in the AIIB Charter include variation in the definition of the Asia region (art 1-2), modification of the 75 percent regional shareholding requirement (art 5-2 and 5-3), financing in non-member territory (art 11-1 (b)), introduction of new types of financing (art 11-2 (vi)), increase in the lending limit (art 12-1) and changing the non-resident status of the Board of Directors (art 27-1).

CHAPTER 6

The Evolving Jurisprudence of the International Administrative Tribunals: Convergence or Divergence?

*Joan S. Powers**

Abstract

Between the late 1940s and 1980, there were two principal international administrative tribunals in operation—the United Nations Administrative Tribunal and the Administrative Tribunal of the International Labor Organisation. Observers at the time noted that certain principles of international administrative law had become well-established in the jurisprudence of these tribunals, and that their judgments reflected a commonality in approach. However, since 1980, a number of new administrative tribunals have been established by various international organizations, including each of the multilateral development banks and other international financial institutions, and the UN has changed to a two-tier judicial system. Now, with over 15 administrative tribunals in operation, can it still be said that there is a general harmonization amongst the tribunals? Or have the tribunals gone in different directions in analyzing the legal framework for the employment relationship within an international organization? This presentation will examine these questions with respect to selected issues considered by administrative tribunals.

1 Introduction

One thing that the diverse array of international and regional intergovernmental organizations have in common is that they provide staff with recourse to an independent administrative tribunal as part of their internal justice system. These tribunals are authorized to adjudicate employment disputes and render final and binding judgments, including remedial measures.

* Joan Powers, formerly Assistant General Counsel of the International Monetary Fund, is currently a consultant to various international organizations on employment-related issues and internal dispute resolution. She may be contacted at: joanspowers@yahoo.com.

In the years between the late 1940s and 1980, there were essentially two major international administrative tribunals in operation—the United Nations Administrative Tribunal (UNAT) serving the UN family of organizations, and the Administrative Tribunal of the International Labor Organisation (ILOAT) serving the ILO and other, mainly European-based, organizations that had accepted its jurisdiction. Contemporary observers at the time spoke of a "common system of law" between the international organizations,[1] and noted that the tribunals applied the same general principles of law and also quoted each other's judgments, cautioning that "the consequences would be very awkward if it were otherwise".[2]

Since 1980, a number of new international administrative tribunals have been established, and there are now over 15 different administrative tribunals in existence.[3] Given these developments, can it still be said that their respective case law and the principles they apply are consistent? Or have the various tribunals gone in different directions, with divergent views on the principles underlying the employment relationship in international organizations? This is a particularly important issue for newly established organizations like the Asian Infrastructure Investment Bank, which have to consider how best to structure their internal justice system and decide what would be the optimal approach.

2 Background

With respect to the administrative tribunals in operation prior to 1980, the ILOAT is the oldest administrative tribunal, having succeeded to the

1 As of the 1960s, scholars such as Prof. Michael Barton Akehurst referred to the "theory of a common system of law" between the international organizations, which was reflected in the tribunals' jurisprudence. M B Akehurst, *The Law Governing Employment in International Organisations* (CUP 1967) 262.

2 The source of these general principles is, however, somewhat murky. According to one leading commentator, "[t]here is very little evidence of how general principles are identified in the judgments of these tribunals, though there are frequent references to such principles, and such principles are in fact often applied." C F Amerasinghe, *The Law of the International Civil Service*, vol I (2nd edn, Clarendon Press 1994) 158, n 46. *See generally* Renuka Dhinakaran, "Law of the International Civil Service: A Venture into Legal Theory" (2011) 8 International Organizations Law Review 137, 137.

3 AfDBAT; ADBAT; BISAT; CoE AT; EBRDAT; EUMETSAT Appeals Board; ESA Appeals Board; ESMAT; IDBAT; ILOAT; IMFAT; NATO AT; OASAT; OECDAT; UNAppT; WBAT. The European Union Civil Service Tribunal was dissolved in 2016.

Administrative Tribunal of the League of Nations in the late 1940s.[4] According to the ILOAT's website, it is currently open to more than 58,000 international civil servants who are current or former officials of 62 international organizations. The ILOAT has issued over 3,800 judgments since 1947.

The UNAT was established in 1950, and its jurisdiction was extended to various UN specialized agencies and other organizations that accepted its jurisdiction.[5] Over the next 30 years, a few other international agencies established their own tribunals, including the Organization for Economic Cooperation and Development (1950), the Council of Europe (1965) and the Organization of American States in 1971. The European Space Agency established its own Appeals Board in the 1970s.

But the largest number of cases during this period, and the relevant jurisprudence, arose mainly at the UNAT and the ILOAT. International law scholars observed that these tribunals recognized and applied general principles of international civil service law, although there was no formal basis for doing so.[6]

The convergence between the various tribunals was noted not only by scholars but also by the tribunals themselves. The World Bank Administrative Tribunal (WBAT), in its very first decision, the landmark *de Merode* case (1981),[7] mentioned the tendency towards a certain *rapprochement* in the solutions provided by other administrative tribunals in comparable situations. Similarly,

4 The first administrative tribunal was established in 1927 by the League of Nations. When the League was dissolved in 1946, the League Tribunal was reconstituted, with minor modifications, by the International Labour Organisation and became the ILOAT. In 1949, the ILOAT statute was amended to enable other international intergovernmental organizations to use the tribunal, and a number of organizations headquartered in Europe have accepted its jurisdiction.

5 The International Civil Aviation Organization (ICAO), the International Court of Justice (ICJ), the International Maritime Organization (IMO), the International Seabed Authority (ISA), the World Meteorological Organization (WMO), and the International Tribunal for the Law of the Sea (ITLOS) all accepted the jurisdiction of the UNAT.

6 Cf Akehurst (n 1) 262–263. According to Prof. Akehurst, "[i]nternational administrative tribunals behave *as if* the internal laws of different organizations formed part of a single system of law"; he observed that the "[t]ribunals seem to regard unwritten sources as constituting a sort of international administrative law, of universal application, which supplements the internal law peculiar to each organization." He concluded that "general principles of law constitute a source of law common to those internal laws and to general international law, so that general international law may rely on some of the precedents established by international ATs, and vice versa."

7 *De Merode and Others v IBRD*, WBAT Decision no 1 (1981), para 28, stating that the Tribunal was "free to take note of solutions worked out in sufficiently comparable conditions by other administrative tribunals, particularly those of the United Nations family," so that it can "take account both of the diversity of international organizations and the special character of the Bank without neglecting the tendency towards a certain *rapprochement*."

Lindsey (1992), the first decision of the Asian Development Bank Administrative Tribunal (ADBAT), spoke of "a large measure of 'common' law of international organizations to which, according to the circumstances, the Tribunal will give due weight."[8]

Others, however, were not so sanguine.[9] As early as 1973, concerns were expressed about the risks of conflicting jurisprudence if there were multiple tribunals serving international organizations. Judge Manfred Lachs of the International Court of Justice wrote at length about this, and urged the creation of a single tribunal for all international organizations. He was of the view that "the problem of uniformity [had] become of great importance."[10] He felt that the best solution would be to merge the UNAT and the ILOAT into a single administrative tribunal, and urged this to the United Nations, which took up the issue. The feasibility of such a merger was studied in detail by both organizations,[11] but, in Judge Lachs's words, "difficulties of a bureaucratic nature surfaced …"

By 1988, Judge Lachs wrote, rather despondently: "it is surely regrettable that notwithstanding the warning I gave 15 years ago, so little progress has been made." He "remained convinced that the goal of creating one Administrative Tribunal for all International Organizations [was] both realistic and desirable, in view of the difficulties and inequities arising out of the existing state of affairs."[12]

Not only did Judge Lachs's hopes for a single, world-wide tribunal never materialize, but also, starting around 1980, new administrative tribunals were

---

8 *Lindsey v ADB*, ADBAT Decision no 1 (1992), para 4. *Lindsey* also made reference to the role and importance of precedent and referred to "the staff practices of international organizations generally, including the decisions of international administrative tribunals dealing with comparable situations. There is, in this sphere, a large measure of 'common' law of international organizations to which, according to the circumstances, the Tribunal will give due weight."

9 C Wilfred Jenks, *The Proper Law of International Organisations* (Oceana Publications 1962) 41. In his 1962 study, Wilfred Jenks favored the creation of a single "World Administrative Tribunal" (his term) to serve all or most of the international organizations. But he also recognized that "the existence of more than one tribunal will, at the present stage of development, prove to be a service rather than a disservice to the development of a satisfactory body of international administrative law."

10 Manfred Lachs, "The Judiciary and the International Civil Service," (1988) Law of Nations, Law of International Organizations, World's Economic Law, Liber Amirocorum honouring Ignaz Seidl-Hohenveldern 301, 307

11 Report of the Secretary-General, "Feasibility of Establishing a Single Administrative Tribunal" (1984) UN Doc A/C.5/39/7

12 *See* Lachs (n 10) 313

created by each of the international financial institutions.[13] NATO transformed its Appeals Board into an administrative tribunal in 2013, and the recently-created European Stability Mechanism established its own administrative tribunal in 2014.

In addition to these new tribunals, the UN introduced major reforms in its internal justice system in 2009. The UNAT was abolished and replaced by a two-tiered justice system,[14] consisting of three Dispute Tribunals that would hear cases in the first instance and one Appeals Tribunal (UNAppT) to conduct an appellate-style review, as the final and binding stage. Notably, both staff members and the Secretary-General may appeal decisions of the Dispute Tribunals to the Appeals Tribunal. The UNAppT has also made clear that the case law of the former UNAT is not necessarily binding on it.[15]

There are now over 15 international administrative tribunals serving either multiple or single organizations under their respective statutes. Collectively, these tribunals have issued well over 7,500 judgments since the late 1940s.

A 2004 report of the International Law Association emphasized the need for consistency and coherence in case law, and the importance of uniform interpretation of identical or similar provisions. The report recommended a common review mechanism over tribunal judgments "in order to achieve the greatest possible consistency of jurisprudence in international administrative law."[16] The report also recommended that the tribunals be encouraged to take account of each other's decisions in efforts to reduce the risk of incompatible case law.

---

13 During the next 25 years, administrative tribunals were established by each of the major international financial institutions: World Bank Group (1980), Inter-American Development Bank (1981), Bank for International Settlements (1987), Asian Development Bank (1991), International Monetary Fund (1992), African Development Bank (1997), and European Bank for Reconstruction and Development (2002).

14 Between its establishment in 1950 and its abolition in 2009, the UNAT issued 1,495 judgments. The UNAppT has issued nearly 800 judgments since 2010.

15 *Obdeijn v Secretary-General of the United Nations*, Judgment no 2012-UNAT-201, para 30. The UNAppT deliberately departed from the jurisprudence of the UNAT, noting that "the jurisprudence of the former Administrative Tribunal, though of persuasive value, cannot be a binding precedent for the new Tribunals to follow." It thus reached the opposite conclusion as the UNAT as to whether the Administration was obligated to provide reasons for the non-renewal of a staff member's contract, and the Administration's refusal to do so shifted the burden of proof from the staff member to the organization.

16 "Accountability of International Organizations: Final Report' in International Law Association Report of the Seventy-first Conference" (Berlin 2004) (International Law Association, London 2004), 48. "International administrative tribunals should be encouraged to take account of each other's decisions in order to reduce the risk of incompatible case law."

Is this happening? Do the tribunals take note of each other's jurisprudence, or are they operating in isolation—and even in divergent ways?

The practice of the tribunals in terms of citing cases from other tribunals varies widely. It is quite uncommon for the ILOAT or the former UNAT to cite other tribunals, perhaps because they each have their own extensive jurisprudence to draw on.[17]

This contrasts with the practice of the tribunals of the World Bank, IMF and ADB, which do occasionally cite cases from other tribunals. In one commentator's view, "[w]hile this is no indication that one tribunal regards the decisions of other tribunals as binding, it is evidence ... that there may be certain general principles of law applicable within the internal legal systems of international organizations pertaining to the employment relationship which extend beyond the limits of the internal system of any one organization."[18]

In recognition of this, Article III of the IMFAT Statute calls upon the Tribunal to adhere to and apply generally recognized principles for judicial review of administrative acts. At the time the IMFAT was established, it was recognized that these principles had already been extensively elaborated in the case law of the international administrative tribunals, particularly with respect to review of decisions taken under discretionary authority.[19] So the objective of harmonization was made part of the IMFAT's statutory mandate.

17 A Triblex search indicates that ILOAT has never cited a judgment of the WBAT, IMFAT or ADBAT (even though an ADBAT case was apparently invoked by one complainant), and has only referred to the UNAT on three occasions. The UNAppT has occasionally cited with approval ILOAT rulings concerning the standard of judicial review of classification decisions, but this is infrequent. In Fuentes, it stated that "we note and endorse, in principle, the jurisprudence of the Administrative Tribunal of the International Labour Organization (ILOAT)." *Fuentes v Secretary-General of the United Nations*, Judgment no 2010-UNAT-105, para 26.

18 CF Amerasinghe (n 2) 18

19 Commentary on the Statute of the Administrative Tribunal of the International Monetary Fund, commentary on Article III <https://www.imf.org/external/imfat/report.htm#commentary_III> accessed 23 November 2017. Nevertheless, the official commentary on the Statute made clear that the reference to general principles should not be construed so as to derogate from the IMF's Articles of Agreement or the Statute. According to the official commentary, "the reference [in Art III] to general principles is not intended to introduce concepts that are inapplicable to, or inappropriate for, the Fund. With respect to the concern that the application of the principles enunciated by other administrative tribunals may have the unintended result of interfering with the responsibilities entrusted to the Executive Board, it should be noted that, to the extent that a tribunal's decision is dependent on the particular law of the organization in question (such as the precise language of a staff regulation), the decision would be regarded as specific to the organization in question and not part of the general principles of international administrative law."

What about the consistency of the rulings issued by these 15+ tribunals—can it still be said that there still a "common law" as regards the international civil service and "general" principles regarding the law of the international civil service?

This is a huge question that deserves a more comprehensive treatment, but it may be instructive to examine a few types of employment-related decisions that are regularly reviewed by administrative tribunals: (i) abolition of position; (ii) disciplinary decisions; and (iii) review of rules of general applicability, or so-called "regulatory decisions."

3 Abolition of Position

One area of convergence, in which the tribunals have remained largely in sync, is in the review of decisions terminating a staff member's employment due to redundancy or abolition of position. Each tribunal has recognized the discretionary nature of such decisions, as well as the limitations on that discretion.[20] The relevant issues are fairly clear and consistent across the tribunals:

- Was there a valid business rationale for making the incumbent redundant (e.g., outsourcing, restructuring, new skills required) and not simply a pretext for discrimination or dealing with substandard performance?
- Were the applicable procedures followed, e.g., notice to affected staff?
- Did the organization make sufficient efforts to find alternative positions for staff who would otherwise lose their jobs?[21]

---

20 E.g., *K v ITER Organization*, ILOAT Judgment no 3770 (2017), Consideration 7: "According to firm precedent, a decision concerning the restructuring of an international organization's services, which leads to the abolition of a post, may be taken at the discretion of its executive head and is subject to only limited review by the Tribunal. The latter must therefore confine itself to ascertaining whether the decision was taken in accordance with the rules on competence, form or procedure, whether it involves a mistake of fact or of law, whether it constituted abuse of authority, whether it failed to take account of material facts, or whether it draws clearly mistaken conclusions from the evidence. The Tribunal may not, however, supplant an organization's view with its own [citations omitted]. Nevertheless, any decision to abolish a post must be based on objective grounds and its purpose may never be to remove a member of staff regarded as unwanted. Disguising such purposes as a restructuring measure would constitute abuse of authority." *See also González Flavell v IBRD*, WBAT Decision no 553 (2017); *Pacheco v Secretary-General of the United Nations*, Judgment no 2013-UNAT-281, para 22.

21 E.g., *P v WHO*, ILOAT Judgment no 3755 (2017); *DI v IBRD*, WBAT Decision no 533 (2016), para 126; *Sachdev v IMF*, IMFAT Judgment no 2012-1 (observing that "the obligation of the organization to assist a redundant staff member in identifying opportunities for

In these types of cases, there is clearly a commonality of approach between the various tribunals, and the principles and standards they have applied are now typically reflected in the staff rules on redundancy (e.g., the organization's obligation of job search assistance to a staff member whose position is abolished), so there is considerable consistency between the organizations' internal legal systems on this as well.

4 Review of Disciplinary Decisions

Again, in general terms, the same analytical framework seems to be widely accepted across the administrative tribunals. Basically, there are three possible grounds for legal challenges to disciplinary sanctions imposed on a staff member who has committed misconduct:

(i) Have the facts been established and do they amount to misconduct under the organization's standards of conduct?

(ii) Was the sanction provided for in the staff rules and not disproportionate to the offense?

(iii) Did the organization follow proper procedures and respect due process?

Although the principles cited by the tribunals in these cases are broadly consistent, they may be applied somewhat differently. This may be due to the fact that the concept of "due process" is anything but self-evident, and by its nature will be very fact-specific in practice. So the tribunals have reached different conclusions even within their *own* jurisprudence as to whether staff members who were investigated for misconduct were given adequate due process, including the opportunity to defend themselves (the adequacy of the notice they received; whether the length of time taken for the investigation and disciplinary process was excessive,[22] etc.).

---

reassignment, which is given expression in the Fund's internal law ..., is supported by generally recognized principles of international administrative law ...").

22 *Compare S.G. G. v WIPO*, ILOAT Judgment no 2698 (2008) (organization did not conduct the investigation with "all due speed," and such unjustified delay warranted moral damages to complainant) *with S. (no 8) v IAEA*, ILOAT Judgment no 3831 (2017), Consideration 27 (holding that a 25-month delay in the completion of the investigation was not unreasonable in the circumstances, given the factual complexity of the case and difficulties securing the availability of witnesses) and *S.N.-S. v FAO*, ILOAT Judgment no 2773 (2009) (although the proceedings took almost four years in total, this was explained in part by the need to thoroughly check the validity of the charges and review the lengthy documentation involved).

But there are perhaps two aspects of disciplinary cases where interesting differences exist between the tribunals, and no uniform practice exists:

(i) the standard of proof to be applied;

(ii) the rights of victims of misconduct, e.g., harassment or retaliation, who have reported such behavior and asked for an investigation of the perpetrator.

With respect to the standard of proof in misconduct cases, the ILOAT has held that, in order to justify dismissal as a disciplinary sanction, the organization must establish misconduct "beyond a reasonable doubt."[23] This is an extremely high standard (derived from criminal law in certain national legal systems). The difficulties it poses were apparent in ILOAT Judgment no 2786 (2009) [WHO].

In this case, a staff member had been dismissed for submitting several fraudulent medical claims for medical services to his family members. However, the ILOAT overturned the termination decision, stating that it was "for the Organization to establish that the [staff member] has knowingly made a false claim". With respect to the allegation that the staff member had fraudulently obtained reimbursement for surgery performed on his wife, the ILOAT found that the organization had not sufficiently established the misconduct alleged beyond a reasonable doubt—even though the hospital in question had confirmed that it had no record of the patient or the treatment for which the staff member had claimed reimbursement. In the Tribunal's view, this evidence was insufficient to overcome the staff member's "entitle[ment] to the benefit of the doubt" (Consideration 16).

It must be said, however, that in its most recent session, the ILOAT dismissed a number of appeals against disciplinary sanctions, and upheld the organization's decision.[24] The Tribunal emphasized that the question was not whether *the Tribunal* was satisfied beyond a reasonable doubt, but rather whether, on the basis of the evidence, the primary trier of fact could have properly found guilt beyond a reasonable doubt. This distinction is perhaps a nuance, but it could be outcome-determinative, since—as ILOAT itself has acknowledged—reasonable minds can differ about the probative value of evidence.[25]

---

23 *See Navarro v WHO*, ILOAT Judgment no 969 (1989), Consideration 16; *see also I. L. v WHO*, ILOAT Judgment no 2699 (2008) and *I. U. v FAO*, ILOAT Judgment no 2849 (2009).

24 *See generally W. (no 2) v FAO*, ILOAT Judgment no 3882 (2017); *F. v CERN*, ILOAT Judgment no 3875 (2017); *K. v WHO*, ILOAT Judgment no 3872 (2017); *L. v OPCW*, ILOAT Judgment no 3852 (2017).

25 *E.g., S. v International Criminal Court*, ILOAT Judgment no 3863 (2017), Consideration 11.

In contrast, the UNAppT has explicitly rejected the ILOAT standard and instead adopted a test of "clear and convincing" evidence in misconduct cases.[26] The World Bank, ADB and the AfDB Tribunals are in line with the UNAppT on this.[27] The UNAppT will generally defer to the Dispute Tribunal's findings as to whether misconduct has been duly proven. The difference in the legal standard of proof between "beyond a reasonable doubt" and "clear and convincing" could be outcome-determinative in certain cases.

A related development is that the UNAppT now reviews decisions by the Dispute Tribunals, which may be challenged by management as well as staff. In disciplinary matters appealed by the Secretary-General, the Appeals Tribunal has shown a willingness to disagree with the Dispute Tribunal's legal conclusions and overturn its ruling, for example, as to whether a sanction was disproportionate and reinstate the Secretary-General's original decision.[28] So the stakes have clearly shifted in a two-tier judicial framework, where management also has the ability to appeal the decisions of the Dispute Tribunals.[29]

With respect to the rights of victims who lodge complaints of harassment or retaliation, this is a relatively new issue for the tribunals, such that it cannot

26 *Molari v Secretary-General of the United Nations*, Judgment no 2011-UNAT-164, paras 1 and 30. In contrast, the UN Appeals Tribunal has stated: "We will not follow [the ILOAT] in holding that the standard of proof in disciplinary cases is beyond a reasonable doubt. *While it is correct that beyond a reasonable doubt is the standard at the ILOAT, this has never been the standard at the United Nations*… . Disciplinary cases are not criminal… . But when termination might be the result, we should require sufficient proof. We hold that, when termination is a possible outcome, misconduct must be established by *clear and convincing* evidence. Clear and convincing proof requires more than a preponderance of the evidence but less than proof beyond a reasonable doubt—it means that the truth of the facts asserted is highly probable." [citation and footnotes omitted].

27 AfDBAT: "The standard of proof in proceedings such these is proof on a balance of probabilities. [citation omitted] The Bank does not have to establish the Applicant's guilt beyond all reasonable doubt. It is sufficient if the Bank can establish on a *balance of probabilities* that it had just cause to terminate the Applicant's employment." *B.O. v AfDB*, AfDBAT Judgment no 95 (2016), para 87. ADBAT: the standard for investigations is "preponderance of the evidence." *Mr. "E" v ADB*, ADBAT Decision no 103 (2014), para 53. WBAT: "higher than a mere balance of probabilities." *Bauman v IBRD*, WBAT Decision no 532 (2016).

28 *See Portillo Moya v Secretary-General of the United Nations*, Judgment no 2015-UNAT-523, para 23, in which the UNAppT reversed the UNDT's conclusion that sanction of termination was disproportionate, where the staff member had engaged in fraud and failed to meet standards required of her position, including safeguarding the quality of distributed food products.

29 *See, e.g., Carrabregu v Secretary-General of the United Nations*, Judgment no 2014-UNAT-485 (allowing Secretary-General's appeal and overturning UNDT's determination that staff member was eligible for conversion to a permanent appointment).

be said that "general principles" have been established.[30] For example, do complainants have the right:

- To see the investigative report, and challenge the statements of the witnesses?
- To be informed of outcome and the sanction, if any, imposed on the perpetrator?
- To appeal a finding of no harassment and a decision not to impose any sanctions?

The tribunals appear to be dealing with these issues on a case-by-case basis, and individual cases are expanding the concept of due process rights for complainants, in additional to the alleged perpetrators of misconduct.

In a 2014 decision,[31] the UNAppT rejected an appeal by the Secretary-General after the Dispute Tribunal had ordered him to inform the victim of retaliation of the nature of the disciplinary measures imposed on the persons responsible for the retaliation. In making this order, the UNDT acknowledged that there was no legal provision requiring the Secretary-General to do so, but it concluded that it would be fair and reasonable to do so, as part of the Secretary-General's responsibility to provide justice for the victim, and the UNAppT agreed.[32]

---

30 The justiciability of claims brought by staff who have complained of harassment is, however, well-established. In *McKinney (no 2) v IBRD*, WBAT Decision no 194 (1998), the WBAT considered the Bank's arguments that allowing complaining staff members to secure administrative and Tribunal review of any investigation undertaken (or not undertaken) by the Bank would have a disruptive impact, and that "[t]here is no obligation owed by the Bank to the complaining staff member ... to resolve his allegations in his favor or to otherwise conduct the investigation in a manner desired by that staff member." The WBAT acknowledged that there is no obligation on the Bank to adopt the course of action urged by a complaining staff member. But in the tribunal's view, "What the Applicant here seeks is not that, but rather review of the investigating official for conduct that is arbitrary or lacking in due process. Such review is appropriate and can properly take account of the needs of the investigating officer for flexibility, confidentiality and the like. There is no reason to believe that allowing such review will seriously impede the operations of the Bank." (para 13)

31 *Rahman v Secretary-General of the United Nations*, Judgment no 2014-UNAT-453, in which the UNAppT agreed with the Dispute Tribunal that "the victim of retaliation is entitled to know whether justice was done to the perpetrators of the retaliation, and that it is fair and reasonable to require the Secretary-General to provide this information, regardless of whether or not there is any legal provision to that effect. As the UNDT held, it is the Secretary-General's responsibility to dispense justice for the victim." (see paras 42–44)

32 *See also Nwuke v Secretary-General of the United Nations*, Judgment no 2010-UNAT-099, in which the UNAppT overturned the UNDT's ruling that it could not review the Administration's decision not to conduct an investigation. The UNAppT held that, although staff members have no right to compel the Administration to conduct an investigation (unless

The ILOAT has gone even further with respect to the due process rights of staff who make claims of harassment. It has held that the organization's duty to a person who makes a claim of harassment means that the claim must be investigated promptly and thoroughly, the facts be determined objectively, the law be applied correctly, and due process be observed. This has meant, in practice, that the organization's refusal to provide the complainant with a copy of the investigative report was a breach of the right to procedural fairness, resulting in the award of moral damages.[33] Similarly, moral damages were awarded to a complainant of harassment because she was not given the opportunity to comment on statements given by her former supervisor and challenge them, if necessary by introducing evidence.[34] The ILOAT has awarded considerable moral damages to complainants in situations where it concluded that the organization had mismanaged their harassment complaints.[35]

The WBAT has been more equivocal as to exactly what due process rights are owed to the accuser. In *DK v IBRD, WBAT* Decision no 552 (2017), a staff member who had complained of sexual harassment wanted the ethics office to reopen its investigation, which had concluded that there was no sexual harassment and that the complainant had engaged in a consensual relationship with the alleged perpetrator. The Bank took the position that under the Staff Rules, the complainant's only rights are to be generally informed of the outcome of the investigation, and that the information provided in this instance went beyond this minimal requirement. The WBAT found that there had been valid reasons for the decision not to reinvestigate the allegations, and these reasons had been given to the complainant. But it pointed out that any investigative findings on allegations of sexual harassment may affect the rights of the complaining staff member as well as the suspect. It therefore encouraged the Bank "to consider whether in conducting such investigations it takes due account

such right is provided in Rules and Regulations), there is a duty to consider requests for investigation (paras 39–40), and the organization will be accountable on this.

33 In S. (*no 8*) *v IAEA*, ILOAT Judgment no 3831 (2017), a staff member claimed that she had been the victim of harassment and requested an investigation. The investigation concluded that harassment had not occurred and closed the case; the organization refused to provide the complainant with a copy of the investigative report, on confidentiality grounds. She pursued the matter to the ILOAT. The tribunal, although acknowledging that the complainant did not have the same due process rights as a staff member who is suspected of misconduct, nevertheless held that the failure to provide her with a copy of the report was a breach of her right to procedural fairness, and awarded her moral damages.

34 See G. v EPO, ILOAT Judgment no 3617 (2016), Considerations 11 and 12.

35 See, e.g., S. F. d M. (nos 1 and 2) v ILO, ILOAT Judgment no 3777 (2017); *E. v FAO*, ILOAT Judgment no 3593 (2016).

of the *rights of the complaining staff member* who claims to be the victim of sexual harassment."[36]

In *Ms. G (no 2)*, ADBAT Decision no 107 (2015), the Applicant claimed that her supervisor had harassed her, and she asked for an investigation, which was done. The investigators interviewed some but not all of the witnesses suggested by the Applicant. The investigation did not find harassment on the part of the supervisor, and the Tribunal did not disturb this finding. However, because the investigation did not interview all of the witnesses named by the Applicant, the Tribunal awarded her damages, at least in part for this reason, as she—the erstwhile victim—had "a right to a proper conduct of the investigation" under the staff rules (Administrative Order 2.04).

In short, the various tribunal pronouncements on the due process rights of both the accused and a complainant in harassment cases have created challenges for international organizations in balancing the interests of all the parties involved in such cases. It is fair to say that harassment and bullying are areas where organizations are struggling with different definitions and procedures, not only in drafting their investigative protocols, but also with respect to the relationship between the disciplinary process and other internal proceedings in which allegations of harassment play a role, which could occur, for example, in challenges to performance assessments or other types of career-related decisions.

5 Review of Regulatory Decisions

All of the tribunals recognize, in one way or another, that decisions taken by the governing bodies of any organization that alter the terms and conditions of employment are subject to judicial review. Although the terminology may differ somewhat, each tribunal has recognized important limitations on this authority, on the basis of such concepts as "acquired rights" or "fundamental terms and conditions" of employment, as well as non-retroactivity and abuse of discretion.[37] These concepts may not have identical meanings, but they

36 *DK v IBRD*, WBAT Decision no 552 (2017), (para 163; emphasis added).

37 *See generally Kaplan v. Secretary-General of the United Nations*, Former UNAT Judgment no 19 (1953); *Poulain d'Andecy v FAO*, ILOAT Judgment no 51 (1960); *Lindsey v ITU*, ILOAT Judgment no 61 (1963); *Elsen and Elsen-Druout v EPO*, ILOAT Judgment no 368 (1979); *de Merode et al v IBRD*, WBAT Decision no 1 (1981); *Pinto v IBRD*, WBAT Decision no 56 (1988); *von Stauffenberg v IBRD*, WBAT Decision no 38 (1987); *Aicher v OECD*, OECD Appeals Board Decision no 37 (1964).

underscore that the tribunals are prepared to review legislative decisions by the governing organs against higher legal norms.

But the ways in which the administrative tribunals go about reviewing decisions of general applicability have some interesting differences. How do staff go about challenging Board decisions? When is a decision of general applicability ripe for review? Since there are no "class actions" as such before administrative tribunals, does a ruling as to one staff member automatically apply to similarly situated staff, or must multiple cases be brought?

These issues are evident in several recent tribunal judgments.

The ILOAT handed down a series of rulings in 2017 concerning a decision by the European Patent Office (EPO) to eliminate the ceiling on employees' contributions to health insurance.[38] The decision was taken by the EPO's Administrative Council in 2010, but it also provided that the ceiling would remain in place for three years, i.e., until 2014, at which point it would be lifted; thereafter, contributions—taken from salary or pensions—could then exceed the ceiling.

More than 1,000 EPO employees appealed this decision, some ultimately turning to the ILOAT. However, the Tribunal dismissed the complaints on receivability grounds. The Tribunal held that staff could not directly challenge a decision of general applicability, as it had no immediate and direct effect on them. This ruling was consistent with several prior decisions[39] in which the Tribunal had held that a general decision that required further individual implementation could only be challenged by impugning an individual decision, such as a change in an individual's salary or pension.[40]

---

38 *See M. R. (no 2) and B.J. (no 4) v EPO*, ILOAT Judgment no 3812 (2017); *H. (no 3) v EPO*, ILOAT Judgment no 3810 (2017); *see also A. (no 75) v EPO*, ILOAT Judgment no 3628 (2016).

39 *E. A. et al v EPO*, ILOAT Judgment no 3291 (2014), Consideration 8. The ILOAT explained that "allowing a complaint against a general decision which does not directly and immediately affect the complainant but which may have a direct negative effect on her/him in the future would cause an unreasonable restriction of the right of defense, as staff members would then have to impugn immediately all general decisions which may have any connection with their future interests, on the basis that a general decision which is not challenged within the established time becomes immune from challenge."

40 The WBAT has taken a similar line regarding challenges to decisions of general applicability. *See BL v IBRD*, WBAT Decision no 446 (2010), para 30: "Furthermore, along with other international administrative tribunals, the Tribunal has consistently held that a claim of non-observance of a staff member's contract of employment or terms of appointment *must be directed not against the Organization's promulgation of some general rule or policy but rather against an application of that rule or policy*—be it reflected in an action or an omission—that directly affects the employment rights of a staff member in an adverse manner. (*Briscoe v IBRD*, WBAT Decision no 118 [1992], para 30)." [emphasis added.] *See generally Andronov v Secretary-General of the United Nations*, Former UNAT Judgment no 1157 (2003) (an "administrative decision" is a unilateral decision taken by the

These complaints were dismissed in 2017—well after the changes at issue had gone into effect and had a financial impact on the complainants individually. The ILOAT pointed out that, when the complaints were initially filed, the ceiling had not been applied to the complainants individually and had not yet affected them. But now—some seven years after the Council decision they are challenging was taken—the complainants have had to go back through the internal appeals process and, essentially, begin anew.[41]

This contrasts sharply with the approach taken by the IMFAT, based on a specific provision in its Statute that was intended to avoid these difficulties. The drafting of this provision (Art VI(2)) was intentionally different than that of existing tribunals at the time, in three respects:

- First, a case challenging the legality of a general decision taken by the legislative organ (referred to as a "regulatory decision") may be brought directly before the Tribunal—no need to exhaust administrative remedies if gravamen of complaint is the legality of the policy itself, as Grievance Committee is not competent to review Executive Board decisions.
- Second, the provision allows for direct review within 90 days of the approval of a new policy—staff need not await application of the policy in an individual case, so long as there will be an adverse impact on them.
- Finally, under the direct review process, a finding of illegality has the effect of annulling the policy at issue, which means that the ruling would automatically apply to similarly-situated staff; no need for multiple applications or erstwhile class action to achieve this result.[42]

administration in a precise individual case, which produces direct legal consequences, and is distinguished from a decision having regulatory power).

41 *Cf Perrin et al v ADB*, ADBAT Decision no 109 (2017) where, as permitted under the ADBAT's Statute, the Asian Development Bank and the applicants agreed to submit the dispute directly to the Tribunal without requiring recourse through prior administrative remedies. At issue was the legality of changes to the educational allowance and whether these changes abrogated fundamental conditions of employment. However, the Tribunal dismissed the case as inadmissible, on the grounds that "The Tribunal cannot review the alleged violation in accordance with the law in the absence of detailed facts and evidence as to the impact of the EA changes in relation to each Applicant under his or her employment contract." (para 59) The ruling left open the possibility that the applicants could bring a subsequent case in which they presented evidence of individual injury as a result of the impugned decision and the remedies sought.

42 Article XIV, Section 3 sets forth the consequences of a ruling in favor of an application directly challenging the legality of a regulatory decision. In that case, the statute provides for "annulment" of the decision, which means that it has no legal effect, and any prior applications of the decision would be null and void.

These principles were incorporated in Articles VI(2) and XIV of the IMFAT Statute.[43] In Daseking-Frank (IMFAT Judgment 2007-1), these provisions were used by staff to directly challenge a decision by the Executive Board introducing major revisions to the methodology for reviewing and adjusting the IMF's salary structure. These changes to the compensation system were systemic in nature;[44] they had no immediate impact on actual salaries or even on the salary structure itself—this would require a separate decision in the context of an annual compensation review. But the direct review process allowed staff to challenge the first decision, that is, the systemic changes in the methodology for reviewing and adjusting the salary structure, directly before the IMFAT.

The IMFAT ultimately concluded that the changes did not infringe a fundamental element of employment, and it upheld the Executive Board's decision. But from a procedural standpoint, the direct review process allowed this issue to be decided relatively quickly; the outcome would automatically apply to all similarly-situated staff and not require individual complaints to be brought. Perhaps most importantly, it achieved the underlying intention of the Statute that a decision of general applicability may be challenged directly, without the need to await its implementation in individual cases. This allows for prompt resolution and avoids lingering uncertainty, which is particularly helpful when major changes are made to the employment framework.

In fact, the Statute of the African Development Bank Administrative Tribunal (Art. IV) goes so far as to authorize the Tribunal to issue advisory opinions upon request by the Board of Governors, presumably even before a regulatory decision is taken (although this provision has not been invoked to date).

6 Observations and Conclusions

It is undeniable that the various tribunals are distinct in the ways they consider and decide cases—even the style of their judgments is quite varied. And the

43 *See* Commentary on the IMFAT Statute (n 19). The official Commentary to the IMFAT Statute on Art VI (2) explained that "[r]egulatory decisions could be challenged by adversely affected staff within three months of their announcement or effective date. It is considered useful to permit the direct review of regulatory decisions within this limited time period. As a result, the question of legality, and any related issues (such as interpretation or application) could hopefully be firmly resolved before there had been considerable reliance on, or implementation of, the contested decision."

44 Such revisions included changes to the cycle for conducting a market review vs. reliance on indexation; the composition of the relevant competitor markets and their weighting in the system; and the parameters of the discretion afforded to the Executive Board in deciding on the new salary structure.

remedies provided, including the amounts and bases for the damages awarded, vary considerably.

But it has to be said that there is still far more convergence than divergence in the tribunals' jurisprudence. This is perhaps not surprising—particularly since the same tribunal judges often sit on more than one tribunal and bring their other experience with them.[45] Moreover, the litigants will typically look for relevant case law to cite to a tribunal, even if it is from another tribunal. All of this reinforces the tendency towards commonality that is reflected in the case law.[46]

But this begs the question whether such convergence is desirable or even appropriate. Does it make sense to aim for commonality in the employment frameworks of organizations as diverse as, say, the OAS and the European Molecular Biological Laboratory? On one hand, the administrative issues faced by international organizations are similar, and their internal staff rules have much in common. So, it seems sensible to try and harmonize the interpretation of that internal law by the various tribunals.

On the other hand, the emphasis on ensuring harmonization raises the question whether this may impede the organizations' ability to work out their own solutions, based on their own assessment of what is in the best interest of the organization. For example, the reliance on fixed-term appointments versus continuing or indefinite appointments varies greatly between international

45 David Ruzié, "L'influence des droits français sur celui de la fonction publique internationale et européene" [1995] L'Internationalité dans les Institutions et le Droit 199, 207, n 62. Prof. David Ruzié observed this tendency with approval, stating that it enables, "to a certain extent, a harmonization of the jurisprudence" notwithstanding differences in the internal laws of the different organizations.

46 Olufemi Elias (ed), *The Development and Effectiveness of International Administrative Law on the Occasion of the Thirtieth Anniversary of the World Bank Administrative Tribunal* (Martinus Nijhoff Publishers 2012) 325. Judge Chris de Cooker, a long-time observer of the international administrative tribunals, noted on the occasion of the 30th anniversary of the WBAT in 2011 that "managers, staff and judges refer more than ever to this system as a body of law." De Cooker commented that "since the 1960's, numerous books have been published on the law of international institutions and that of the international civil service. They all recognize the differences that do exist between the organizations in terms of objectives, purpose, size and rules, but also emphasize the fact that the organizations have much in common in terms of institutional law. Internal laws are very similar in most situations in most organizations, and so are the problems that they are facing. This communality is only increasing to the extent that today, easy reference is made by many to international administrative law, and to the international administrative law as a corpus juris." ibid, 320.

organizations.[47] Whereas some organizations stress the need for continuity, others may want more flexibility and fewer constraints regarding non-renewal of fixed-term contracts, particularly in situations where the use of fixed-term contracts is intended to facilitate turnover and reflect fluctuations in the level and nature of projects as well as budgetary resources. Thus, a "one size fits all" approach in terms of the legal standards for review of non-extension of fixed-term appointments would be inappropriate.

Moreover, if each tribunal looks to the others as to what constitutes the highest or strictest level of due process, is that necessarily "best practice"? In particular, the requirement that harassment must be established beyond a reasonable doubt in order to justify termination of employment may be counterproductive to ensuring zero tolerance of unacceptable behavior in the workplace.

In conclusion, it may be useful from time to time to re-examine the long-standing assumption that international administrative law *should be* a cohesive body of law or *corpus juris*, if only to confirm its continuing importance and utility in protecting the employment rights of international civil servants, while providing sufficient flexibility to recognize distinctions in the internal law of international organizations.

---

47 Secretary-General Bulletin, "Continuing Appointment" (2011) UN Doc ST/SGB/2011/9. In 2011 the United Nations introduced new criteria and eligibility requirements for offering a continuing appointment, which will have the result of increasing the organization's reliance on fixed-term appointments.

PART 3

The Governance Vocation of International Financial Institutions

CHAPTER 7

Open Data for Development: The World Bank, Aid Transparency, and the Good Governance of International Financial Institutions

*Catherine E. Weaver**

Abstract

Development scholars and practitioners today see progressive access to information and transparency policies as necessary preconditions for improved effectiveness of international development aid and the legitimacy of modern international financial institutions. This chapter examines the evolution of access to information and broader open data policies in international development institutions. Drawing from the case of the World Bank as a "first mover," this chapter examines the complex internal processes and factors that shape the adoption and implementation of access to information policy reforms. While challenges to achieving robust information disclosure and open data policies across all multilateral and bilateral aid agencies persist, transparency is now a benchmark for good governance in global development finance and the proverbial genie that cannot be put back in the bottle.

1 Introduction

International development is experiencing a transparency revolution. Since the first high level forum on aid effectiveness in Paris in 2003, there has been a proliferation of declarations, initiatives, and organizations dedicated to improving access to information on donor agencies' own projects and programs. The presumed benefits of such transparency include the centralization of information for better donor coordination, better development planning and management, and the empowerment of aid stakeholders to push for greater

* Associate Professor, LBJ School of Public Affairs and Co-Director, Innovations for Peace and Development, The University of Texas at Austin, US; ceweaver@austin.utexas.edu. I would like to thank Liz Teare for valuable assistance in gathering data on the current information disclosure policy of bilateral and multilateral development aid agencies.

 | DOI:10.1163/9789004408326_008

voice and feedback.[1] Instrumentally, transparency, helps to makes aid more accountable and more effective. Normatively, transparency is a hallmark of modern, legitimate institutions in global governance.

Beneath the complex debates over transparency's normative theory of change[2] lies a pragmatic challenge. Donor agencies have enjoyed relative opacity for most of their existence. For years, efforts to enact fundamental changes in national freedom of information acts (FOIAs) and organizations information disclosure policies were met with resistance and persistent delays.[3] Numerous published analyses and interviews repeatedly point out pervasive problems of organizational inertia, technological and economic barriers to change, and staff's cultural fears surrounding transparency.[4] Yet over the past ten years, this landscape has shifted dramatically.[5] Why are donors' information disclosure and transparency reforms progressing now?

---

1 Ann Florini, "Increasing Transparency in Government" (2002) 19 *International Journal on World Peace* 3; Ann Florini (ed) *Transparency for an Open World* (Columbia University Press 2007). M Collin, A Zubairi, D Nielson, and O Barder "Costs and Benefits of Aid Transparency" (AidInfo 2009); Publish What You Fund "Briefing Paper 1: Why Aid Transparency Matters, and the Global Movement for Aid Transparency" <www.publishwhatyoufund.org/files/BP1_final.pdf> access 25 January 2018; Sarah Mulley "Donor Aid: New Frontiers in Transparency and Accountability" (Transparency & Accountability Initiative 2010); Thomas Carothers and Saskia Brechenmacher "Accountability, Transparency, Participation and Inclusion: A New Development Consensus" (Carnegie Endowment for International Peace 2014); Sheila Herrling "The Business Proposition of Open Aid Data: Why Every US Agency Should Default to Transparency" (*Publish What You Fund Blog*, 30 June 2015) <www.publishwhatyoufund.org/updates/by-country/us/business-proposition-open-aid-data-why-every-u-s-agency-should-default-transparency/> accessed 25 January 2018; Owen Barder "Aid Transparency: Are We Nearly There?" (*Center for Global Development Views from the Center,* 14 April 2016) < https://www.cgdev.org/blog/aid-transparency-are-we-nearly-there> accessed 25 January 2018.

2 Jonathan Fox "The Uncertain Relationship between Transparency and Accountability" (2007) 17 *Development in Practice* 663; Archon Fung, Mary Graham, David Well, and Elena Fagotto "What Makes Transparency Work?" in Archon Fung, Mary Graham, and David Well (eds), *Full Disclosure: The Perils and Promise of Transparency.* Cambridge University Press 2008); Carothers and Brechenmacher (n1).

3 Paul J. Nelson (2001) "Transparency Mechanisms at the Multilateral Development Banks" 29 *World Development*, 1835; Florini (2007) (n1); Carothers and Brechenmacher (n1).

4 Rodney Bent "A Sad State of Affairs: Is Transparency a Solution?" (Publish What You Fund Blog, 23 September 2015) <www.publishwhatyoufund.org/updates/by-country/us/state-transparency-solution/> accessed 25 January 2018. George Ingraham "Making Aid Transparency a Reality" (Brookings Institution Blogpost, 11 February 2015), https://www.brookings.edu/blog/up-front/2015/02/11/making-aid-transparency-a-reality/> accessed 25 January 2018.

5 For reviews of transparency and accountability initiatives in global development, including campaigns and initiatives focused on aid transparency, see Sefton Darby *Natural Resource Governance: New Frontiers in Transparency and Accountability* (London: Transparency &

Twenty years ago, it was relatively easy to access information on aggregated aid data, as long as one had access to the internet and the capacity to search and decipher the dense online spreadsheets offered by the Organization for Economic Cooperation and Development (OECD) Development Assistance Committee (DAC). However, if one wanted to attain detailed information on the specific aid programs, such as information on subnational project locations, budget, implementing partners, and contracting information, it would require a physical trip to one of the few public information centers of institutions such as the World Bank (where some—but hardly all—hardcopy projects documents were available for purchase) or a patient Freedom of Information Access (FOIA) request for USAID files. Even then, much of the information would be missing.

Today, this information landscape is dramatically different. Since the second and third High Level Forums on Aid Effectiveness in Paris in 2003 and Accra in 2008, several specific definitions and standards on aid transparency have emerged, as well as numerous efforts to construct monitoring and verification systems around compliance with international agreements and national transparency guarantees. At the Fourth High Level Forum on Aid Effectiveness in Busan, South Korea in November 2011, most major donor countries and agencies—including many from the global south—committed themselves to reporting their aid information to a common standard that combined three complementary systems: the Organization for Economic Cooperation and Development (OECD) Development Assistance Committee (DAC) Creditor Reporting System (CRS++),[6] the OECD DAC Forward Spending Survey (FSS)[7] and the International Aid Transparency Initiative.[8] Over this time period, international principles and standards for aid effectiveness, transparency and accountability has grown by leaps and bounds, constituted by a rich set of

Accountability Initiative, Open Society Foundation 2010); Matthew Martin "Review of Progress in International and National Mutual Accountability and Transparency on Development Cooperation" Background Paper for the UN Development Cooperation Forum High-Level Symposium 7/2010 < http://www.un.org/en/ecosoc/newfunct/pdf/ma_study-status_and_progress.pdf> accessed 25 January 2018; Carothers and Brechenmacher (n1); Rosemary McGee and John Gaventa "Review of Impact and Effectiveness of Transparency and Accountability Initiatives" Synthesis report prepared for the Transparency and Accountability Initiative Workshop 10/ 2010 <http://www.transparency-initiative.org/wp-content/uploads/2017/03/synthesis_report_final1.pdf> accessed 25 January 2018.

6 <https://stats.oecd.org/Index.aspx?DataSetCode=CRS1> accessed 25 January 2018.

7 <https://stats.oecd.org/Index.aspx?DataSetCode=FSS> accessed 25 January 2018.

8 <http://www.aidtransparency.net/> accessed 25 January 2018.

supranational initiatives,[9] national level policies and open data systems,[10] and international non-governmental organizations and networks devoted specifically to the advocacy and production of transparent and open aid data.[11]

Critically, a number of major development agencies launched aggressive reforms to their informational disclosure policies, which directly contributed to the open data initiatives we see today. At the forefront was the World Bank, which is examined closely in this chapter as case study of the complex processes of organizational change that such transparency reforms have entailed (see Section 3). The World Bank's Access to Information Policy was established in 2009, and most other major multilateral and bilateral institutions quickly followed suit. As a result, nearly ten years later such transparency policies are widely seen in the international community as the benchmark for good governance in international financial institutions.

Most recently, the launch of the United Nations post-2015 Sustainable Development Goals included a distinct call for a "data revolution" in international development. Specifically, the UN established the Independent Expert Advisory Group on the Data Revolution for Sustainable Development (IEAG). In 2014, the IEAG issued a major report, entitled *A World That Counts: Mobilizing the Data Revolution for Sustainable Development.*[12] The report called for investments in new technologies and capacity building to improve the quantity and quality of data, including information on international aid flows, to address the inequalities in data access between countries and to promote the use of data in development decision-making, participation and accountability. Explicit references to transparency around aid also found in the 2013 G8 Open Data Charter. The 2015 African Data Consensus calls for a "partnership of all

9 See, e.g., the EU Aid Transparency Guarantee and the Global Partnership for Effective Development Cooperation.

10 For example, many countries—especially lead countries such as Sweden, Britain, Denmark and the US—adopted National Transparency Guarantees with specific references to aid (Sweden, Britain), integrated aid transparency commitments within their Open Government Partnership National Action Plans, and similar open aid data strategies and policy papers. For examples of aid transparency systems, see the UK Department for International Development's DevTracker, Sweden's openaid.se, Denmark's Danida Open Aid USAID's Global Aid Explorer, and the US Government's Foreign Assistance Dashboard. See also Ali Clare, Stefaan Verhulst and Andrew Young *OpenAid in Sweden: Enhanced Transparency and Accountability in Development Cooperation* (Report for the GovLab, in collaboration with the Omidyar Network 2016) <http://odimpact.org/case-openaid-in-sweden.html> accessed 9 February 2016.

11 See, e.g., AidData, Aidwatch, aidinfo, Development Gateway, DevInfo, Development Initiatives, Data2X, Interaction, Modernizing Foreign Assistance Network, Open Aid Partnership, Oxfam International, and many others.

12 < http://www.undatarevolution.org/report/> accessed 12 June 2017.

data communities that upholds the principles of official statistics as well as openness across the data value chain, which creates a vibrant data ecosystem providing timely, user-driven and disaggregated data for public good and inclusive development.[13]

2 Why AID Transparency now? The Global Movement Towards Access to Information

One can trace the roots of movements to open access to information and the contemporary transparency and accountability initiatives to the rise of national Freedom of Information Acts.[14] Sweden was the first country to adopt an access to information legislation in 1766, but the diffusion of such policies over time has been very slow. The US was the second country to adopt FOIA legislation in 1966 (amended in 1971), with supporting legislation that followed in the form of the Sunshine in Government Act (1976), Presidential Records Act (1978), Whistleblower Protection Act (1989) and Foreign Corrupt Practices Act (1977). The rise of FOIAs and access to information legislation outside of advanced democracies is a recent phenomenon. Only 14 enacted such legislation prior to 1990 and 35 by 2000. Yet by February 2014, 107 countries had adopted Access to Information or FOIA provisions in their national or federal laws and actionable decrees.[15]

The spread of FOIAs represents the spread of public values in political life that encapsulate the desire to counter corruption, open up decision-making

13 African Data Consensus, signed 29 March 2015 in Addis Ababa, Ethiopia.

14 Ana Bellver and Daniel Kaufman "Transparenting Transparency: Initial Empirics and Policy Applications" (WBI Working Paper 8/2005), <http://siteresources.worldbank.org/INTEAPREGTOPRURDEV/Resources/573691-1175901454225/seminar1_background_reading.pdf> accessed 25 January 2018; Florini 2007 (n1); Carolyn Ball "What is Transparency?" (2009) 11 *Public Integrity* 293; R Calland "Annex 3 Freedom of information. Review of impact and effectiveness of transparency and accountability initiatives" (Institute of Development Studies 5/2011) <http://www.transparencyinitiative.org/wp-content/uploads/2011/05/impacts_annex3_final1.pdf> accessed 25 January 2018; R Calland and K Bentley "The Impact and Effectiveness of Transparency and Accountability Initiatives: Freedom of Information" (2013) 31 *Development Policy Review* s69.

15 Open Society Justice Initiative. *List of Countries with Access to Information (ATI) Provisions in their National/Federal Laws or Actionable Decrees, and Dates of Adoption & Significant Amendments* (2014) <www.right2info.org/resources/publications/national-security-page/countries-with-ati-provisions-02.2014> accessed 7 July 2016. See also Stephen Kosack and Archon Fung "Does Transparency Improve Governance?" (2014) 14 *Annual Review of Political Science*: 65; Open Society Foundation *Access to Informational Laws: Overview and Statutory Goals* (Open Society Justice Initiative 2012).

processes by public officials and in general adhere to the principles of good governance that were the focus of many development programs in the 1990s.[16] Similar transparency legislation emerged in other areas of global governance. This included international conventions focused on promoting financial transparency and anti-corruption, such as the OECD's Anti-Bribery Convention (1996) and the UN Convention Against Corruption (2003).[17] The demand for transparency is multidirectional. For example, international financial institutions are demanding more transparency from their member governments. In turn, they themselves face increasing pressures from civil society groups to open up their own data and decision-making processes.[18]

The rise of FOIAS, information disclosure and right to information (RTI) policies by themselves represent "reactive transparency," meaning that citizens can request information, but that information is not provided a priori.[19] By contrast, more recent TAIs have shifted focus to "proactive transparency," access to information (AI) and open data initiatives, which entail the presumption not just of disclosure upon request, but the forthwith publication of data as an automatic part of the data production process.

In the development industries' parlance, this broader movement is encapsulated in the notion of "Open Data for Development" (OD4D).[20] OD4D rests upon clear principles and objectives: promote the development of open data "ecosystems" that promote the production, awareness and demand for user-driven and disaggregated data to improve decision-making, accountability and participatory, inclusive development). The movement also places emphasis on making data open, meaning that data is accessible and usable by all and follows established practices for producing data, including use of common standards and public application programming interface (API) for data reporting and publication.

Today, this international regime complex around open data for development presents a strong international normative framework for proactive information disclosure and open data policies. The regime includes transparency and accountability initiatives such as the 2002 Extractive Industry Transparency Initiative; Global Initiative on Fiscal Transparency (GIFT), the International

16 Florini 2002 (n1); Ball (n 14) 298; C Darch and P Underwood *Freedom of Information in the Developing World: Demand, Compliance and Democratic Behaviours* (OUP 2010). McGee and Gaventa (n5), Calland 2011 (n14).

17 Bellver and Kaufman (n14) 4–5.

18 Florini 2002 and 2007 (n1), Carothers and Brechenmacher (n1) 7–9.

19 Timothy Davies, Perini Fernando and Jose Alonso, *Researching the Emerging Impacts of Open DataODDC Conceptual Framework* (World Wide Web Foundation 2013), 17.

20 See opendatacon.org.

Budget Partnership (2007) and Open Budget Initiative (2006); the 2011 Open Government Partnership, and the 2012 Open Contracting Partnership and Construction Sector Transparency Initiative.

The aid transparency movement emerged synergistically with the rapidly shifting donor landscape of development aid over the past decade. By the early 2000s the international development community included a growing number of public and private donor agencies, NGOs, civil society organizations, and foundations, in addition to the bilateral and multilateral governmental organizations that included many donors who were not members of the OECD's Development Assistance Committee (the so-called "south-south cooperation" agencies). This expanding industry of aid prompted reforms in existing processes to improve cooperation and better leverage development resources between all these new actors. In 2002, over 50 heads of state, along with representatives from the United Nations, the International Monetary Fund, the World Bank, and the World Trade Organization, convened in Mexico for the Monterrey Conference. The resulting Monterrey Consensus encapsulated the tenets of modern international development cooperation, with a focus on renewed funding commitments and better mobilization of financial resources for development, including foreign aid.

While the Monterrey Consensus set the stage for increasing cooperation in aid allocation, subsequent High Level Forums on Aid Effectiveness set the stage for setting the specific agenda around aid transparency and accountability.[21] Following the first forum in Rome in 2003 and the Rome Declaration on Aid Harmonization, the 2005 conference in Paris underscored the importance of aid transparency in achieving development results. The Paris Declaration on Aid Effectiveness was signed in 2005 by over 100 bilateral and multilateral donor agencies, developing-country governments, and international donor organizations. While the transparency agenda was not front and center in the Paris Declaration, the need for greater transparency was implicit in the commitment to achieving improved harmonization between donors and greater alignment between donors and recipient government in establishing development agendas.[22]

At the Third High Level Forum on Aid Effectiveness held in Accra, Ghana in 2008, donors sought to create implementation and monitoring plans to enforce the goals set by the Paris Declaration. The Accra Agenda for Action specifically pointed to transparency and accountability as essential to holding donors and recipient governments accountable for aid spent and its impact. Central to this

21 These includes forums in Rome (2003), Paris (2005), Accra (2008), and Busan (2011).

22 Mulley (n1), 19.

goal was a strong focus on improving access to statistical and data information systems to better track, monitor and evaluate development results.

The International Aid Transparency Initiative (IATI) was launched in Accra in September 2008, the International Aid Transparency Initiative. IATI was designed as a multi-stakeholder, voluntary initiative, designed to improve upon prior donor report practices (through forums such as the OECD) through the inclusion of reporting by more donors and relevant actors (including non-DAC sovereign donors, NGOs, foundations and aid implementing partners), IATI also sought to establish a more robust system of comparability among donors by establishing a common standard for reporting and promoting the principles of open aid by making all data entered into IATI publicly accessible, machine readable and easily downloadable for replication and integration with other datasets. The establishment of IATI was accompanied by the creation of Publish What You Fund, a small but critically influential NGO based in London that created the annual Aid Transparency Index to monitor donor commitments to access to information reforms and compliance with IATI and other aid transparency commitments through an annual Aid Transparency Index.

The Fourth High Level Forum on Aid Effectiveness in Busan, South Korea, and the resulting Busan Partnership for Effective Development Cooperation was a tipping point in the aid transparency agenda in terms of eliciting a critical level of political commitment. More than 3,000 government officials, NGOs, official donors and other groups were present, including UN Secretary General Ban-Ki Moon, former UK Prime Minister Tony Blair, and US Secretary of State Hillary Clinton. One of the most important events was then Secretary of State Hillary Clinton's announcement that the US would become a signatory to IATI and reach full compliance with open data reporting by 2013. As the largest bilateral donor, US inclusion in IATI brought IATI membership up to 75 percent of global aid.[23] The Busan agreement also established the Global Partnership for Effective Development Cooperation (GPEDC), supported by the OECD and UNDP, which identified transparency and accountability within and among donors to be one of four key objectives of the partnership (Busan Declaration 2011).[24]

23 Owen Barder, "What Happened in Busan?" (Owen Abroad, 11 December 2011) <www.owen.org/blog/5131> accessed 3 March 2014.

24 During this same period, aid- receiving countries were adopting domestic aid information systems to track incoming aid flows. By 2013 (when IATI reached 200 signatories), 25 countries hosted aid management platforms (AMPs), 35 countries had development assistance databases (DADs), and numerous other developing countries had "home grown" aid information systems housed in their Ministries of Finance or Planning. Furthermore, between 2013–2015, most major donors incorporated transparency initiatives into their

In 2014, UN Secretary-General Ban Ki-moon announced the need for a data revolution to support the forthcoming post-2015 Sustainable Development Goals. At the same time, the Independent Expert Advisory Group was formed to provide recommendations for this agenda. This UN Data Revolution, as it became known, calls for the full integration of data and statistics in decision-making, closing of data gaps, as well as building technological capacity and data literacy in small and big data analytics. Most recently, international commitments to aid transparency have been reified by renewed pledges under the auspices on the UN post-2015 Sustainable Development Goals summit in 2015 and the mutual accountability pact of the 2015 Third International Conference on Financing for Development in Addis Ababa, Ethiopia—both of which call for an enhanced commitment from both donors and recipient governments to transparent and timely reporting of all developed-related financial flows, including aid, in as close to real-time as possible.[25]

3 Opening from within: Explaining how Transparency Evolves at the Donor Agency Level[26]

The above account of the broader global movement towards aid transparency helps to explains why aid organizations have now—after many decades of incremental steps towards openness—signaled a strong commitment to transparency norms. Yet it says little about how these policies within aid agencies evolved from relatively restrictive information disclosure policies to quite liberal and proactive AI and open data policies. This account of internal reforms is important, insofar as it reveals specific strategies that may be more or less effective in overcoming initial concerns and organizational inertia and may provide insights for new organizations currently developing their own Access to Information policies, such as Asian Infrastructure Investment Bank (AIIB).

The analysis provided here draws extensively upon findings from primary research conducted on the World Bank (hereafter the Bank). In late 2009, the

strategic operating plans and had either launched or made plans to release publicly accessible external databases with detailed information on their ODA projects and spending.

25 ONE, The 2015 Data Report: Putting the Poorest First, 2015. <www.one.org/international/policy/data-report-2015/> accessed 15 January 2018.

26 For a more detailed account of the evolution of the World Bank's informational disclosure policy reforms, see Catherine Weaver and Christian Peratsakis "Engineering Policy Norm Implementation: The World Bank's Transparency Transformation," in Alexander Betts and Phil Orchard (eds) *Implementation and World Politics: How International Norms Change Practice* (Oxford University Press 2014).

Bank was the first multilateral development bank to shift its more reactive information disclosure policy towards a more proactive access to information policy, and to take the dramatic steps of publishing extensive information on its projects, development data and budgets. The Bank shifted from a "positive list" of limited materials available for disclosure to a "negative list," which presumed automatic access to all materials except those on a carefully defined list of exceptions. This represented a "transformative change" in the Bank's culture and approach towards organizational transparency.[27] According to Barbara Lee, Manager of the Aid Effectiveness Unit at the Bank, the Bank shifted "from a hush-hush place to an era of openness" as the result of this policy.[28]

The Bank's embrace of transparency was by no means spontaneous. Instead, it was the result of a protracted debate over its information disclosure policy since the early 1990s. The timing of the Bank's long awaited reversal of its information policy reflects, in some sense, a dramatic alignment of ideational and material pressures for greater transparency in the mid-2000s described in the previous section. But it also reflects the fact that those championing transparency at the Bank were well aware of the potential pitfalls of pushing transparency too far, too fast. Advocates worked to ensure the passage of an "airtight [access to information, or AI] policy"[29] by the Bank's Board of Executive Directors that would minimize internal and external resistance to the AI policy. They also sought to cultivate an environment for nervous staff wherein compliance would be strictly enforced, while recognizing that "mistakes will happen."[30] The design of the AI policy and implementation plan also included extensive involvement of key actors inside the Bank, as well as some of its most vocal external critics. There was a seven-month preparation period between 2009, when the Board passed the new AI policy, and July 2010, when the policy went into practice, during which management sought to identify and deal with capacity constraints and resistance.

The ensuing integration of the AI policy into Bank standard operating practices was both more rapid and smooth than its architects, advocates and

27 Interviews with Caroline Anstey, World Bank Managing Director, Washington, DC (Washington, DC January 2012); Jeff Gutman, former World Bank Director of Operational Policy and Country Services (December 2011), Chad Dobson Director of the Bank Information Center (Washington DC, December 2011); and Owen Barder Senior Fellow at the Center for Global Development (Washington, DC, December 2011).

28 Quoted in Rebecca Harris, "Knowledge is Power: Transparency and Participation Will Be the Drivers of Effective Development" *Huffington Post* (19 April 2011).

29 Interview with Gutman (n26).

30 Interviews with Anstey (n26) and Gutman (n26).

even critics expected.[31] Moreover, from the perspective of many Bank staff and managers, the surprisingly unproblematic implementation of the AI policy "opened the door" for a broader transparency agenda and "set the ball rolling down the hill"[32] for the "democratization of development.'[33] In turn, the Bank's transparency agenda started to diffuse (albeit unevenly) to other aid agencies, who adopted similar AI and open data policies in response to changing public expectations regarding aid transparency.[34]

The evolution of the Bank's access to information policy reflects a long history of moving from a relatively closed to quite open institution. The first discussion of AI policies began in 1985, when the Bank established its first set of staff guidelines on public information disclosure in response to demands of environmental activists concerned about the social and ecological impact of the Bank's lending programs. Over the next 20 years, the Bank made three significant revisions to its information disclosure policies. The first was in 1994 (the year of the "Fifty Years is Enough" campaign), when the Bank established its first official disclosure policy. This coincided with the creation of the Independent Inspections Panel and the opening of the Bank's Public Information Center.[35] The 1994 policy ostensibly worked on a presumption of disclosure. But in fact all Bank data and documents were <u>not</u> eligible for disclosure unless they were on a short list of permissible items—a so-called "positive list." For example, in 1993, it was nearly impossible for an interested party to obtain through official channels timely and detailed information on lending agreements, individual projects, or even announcements (much less minutes or transcripts) of Board meetings.

In response to shifting demands regarding informational disclosure, the World Bank incrementally revised its "positive list," roughly every two years. For example, in 1998, the Bank made Country Assistance Strategy papers public, albeit only with the permission of the country in question. In 2001 the Board expanded the list quite substantially, and also revised the Archival policies to make it slightly less difficult to access historical materials.[36] By 2002, the Bank's

31 Interviews with Anstey (n26), Gutman (n26), Dobson (n26), and Barder (n26).

32 Interview with Gutman (n26).

33 Robert Zoellick "Democratizing Development Economics," Speech delivered at Georgetown University, 29 September 2010.

34 Mulley (n1).

35 Richard E. Bissell "Regarding the World Bank's Policy on Disclosure of Information," *Committee on Financial Services, US House of Representatives* (Washington, DC, 10 September 2009).

36 World Bank *World Bank Disclosure Policy: Additional Issues: Follow-Up Consolidated Report (Revised)* (World Bank Operations Policy and Country Services, 14 February 2005).

management began to discuss deeper policy changes.[37] In 2003, the Board of Executive Directors debated the disclosure of Board minutes and other deliberative process materials. However, the "presumption in favor of disclosure" remained limited by the existence of the cumbersome positive list, which many within the Bank felt to be ambiguous and difficult to interpret.

Nonetheless, in 2004 several Executive Directors continued to push for more open access with respect to policy and strategy papers related to operations.[38] Of particular importance were the internal discussions over disclosure of documents related to Board deliberations. In a series of meetings between 2004 and 2005, the Executive Directors discussed the disclosure of Board minutes, drawing on the experience of other international financial institutions (such as the Inter-American Development Bank and Asian Development Bank). Informal notes between the Executive Directors in 2005 indicate "an emerging consensus to move toward greater transparency in this respect, with the understanding that the content of Board minutes would not change from its present form.'[39] The proposal to increase the transparency of Board discussions was approved, but with several caveats: material deemed by the Board to be too sensitive would be redacted prior to disclosure, and Board transcripts, summaries of discussion, committee minutes and reports to the Board (called "green sheets") would not be disclosed. The Board also solicited a cost-benefit study of simultaneous disclosure designed to assess the possibility of further disclosure creating opportunities for "undue pressure from special interest groups" or risks of "loss of candor." While there was some reluctance on the part of Board to go the distance on the release of deliberative documents, the progressive discussion of disclosure reform attracted some much desired praise from external watchdog groups.[40]

By the mid-2000s, momentum was building. Externally, the aforementioned influence of parallel transparency movements in areas such as extractives industries (EITI) and the growth in FOIAs clearly was influencing the Board's discussion of the Bank's information disclosure policies between 2001 and 2009. Both internal documents and interviews reveal that Executive Directors from countries with strong FOIA traditions—particularly India, Mexico and the US—were vocal proponents of similar freedom of information policies at the

37 In 2002, the Bank also established a global network of Public Information Centers to enhance public access outside of the US, by filling requests for information when documents could be disclosed.

38 Word Bank (n35).

39 Ibid, 4.

40 H Kovach, C Neligan, and S Burall *Global Accountability Report: Power without Accountability?* (One World Trust 2003).

Bank. At the same time, these countries advised the Bank to approach freedom of information slowly and incrementally, as if "peeling an onion," in order to build broad support and develop the institutional capacity to manage a robust freedom of information system.[41]

The Board's internal discussions also reflected the mounting pressure of NGO campaigns. NGO demands for greater transparency were especially prominent at the Gleneagles G8 Summit in 2005.[42] The following year, the Global Transparency Initiative (GTI), a network of civil society organizations promoting openness in the international financial institutions (IFIs), was established. GTI went so far as to draft a model policy for the World Bank's Access to Information Policy in early 2009, parts of which later appeared in the official policy adopted by the Bank (GTI 2009).[43] The Bank Information Center (BIC), a leading DC-based NGO aid watchdog group within the GTI, was a central player running up to and during the 2009 AI policy negotiations. For years, BIC had pushed the Bank to move from a positive to negative list, and also advocated for the disclosure of particularly sensitive materials such as draft country programming plans, project appraisal and policy documents, and access to Board documents.[44]

In late 2007, the Bank reached out to BIC to help coordinate the Bank's external consultations in 33 countries of its new draft AI policy paper. Carolyn Anstey, one of the key architects of the new AI policy and (as of June 2013) one of the Bank's three Managing Directors, argued that having an NGO partner like BIC as a standard bearer was helpful to the Bank's evolving stance on its own AI policy and building external support for the policy.[45] BIC later became

41 Interview with Gutman (n26) and Anstey (n26). See also World Bank *FY2011 Access to Information Annual Report* (World Bank 2012).

42 Mulley (n1).

43 In addition to the NGOs and campaigns already mentioned, some of the most prominent watchdog NGOs with respect to the aid transparency and accountability movement include AidInfo, Aid Watch, BetterAid, Bretton Woods Project, EURODAD, and Reality of Aid Initiative.

44 Bruce Jenkins "World Bank and IMF Launch Disclosure Reviews" 65 *Bretton Wood Project Update* 23 April 2009. See also Jonathan Fox "Transparency for Accountability: Civil Society Monitoring of Multilateral Development Bank Anti-Poverty Projects," (1997) 7 *Development in Practice* 167; Jonathan Fox and L.D. Brown (eds) *The Struggle for Accountability: The World Bank, NGOs, and Grassroots Movements* (MIT Press, 1998); D. Clark, J. Fox, and K. Treakle *Demanding Accountability: Civil Society Claims and the World Bank Inspection Panel* (Rowman & Littlefield 2003).

45 Interview with Anstey (n26).

a member of the AI Working Group, in charge of preparing for the Bank's policy implementation in 2010–2011.[46]

Simultaneously, the growing attention to good governance in the Bank's programming was reverberating in terms of the institution's internal governance. The Bank's 2007 Governance and Anticorruption strategy paper specified the need for more transparency and accountability in the Bank's own internal conduct. The aim was to set an example for others and to demonstrate that the Bank lived up to its own ideals.[47] In the words of Shaida Badiee, then Director of the Bank's Development Data Group and now the Executive Director of Open Data Watch, "if we are going to support Open Data and Open Government in countries, the World Bank must not only preach it, but also do it."

Arguably, the final and most important impetus for the 2009 AI Policy shift came from Bank management. Arriving in the wake of the Wolfowitz scandal,[48] President Robert Zoellick proclaimed the Bank's transparency and accountability would be a key tool in restoring good governance. He quickly set about to revitalize the Bank from the inside out.[49] Interviews with Bank staff reveal that Zoellick and other senior managers[50] were keen to solidify the Board's support for the transparency agenda and willing to exercise authority to overrule reticent managers and staff. Resources needed for this (and later

46 Jenkins (n43); World Bank *FY2011 Access to Information Annual Report* (World Bank 2012). Interviews with Bruce Jenkins (Washington, DC, June 2009), Dobson (n26), Gutman (n26), and Anstey (n26).

47 World Bank, *Implementation Plan for Strengthening World Bank Engagement on Governance and Anticorruption* (The World Bank 2007); Paul A. Volcker, et al. *Independent Panel Review of the World Bank Group Department of Institutional Integrity* (World Bank 2007); World Bank, *Towards Greater Transparency: Rethinking the World Bank's Disclosure Policy: Approach Paper* (World Bank Operations Policy and Country Services, 29 January 2009); World Bank 2012 (n45).

48 Catherine Weaver, *Hypocrisy Trap: The World Bank and the Poverty of Reform* (Princeton University Press 2008).

49 Sebastian Mallaby, "The Quiet Revolutionary Who Saved the World Bank," (Council on Foreign Relations 17 February 2012) <http://www.cfr.org/international-finance/quiet-revolutionary-saved-world-bank/p27398> accessed 25 January 2018.

50 Zoellick was supported by a cadre of Bank managers in External Affairs (EXT) and Operations Policy and Country Services (OPCS). Carolyn Anstey was especially important in mobilizing internal resources for the AI policy reform and later the Open Data Initiative. Anstey formally served as a country director for Haiti, where she worked extensively with NGOs on the monitoring of government budget transparency. That experience made her keenly aware of the power of involving citizens in transparency and accountability movements, and is one reason she reached out to BIC and supported an extensive external consultation process during the drafting and implementation of the AI policy. Interview with Antsey (n1).

for the Open Data Initiative) were reallocated from existing budgets, already suffering from seven years of zero percent growth. Moreover, there was little tolerance for noncompliance. Vice Presidents reported directly to Zoellick on the progress of the AI policy implementation and were held responsible for lax enforcement within their units.

According to the World Bank's 2009 Approach Paper, "the disclosure policy and its effective implementation rank[ed] high in the Bank's corporate agenda":[51]

> ...the existence of such a positive list has limited the Bank's ability to implement the expressed presumption in favor of disclosure. The policy is also not clear about what cannot be disclosed, and there are many ambiguous and overlapping rules that are cumbersome and difficult for Bank staff to implement, and for the public to understand. At the same time, public interest in transparency has been growing. Many countries have adopted freedom of information legislation and the transparency standards of international financial institutions are subject to increased public scrutiny. Both within and outside the Bank, many feel that the Bank's disclosure policy framework still does not go far enough.[52]

The resulting policy, renamed Access to Information,[53] was passed by the Board in December 2009. The new policy maintained critical exemptions to disclosure that reflect continued concerns over the need to protect client confidences and preserve candor in key deliberations. Many of the exemptions, particularly related to Board documents,[54] were not warmly received by external critics, but were largely seen as a necessary compromise in order to "strike an appropriate balance between the need to grant maximum public access to

51 World Bank (n46).

52 World Bank (n46), 1.

53 Several interviewees noted that the term "information disclosure" was considered out of fashion by 2009. "Access to information" is considered to be better aligned with democratic principles, insofar as it highlights citizen's rights to information, not only governments' (or organizations') obligations to provide information.

54 Specifically, the old policy barred the simultaneous disclosure of confidential information pertaining to Board proceedings, verbatim transcripts of Board and committee discussions and documents prepared by staff for the Board. The new policy presumes that Board papers would be disclosed at the end of the deliberative process, but any materials classified as confidential or strictly confidential would not be disclosed unless the Board specifically provides authorization. World Bank 2009 (n46) 7–8. Classified materials are subject to disclosure after 20 years.

information in the Bank's possession, and its obligations to respect the confidentiality of its clients, shareholders, employees, and third parties."[55]

Overall, the proposed policy was nothing less than a "paradigm shift."[56] It moved the Bank away from the infamous "positive" list to a "negative" list, consciously limited to narrow set of items exempted from automatic disclosure. The policy was intended to align the Bank with its espoused commitment to the "presumption of disclosure" and make publicly available vast numbers of previously closed documents, including those related to ongoing aid projects (e.g., Implementation Status Reports). It was also designed to mirror disclosure policies adopted in numerous countries through FOIAs, and "put the Bank at the forefront of other multilateral agencies with respect to disclosure."[57]

Herein lies the key not only to the successful adoption of the AI policy, but also the successful *implementation*. The six-month pre-implementation period was consciously designed to give the Bank time to put into place sufficient institutional resources, oversight mechanisms, and compliance measures. Strategic planning for the policy implementation included extensive consultation with NGOs (especially the aforementioned BIC) and their participation in testing the new system.[58] In addition, the new AI policy established an appeals process that ensured continued NGO participation in the Bank's development and initial implementation of the policy.[59] The preparation period between December 2009 and September 2010 further focused on securing Board approval to declassify more than 17,000 documents. In addition, the 2010 AI Policy moved the locus of the Bank's documents from the Public Information Centers to the World Bank's external website; using the preparation period to build and strengthen its technical infrastructure and in-house information management systems.

Predictably, there was considerable anxiety regarding how the Bank staff and management would respond to the new policy. The implementation architects were quite concerned that staff would resist the new policy. This was not because staff did not believe in making the Bank more transparent, as there was very little dissent on this general principle. Instead, staff reluctance stemmed from concerns regarding resources, loss of candor and uncertainty about how this would affect client relations with borrowing governments who

55 World Bank (n46), 2.

56 World Bank 2009 (n46); World Bank, "New World Bank Access to Information Policy Takes Effect July 1," (Press Release no. 2010/448/EXC, 3 June 2010).

57 World Bank 2009 (n46), 15.

58 World Bank 2010 (n.55).

59 Ibid.

did not favor such transparency.[60] Some Bank staff also feared that opening the Bank would mean a loss of revenue in instances where the Bank charged for access to information and data. This was particularly the case within the Development Economics Vice Presidency (DEC) and its Development Data unit, which used the sale of development indicators (now accessible through the Open Data Initiative) to help offset the cost of collecting, compiling, analyzing and reporting data. Zoellick, however, assured DEC that the Bank would suffer no revenue loss (and would even experience a revenue gain) by releasing the data.[61]

Staff were also concerned that public exposure would diminish honest discussions in key project documents like Implementation Status Reports, which were critical for mid-course corrections in lending programs. The AI policy team defended the disclosure by arguing that disclosure would *improve* candor by promoting greater accountability and access to third party information and incentivizing staff to produce higher quality reports. But more compelling was the built-in oversight mechanism:

> …the main indicator of candor is the "realism index" which measures the extent to which the current ratings of projects in the portfolio reflect the average rating of projects at exit over the recent past. But, at any point in time, the number of operations classified as being in 'problem' status is well below the average for the projects that exit the portfolio. During the first 18 months following the adoption of the revised policy, Management [will] closely monitor the implications of the changes in the policy on candor, including the realism index.[62]

60 See also David Shaman, *The World Bank Unveiled: Inside the Revolutionary Struggle for Transparency* (Parkhurst Brothers Publisher 2009).

61 A similar debate occurred within the context of the Zoellick's effort to "democratize development economics" (Zoellick 2010) by not only opening public access to key development databases like the World Development Indicators, but also by supporting the creation of open source analytical tools (such as PovcalNet and ADePT) that would empower people outside of the Bank to access datasets and draft publications, and replicate the Bank's analytical work in areas such as calculations of global poverty figures. Martin Ravallion, Senior Economist at DEC, calls this the "wholesale retailing" of development economics. Bank economists feared this will interfere with their first mover advantages in publishing the results of their data collection and analysis and run up against copyright rules in peer-reviewed journals where they are encouraged to publish. Martin Ravallion "Wholesaling Research for Development," World Bank Blog, 29 September 2010. <http://blogs.worldbank.org/developmenttalk/wholesaling-research-for-development> accessed 2 March 2012; interviews with Anstey (n26) and Gutman (n26).

62 World Bank 2009, (n46), 20.

Arguably, the most important part of the implementation plan focused on preparing staff for the policy change. This was a daunting task in an organization that includes over 15,000 staff, with high turnover, with a large DC headquarters and over 100 mission offices worldwide. To prepare staff, senior Bank managers enacted a series of measures to educate staff on the new AI policy. For example, numerous materials were compiled and disseminated, and an internal AI website with helpdesk was created. Training sessions were held on how to classify and declassify materials. Bank Vice Presidents designated 189 staff to serve as AI focal points to provide staff support as well as provide feedback on implementation challenges.

Rigorous oversight and compliance measures were put in place. Most prominent was the *mandatory* AI e-learning program during the first few months after the formal adoption of the AI policy. Completion reports were compiled and distributed every two weeks to all the Vice Presidents, who publicized a list of those who had not yet completed the training. Severe sanctions were threatened: staff were repeatedly told that failure to complete the e-learning program would result in the loss of their email privileges.[63] This proved extremely effective. One staff member we spoke with said, "I can confirm the seriousness with which the staff awareness of the policy was approached. Within my VPU, we were regularly reminded of the need to do the training module, lists of noncomplying staff were circulated on several occasions and the VPs office did pursue staff who had not done the training module. The threat to cut off email access was taken seriously. The training module was actually not bad either."[64]

Overall, the preparation for the implementation period involved an impressive amount of foresight and attention to detail. The AI Working Group (now AI Committee) established vigilant monitoring mechanisms and the published detailed progress reports every quarter during the first year and annually thereafter. The progress reports, produced by the Bank's Legal Department and published online, provide extensive information on internal compliance rates with the mandatory e-learning program (now near 100 percent) as well as a precise list of all public access requests (with time taken for the requests to be filled) and all appeals (with data on which appeals were granted and reasons provided for those that were not).[65]

---

63 Interviews with Gutman (n26) and Anstey (n26). See also World Bank "World Bank Policy on Access to information Progress Report, October through December 2010," (Legal Vice Presidency, 28 March 2011).

64 Email correspondence with Jeff Chelsky, World Bank, 10 March 2012.

65 World Bank 2010 (n55) and 2012 (n45).

Thus, by the time the 2010 Policy was formerly adopted, everything was in place for a smooth transition. A strong consensus was built, reinforced by oversight and control mechanisms and a clear delegation of responsibilities regarding policy enforcement. The architects of the AI implementation plan were nonetheless surprised a year later to see how smoothly and quickly the AI policy took hold.[66] According to one interviewee, "change does not usually come that quickly in the Bank!"

4 Conclusions: The Path Towards AID Transparency

The Bank's 2011 Access to Information Annual Report opens by calling the AI policy a "radical policy shift" which "has heightened the World Bank's interaction with the public…and positively impacted the development community by broadly encouraging other development institutions to adopt similar public access policies, which has helped to push forward the objective of aid transparency and accountability."[67] Once seen as the bastion of secrecy, the Bank was held up in these early years of the current donor transparency as a model of best practice.[68]

The embrace of transparency through its AI policy has contributed to the growth of other major aid transparency initiatives within the Bank and other institutions. The most prominent of these agendas is the aforementioned Open Data Initiative, which makes available to the public—at no cost—the Bank's immense collection of development data, including the once pricey World Development Indicators. The World Bank also initiated a data visualization campaign by mapping all of its active aid projects worldwide through its "Mapping for Results" program. This is an unprecedented exercise in transparency, widely lauded in the press, and has spurred a virtual geomapping race between international aid agencies aspiring to attract similar accolades.

66 Interviews with Gutman (n26), Dobson (n26), and Anstey (n26). See also Hannah George, "Raising the Bar on Transparency, Accountability and Openness," (Blog entry on World Bank's "Inside the Web," 16 February 2012); World Bank, "World Bank's Financial Data, Open and Transparent," World Bank Press Release No. 2012/148/CTR, 9 November 2011.

67 World Bank (n45), 1. See also Bank Information Center. *Unlocking the World Bank's Access to Information Policy: Your Key to the Vault* (Bank Information Center, September 2010) <www.bicusa.org/en/Document.102341.aspx> accessed 10 June 2015.

68 According to Chad Dobson, Executive Director of the BIC, in 2012 "the World Bank's Access to Information Policy continues to set the standard for other institutions to strive for" [quoted in *George* (n65)].

Early information disclosure and accountability policy shifts at the World Bank did not spontaneously diffuse to other regional development banks (RDBS), but have had some spillover effects. As Paul Nelson (2001) documents in his excellent review of earlier disclosure reforms,[69] in the 1990s, the RDBS diverged from the path taken by the World Bank, creating initially weaker disclosure rules and less independent investigation mechanisms. Others, however, argue that since this period "the [World Bank's] policy has encouraged other development institutions to adopt similar public access policies, and, equally important, fosters more systematic engagement with civil society organizations… For example, local civil society organizations have leveraged the AI policy to monitor project procurement plans, encourage access to information initiatives from their own government, and conduct independent review of development outcomes."[70]

There are clear trends in terms of the diffusion of AI policies. Annex 1 below ("Summary of Access to Information Policies in Bilateral and Multilateral Development Banks") overviews the current set of access to information policies at other major multilateral and bilateral development banks. Most of these institutions have overhauled their information disclosure policies and opted for more proactive access to information and open data policies over the past 10 years.

This growth of AI policies in bilateral and multilateral development agencies signals a strong convergence around transparency norms in international development aid. Moreover, the transparency and accountability movement as a whole has resulted in a number of national and agency level initiatives around open aid data. For example, Sweden and the UK passed Aid Transparency Guarantees in January and June 2010, respectively. Each also developed open data platforms (Sweden's openaid.se and UK's DevTracker), which were followed by others, including Denmark's Open Aid website, the US Department of States' Foreign Assistance Dashboard and USAID' Foreign Aid Explorer.

In sum, the past ten years of aid agencies' experiences in adopting proactive AI and broader open data policies offers several key lessons for other development institutions seeking to follow suit. First, strong organizational leadership is needed to initiate transparency initiatives and to overcome the "cultural fear" among staff regarding what open data standards will mean for daily work routines and relationships with client governments. Management and staff of organizations understandably also have concerns that data may be

69 Nelson (n3).
70 George (n65).

misinterpreted and misused by the public.[71] AI policy reforms may be easier in multilateral and bilateral institutions whose political principals are in countries with preexisting FOIA and commitments to other open data initiatives. Second, agencies (and their respective principals) must be able and willing to devote time and resources to developing systems to support such policies. Interviews with numerous staff of development aid agencies over the past seven years, at both headquarters and mission officers, reveal that there are often unanticipated technological challenges and hidden costs in replacing established data systems.

Moreover, the human element of switching over to new data standards and norms cannot be neglected. Organizational learning and change takes time and constant monitoring to ensure full compliance with new policies. This is especially true for agencies with more decentralized structures. For example, key informant interviews suggested that agencies with more centralized data systems (e.g., in UK DFID) have fewer—albeit not insignificant—barriers to entry than less centralized organizations. For example, for USAID, most of the required data is held at the mission level in different software systems, all of which have to converge towards a common standard. This represents significant transaction costs. Similarly, as Rodney (2015) points out, "the [US] State Department is decentralized, with spending authority, contracting authority and procurement norms that vary greatly by bureau and office. If mapped, the State Department would resemble pre-1870 Germany, a colored jigsaw puzzle of different regions, each jealous of its unique culture and authorities." The State Department's bifurcated budget system (with a separation of operational and program spending) and ingrained commitment to upholding "intent and symbolism of its spending" makes the agency more hesitant to reveal spending data that may conflict with its project image. Likewise, the US Millennium Challenge Corporation (which, since 2015 has been at the top or near top of the Aid Transparency Index) reported significant challenges in internal changes around open data policies that were more attributable to technical challenges than any other factor: "The construction of internal data management tools to structure, store and public complex datasets in consumable formats often requires specialized skills not found among the policy staff charged with deciding on agency publication priorities. At the same time, in order to release data responsibly—in a way that allows the public to utilize the data to correctly

71 Heather Hansen, Heather and Catherine Marschner, "Millennium Challenge Corporation: Principles into Practice," Millennium Challenge Corporation 2015) <https://assets.mcc.gov/reports/paper-2015001163301-principles-transparency.pdf> accessed 25 January 2018.

understand the reality that the data represents—care has to be taken at each stage of the decision-making process to ensure a balance between data quality, openness and potential risks."[72]

Despite what appear to be formidable challenges to organizational reform, the transparency revolution is described by many in the international development community as "the genie you can't put back in the bottle." The growth of NGOs and other organizations devoted to monitoring and promoting aid transparency also reinforces this shift in development norms. If development institutions are not proactive in their information policies, it is highly likely that others will seek to fill in the gap with data generated through other means.[73] At a minimum, progressive access to information—and even "right to information" and open data policies—are now integrated centrally into the expectations and goals of international treaties and commitments such as the 2030 UN Sustainable Development Goals. Ultimately, while aid transparency may not be the silver bullet for alleviating poverty or inciting economic growth, it at least holds forth the promise of accountability and enhanced legitimacy for the global governance of development.

---

72 Ibid.

73 See, for example, the efforts by AidData to track Chinese development finance: < http://china.aiddata.org/> accessed 26 January 2018.

ANNEX 1: Summary of Access to Information Policies in Bilateral and Multilateral Development Banks

Donor	ATI Index Rating	Information Disclosure Policy	Summary of policy	Adoption Date of policy	URL to Policy
UNDP	Very good	Yes, clear information disclosure policy in place	Presumption in favor of disclosure unless information falls under confidentiality exceptions which are provided in the policy. Information defined as printed or electronic materials that provide knowledge about UNDP activities, including, but not limited to, programs and operations of UNDP. Four principles guiding policy: Maximize access to information; limited exceptions; simple and broad access to information; explanation of decisions and right to review. Has an information disclosure oversight panel "to oversee the implementation of the Information Disclosure Policy and to consider and review appeals relating to information disclosure."	10 January 1997; major revision in August 2004	http://www.undp.org/content/undp/en/home/operations/transparency/information_disclosurepolicy.html

Donor	ATI Index Rating	Information Disclosure Policy	Summary of policy	Adoption Date of policy	URL to Policy
US, MCC	Very good	Yes, some form of information disclosure policy in place through the Open Government Plan	"Decisions on public release of information are based on a presumption of disclosure. If information does not meet any of the exceptions laid out by the Freedom of Information Act (FOIA) or in other regulations or presidential memos, MCC works to disclose the information." There is a Policy on Access to Information and Materials that outlines exceptions to disclosure and "provides internal guidance to MCC staff on how to effectively disclose information." The Open Government Plan outlines how the MCC works towards proactive disclosures. The section states that the MCC works to share its wealth of data and information with the public; the MCC releases complete financial	17 March 2017	Open Government Initiative https://www.mcc.gov/initiatives/initiative/open https://www.mcc.gov/resources/doc/policy-for-monitoring-and-evaluation

			and program performance information, monitoring and evaluation data, independent evaluations, economic analysis, country selection and procurement information to the public.		
UNICEF	Very good	Yes, clear Information Disclosure Policy under UNICEF's Legal information	Information should be accessible as much as possible, reasonable and practical, on one or more of the UNICEF public-access websites or websites of the United Nations System and disclosed except for confidential information. Information is any produced content, whatever its medium (paper, electronic or sound, visual or audiovisual recording) concerning a matter relating to the policies, activities and decisions of UNICEF.	Adopted in September 2010; updated in May 2011	https://www.unicef.org/about/legal_58506.html https://www.unicef.org/publicpartnerships/files/UNICEF_Transparency_and_Accountability_-_UNICEF_Information_Disclosure_Policy.pdf
UK, DFID	Very good	There is a Freedom of Information Act	Under the Freedom of Information Act 2000, every public body in the UK must produce a publication scheme. The scheme makes it easy for you to access information about our activities.	2002	https://www.gov.uk/government/organisations/department-for-international-development/about/publication-scheme

Donor	ATI Index Rating	Information Disclosure Policy	Summary of policy	Adoption Date of policy	URL to Policy
Global Fund	Very good	Yes, there is a Policy for the Disclosure of Reports Issued by the Office of theInspector General. There is also an information disclosure policy in the Core Documents Policy	The Global Fund will make the fullest disclosure of records possible, consistentwith the rights of individuals to privacy, the property rights of persons in trade sects and confidential commercial or financial information, and the need of the Global Fund to promote frank internal deliberations. There are disclosure categories included in the Core Documents Policy as well as exceptions to the disclosure policy.	The Documents Policy was published in May 2007.	https://www.theglobalfund.org/media/3042/oig_disclosureofreportsissuedbyoig_policy_en.pdfhttps://www.theglobalfund.org/media/5715/core_documents_policy_en.pdf
World Bank, IDA	Very good	Yes, there is the World Bank Policy on Access to Information and The World Bank Policyon Disclosure of Information	The World Bank Policy on Access to Information: Underlying the policy is the principle that the World Bank (namely the International Bank for Reconstruction and Development and the International Development Association) will disclose any information in its possession that is not on its list	World Bank Policy on Access to Information: adopted on July 1, 2010. The URL links to a	http://pubdocs.worldbank.org/en/393051435850102801/World-Bank-Policy-on-Access-to-Information-V2.pdf

			of exceptions. The policy also outlines a clear process for making information publicly available and provides a right to appeal if information-seekers believe they were improperly or unreasonably denied access to information or there is a public interest case to override an exception that restricts access to certain information. Based on five principles: Maximizing access to information; Setting out a clear list of exceptions; Safeguarding the deliberative process; Providing clear procedures for making information available; and Recognizing requesters' right to an appeals process.	document that reflects revisions made on June 30, 2015	
IADB	Very good	Yes, there is an Access to Information Policy document	The policy will apply to information produced by the Inter-American Development Bank and to specific information that is in the possession of the Bank, subject to a list of	4/26/2010; supersedes a policy dated August 17, 2006	http://idbdocs.iadb.org/wsdocs/getdocument.aspx?docnum=35167427

Donor	ATI Index Rating	Information Disclosure Policy	Summary of policy	Adoption Date of policy	URL to Policy
			exceptions. The policy will cover information on Bank activities produced by the Bank in connection with its Office of Evaluation and Oversight, its Office of Institutional Integrity (OII), its Sanctions Committee and the Independent Consultation and Investigation Mechanism (ICIM). Based on four principles: Maximize access to information; Narrow and clear exceptions; Simple and broad access to information; Explanations of decisions and right to review.		
ADB	Very good	Yes, there is the 2011 Public Communications Policy (PCP) of the Asian Development Bank: Disclosure and Exchange of Information	ADB's Public Communications Policy (PCP) expands the scope and type of information ADB makes publicly available. It also allows for earlier disclosure of most Board documents, and offers a more effective framework for proactively disclosing information and responding to information requests on a timely basis.	October 2011; revised a 2005 Public Communication Policy	https://www.adb.org/documents/pcp-2011 https://www.adb.org/site/disclosure/main

			Based on the following principles: presumption in favor of disclosure; accountability and transparency in ADB operations; proactive sharing of knowledge and lessons learned; improved access to operational information; promotion of an information and knowledge-sharing culture; greater two-way information exchange to promote participatory development; timely response to requests for information and documents.		
Sweden, MFA-Sida	Very good	Could not find a policy but there is an Sweden Open Aid Website		2011	https://openaid.se/aid/2016/
AfDB	Very good	Yes, there is a Policy on Disclosure and Access to Information	The objective of the new Policy on Disclosure and Access to Information (DAI) is to provide aclear framework for ensuring greater awareness and understanding of the Bank's developmentmandate and activities through	Adopted in 1997; revised in 2004 and 2005	https://www.afdb.org/fileadmin/uploads/afdb/Documents/Policy-Documents/Bank_Group_Policy_on_Disclosure_and_Acess_to_Infomation.pdf

Donor	ATI Index Rating	Information Disclosure Policy	Summary of policy	Adoption Date of policy	URL to Policy
			public outreach, and providing better access to information,particularly on the Bank's operations. The revised policy constitutes a major change from a list-based eligibility approach for disclosure, to one under which the presumption of disclosure applies to any information in the Bank Group's possession that is not on a list of exceptions. Based on guiding principles: Maximum disclosure; Proactive disclosure; Limited exceptions to disclosure; Enhanced access to information; Consultative approach; Safe-guarding the deliberative process; Right to Appeal		
GAVI	Good	yes, there is the Gavi Access to Information Policy	The purpose of this policy is to enhance Gavi's accountability towards Alliance partners and stakeholders, as well as the general public who may be interested in Gavi's work, by providing access to the information that will	Approved 5 March 2015	https://www.gavi.org/library/gavi-documents/corporate-policies/gavi-access-to-information-policy/ http://www.gavi.org/about/governance/corporate-policies/

			enable Gavi partners and stakeholders to understand its governance, strategies, policies and activities. Guiding principles: Transparency; presumption in favor of disclosure; easy access to information. Policy includes disclosure categories and exceptions to the presumption in favor of disclosure. Also includes appeals process.		
Canada, (CIDA->Global Affairs Canada?)	Good	There is an Access to Information Act under the Canadian government. I had trouble finding the document itself			
EC, NEAR	Good	Sort of, in the EU (so in the European Commission I assume) there is a commitment to transparency and Freedom of Information under	In the spirit of transparency, EU residents can access and obtain documents directly online, through registers and databases or by individual requests. Under Article 15 of the Treaty on the Functioning of the	2003	https://ec.europa.eu/info/about-european-commission/service-standards-and-principles/transparency/freedom-information_en

Donor	ATI Index Rating	Information Disclosure Policy	Summary of policy	Adoption Date of policy	URL to Policy
		Article 15 of the Treaty of the Functioning of the European Union	European Union, citizens and residents of EU countries have a right of access to the documents of the European Parliament, the Council and the European Commission. Each institution, body, office or agency shall ensure that its proceedings are transparent and shall elaborate in its own Rules of Procedure specific provisions regarding access to its documents, in accordance with the regulations referred to in the second subparagraph.		
EC, ECHO	Good	Sort of, in the EU (so in the European Commission I assume) there is a commitment to transparency and Freedom of Information under Article 15	In the spirit of transparency, EU residents can access and obtain documents directly online, through registers and databases or by individual requests. Under Article 15 of the Treaty on the Functioning of the European Union, citizens and residents of EU countries have a right of access to	2003	https://ec.europa.eu/info/about-european-commission/service-standards-and-principles/transparency/freedom-information_en

		of the Treaty of the Functioning of the European Union	the documents of the European Parliament, the Council and the European Commission. Each institution, body, office or agency shall ensure that its proceedings are transparent and shall elaborate in its own Rules of Procedure specific provisions regarding access to its documents, in accordance with the regulations referred to in the second subparagraph.		
EC, DEVCO	Good	Sort of, in the EU (so in the European Commission I assume) there is a commitment to transparency and Freedom of Information under Article 15 of the Treaty of the Functioning of the European Union	In the spirit of transparency, EU residents can access and obtain documents directly online, through registers and databases or by individual requests. Under Article 15 of the Treaty on the Functioning of the European Union, citizens and residents of EU countries have a right of access to the documents of the European Parliament, the Council and the European	2003	https://ec.europa.eu/info/about-european-commission/service-standards-and-principles/transparency/freedom-information_en

Donor	ATI Index Rating	Information Disclosure Policy	Summary of policy	Adoption Date of policy	URL to Policy
			Commission.Each institution, body, office or agency shall ensure that its proceedings are transparent and shall elaborate in its own Rules of Procedure specific provisions regarding access to its documents, in accordance with the regulations referred to in the second subparagraph.		
Netherlands, MFA	Good	Could not find a policy			
Denmark, MFA	Good	There is the Danish Access to Public Administration Files Act	Under the Access to Public Administrations Files Act, the public can request access to administration files. This applies to missions abroad. The default option is disclosure of both physical and digitally stored information, but the public right of access to information may be subject to limitations when the specific information in question is "internal case material"	19 December 1985	http://workingfordenmark.um.dk/en/mfa-at-work/political-and-legal-mandate/our-legal-foundation/public-access-to-information/http://legislationline.org/documents/action/popup/id/6833

			or when protection of information is essential with regard to national security or economic or foreign policy interests. The Legal Department at the MFA has issued internal guidelines on how to respond to requests for access to public administration files and organizes internal courses for staff of the MFA. The act includes exemptions and a duty to take notes.		
Germany, BMZ-GIZ	Good	Yes, there is an is a Transparency and Information Policy.	The policy is designed not only to provide the public with data and documents on GIZ's work and results, but also to foster an intensive exchange of information with partners in project countries, clients and cooperation partners. Based on the principles of transparency, confidentiality, copyright,	Document published October 2011	https://www.giz.de/en/downloads/giz2011-en-policy-transparency.pdf

Donor	ATI Index Rating	Information Disclosure Policy	Summary of policy	Adoption Date of policy	URL to Policy
			economic efficiency, reciprocity. GIZ is bound by the provisions of the German Government's Public Corporate Governance Code and guided by the Code's recommendations on transparency.		
US, USAID	Fair	There is a Freedom of Information Act (FOIA)	The Freedom of Information Act (FOIA), enacted in 1966, generally provides that any person has the right to request access to federal agency records or information. Federal agencies are required to disclose records upon receiving a written request for them, except for those records that are protected from disclosure by any of the nine exemptions or three exclusions of the FOIA. This right of access is enforceable in court.	1966	https://www.usaid.gov/foia-requests
Germany, BMZ-KfW	Fair	Could not find a policy			
US, Treasury	Fair	There is a Freedom of Information Act (FOIA)	The Freedom of Information Act (FOIA), enacted in 1966, generally	1966	https://www.treasury.gov/FOIA/Pages/index.aspx

			provides that any person has the right to request access to federal agency records or information. Federal agencies are required to disclose records upon receiving a written request for them, except for those records that are protected from disclosure by any of the nine exemptions or three exclusions of the FOIA. This right of access is enforceable in court.		
US, PEPFAR	Fair	I did not find much information, but I did find an interesting blog-post on the Center for Global Development.			https://www.cgdev.org/blog/improving-pepfar%E2%80%99s-data-management-and-disclosure
US, State	Fair	There is a Freedom of Information Act (FOIA)	The Freedom of Information Act (FOIA), enacted in 1966, generally provides that any person has the right to request access to federal agency	1966	https://foia.state.gov/Request/Guide.aspx

Donor	ATI Index Rating	Information Disclosure Policy	Summary of policy	Adoption Date of policy	URL to Policy
			records or information. Federal agencies are required to disclose records upon receiving a written request for them, except for those records that are protected from disclosure by any of the nine exemptions or three exclusions of the FOIA. This right of access is enforceable in court.		
EIB	Fair	Yes, there is the EIB Public Disclosure Policy also a Transparency Policy	This Policy is guided by openness and the highest possible level of transparency with the underlying presumption that information concerning the Group's operational and institutional activities will be made available to third parties (the public) unless it is subject to a defined exception ("presumption of disclosure"). Policy includes list of types of documents it will publish, how and where it will	Adopted in 2002; revised in 2007 and 2015	http://www.eib.org/attachments/strategies/eib_group_transparency_policy_en.pdf

			publish them, in a variety of languages, and the restrictions of this policy. The policy document includes a section on the disclosure of information and exceptions, as well as procedures for handling requests.		
Australia	Fair	There is Freedom of Information Act 1982 under the Australian government. There is also a Principles on open public sector information.	The Freedom of Information Act 1982 enforces the right of citizens to access information held by the government, restricted only where there is a stronger public interest in withholding access. There is a process for citizens to request information. There is also the Office of the Australian Information Commissioner (OAIC) advises the Australian Government on how to be more open, accountable and transparent; make public sector information accessible, discoverable and useable; collect, use and manage public sector information efficiently; make public	Adopted in 1982	https://www.oaic.gov.au/information-policy/about-information-policyhttp://dfat.gov.au/about-us/corporate/freedom-of-information/pages/freedom-of-information.aspx https://www.oaic.gov.au/resources/information-policy/information-policy-resources/principles-on-open-public-sector-information.pdf

Donor	ATI Index Rating	Information Disclosure Policy	Summary of policy	Adoption Date of policy	URL to Policy
			sector information more readily and freely available to the public to maximize its reuse and value give citizens new opportunities to engage in, and develop, Australian Government processes and policies. There are also the Principles on open public sector information: Open access to information—a default position; Engaging the community; Effective information governance; Robust information asset management; Discoverable and useable information; Clear reuse rights; Appropriate charging for access; Transparent enquiry and complaints processes.		
EBRD	Fair	Yes, there is a EBRD Public Information Policy	The EBRD is guided by the underlying presumption that, whenever possible, information concerning the Bank's operational and institutional activities will be made available to the public in the absence of a compelling reason for confidentiality	May 2014	http://www.ebrd.com/what-we-do/strategies-and-policies/public-information-policy.html

			Based on the following principles: Transparency; Accountability and governance; Willing to listen and receptive to comment; Safeguarding the business approach to implementing the mandate; Requesting Board Reports for public sector projects. The website also publishes yearly reports on the implementation of the policy.		
Belgium, DGCD	Fair	There is a commitment to transparency and communication; member of IATI	There is a section on transparency between the Belgian public and stakeholders and the international community. Our vision of a transparent development policy consists of: adequately collecting information and documentation related to the policy, activities, results and partners of Belgian development cooperation; systematically communicating this information to the Belgian population,	signed IATI in 2012	https://diplomatie.belgium.be/en/policy/development_cooperation/who_we_are/our_organisation/aid:transparency https://diplomatie.belgium.be/en/policy/development_cooperation/how_we_work/effectiveness_of_aid

Donor	ATI Index Rating	Information Disclosure Policy	Summary of policy	Adoption Date of policy	URL to Policy
			to stakeholders and beneficiaries of the Belgian development cooperation in the South.As laid out in the Aid Effectiveness Agenda, the DGCD believes that Effective transparency requires: that information is easily accessible for interested parties which means it should be published somewhere online, and that (as far as possible worldwide) standards are used both in terms of content (which parameters, which information) as well as in terms of format (specific classifications, codes, deadlines when new data can be expected to be published, agreements on software).		
US, Defense	Fair	There is a Freedom of Information Act (FOIA)	The Freedom of Information Act (FOIA), enacted in 1966, generally provides that any person has the right to request access to federal agency	1966	http://open.defense.gov/Transparency/FOIA.aspx

records or information. Federal agencies are required to disclose records upon receiving a written request for them, except for those records that are protected from disclosure by any of the nine exemptions or three exclusions of the FOIA. This right of access is enforceable in court.

Open and Transparent Government expands upon the principles of full disclosure of information from the government to its citizens, established in the Freedom of Information Act, to further provide a culture in which agencies are responsible for reporting their plans, successes and failures to the citizens they serve. The Department of Defense (DoD) is committed to the Open Government initiative and FOIA is at the core of government transparency at the DoD

Donor	ATI Index Rating	Information Disclosure Policy	Summary of policy	Adoption Date of policy	URL to Policy
Spain, MAEC-AECID	Fair	Under the 2014-2017 Strategic Plan there is the SG7: Improving communication with citizens on development, cooperation and the Agency. There is also the Law 19/2013, on transparency, access to public information and good governance.	The Law on Transparency, Access to Public Information and Good Governance will in general terms be a useful tool for citizens and organizations interested in inquiring on the government's actions in this area. Consequently, they will be able to demand that public institutions be accountable for the obligations they contracted.Several measures are laid out in the Strategic Plan regarding accountabilty and transparency. Under transparency, the AECID there is the Consolidation of "Info@od," which consists of a tool that facilitates coordination among the actors of the Spanish Cooperation for data collection. There is also a commitment to complement previously described measures, and endeavor to publish and explain the logic behind all documents related to strategic planning.	2013	http://www.aecid.es/Centro-Documentacion/Documentos/Planificaci%C3%B3n/Plan_Estrategico_AECID_2014-2017_%20EN.pdfhttp://www.aecid.es/Centro-Documentacion/Documentos/Planificaci%C3%B3n/iv_master_plan_spanish_cooperation.pdf#search=Law%2019%2F2013%2C%20on%20transparency%2C%20access%20to%20public%20information%20and%20good%20governance

Gates Foundation	Fair	Yes, there is the BILL & MELINDA GATES FOUNDATION OPEN ACCESS POLICY	There is an Open Access policy that enables the unrestricted access and reuse of all peer-reviewed published research funded, in whole or in part, by the foundation, including any underlying data sets. The policy contains the following elements: Publications Are Discoverable and Accessible Online; Publication Will Be On "Open Access" Terms; Foundation Will Pay Necessary Fees; Publications Will Be Accessible and Open Immediately; Data Underlying Published Research Results Will Be Accessible and Open Immediately.	January 1, 2015	https://www.gatesfoundation.org/How-We-Work/General-Information/Open-Access-Policy
Switzerland, SDC	Fair	There is a Freedom of Information Act (FOIA) and many commitments to transparency	Like the rest of the federal administration, the SDC is subject to the Freedom of Information Act (FoIA), which entered into force on 1 July 2006. The law grants any citizen the right to inspect official documents and to	July 1 2006	https://www.eda.admin.ch/deza/en/home/activities-projects/grundsaetze-transparenz.html

Donor	ATI Index Rating	Information Disclosure Policy	Summary of policy	Adoption Date of policy	URL to Policy
			obtain information from the authorities without the need to state a reason for the request. The requests must be processed within 20 days.		
France, AFD	Fair	Could not find a policy			
Japan, JICA	Fair	No clear access to information policy, I include a link to Compliance and Anti-Corruption policies.			https://www.jica.go.jp/english/our_work/compliance/index.html
Norway, MFA	Fair	Could not find a policy			http://ati.publishwhatyoufund.org/2014/donor/unocha/
Finland, MFA	Poor	Could not find a policy			
France, MAEDI	Poor	Could not find a policy			

UN OCHA	Poor	Could not find a policy	From the ATI website: It should publish a disclosure policy in line with best practice on presumption of disclosure, exceptions, public interest overrides and independent appeals processes.		
Ireland, IrishAid	Poor	There is are the Freedom of Information Acts of 1997 and 2003	The Freedom of Information Acts 1997 and 2003 allows you to access, to the greatest extent possible, information held by the Department. It gives you the right to have your personal data corrected or updated and to get reasons for decisions taken by the Department that affect you. For transparency and openness, we post FOI requests for non-personal information and the subsequent reply on our Freedom of Information Request Database. The database is ordered by year and month.	1997; 2003	https://www.irishaid.ie/accountability/how-we-are-accountable/

Donor	ATI Index Rating	Information Disclosure Policy	Summary of policy	Adoption Date of policy	URL to Policy
IMF	Poor	Yes, Funds Trasparency Policy - Archives Policy. There is also a Transparency at the IMF fact sheet outlining internal policies to ensure transparency.	Publication of country documents prepared for consideration by the IMF Executive Board ("Board documents") is typically "voluntary but presumed," meaning that, while voluntary, the publication of these documents is encouraged. An even stronger presumption applies to publication of documents relating to the use of Fund resources, though their publication is voluntary. Outside persons, on request, will be given access under the terms specified in this Decision to documentary materials maintained in the Fund's archives	IMF Fact Sheet published in October 2017; The Funds Transparency Policy - Archives Policy became effective on March 17, 2010.	http://www.imf.org/About/Factsheets/Sheets/2016/07/27/15/35/Transparency-at-the-IMF?pdf=1

World Bank, IFC	Poor	Yes, there is a IFC access to information policy	This document sets out the policy of the International Finance Corporation (IFC) regarding the scope of information that it makes available to the public either as a routine matter or upon request. IFC believes that transparency and accountability are fundamental to fulfilling its development mandate. Transparency is essential to building and maintaining public dialogue and increasing public awareness about IFC's development role and mission. It is also critical for enhancing good governance, accountability, and development effectiveness. This policy reaffirms and reflects IFC's commitment to enhance transparency about its activities, improve development effectiveness, and promote good governance.	January 1, 2012	http://documents.worldbank.org/curated/en/232091480670640577/pdf/110692-AIP-English-2012.pdf

Donor	ATI Index Rating	Information Disclosure Policy	Summary of policy	Adoption Date of policy	URL to Policy
			The policy lists exceptions to the policy and what information should be made routinely avaiable, including institutional, financial, investment, advisory-services related documents. It also includes implementation information of the policy like how to access the information and appeals processes.		
Korea, KOICA	Poor	Sort of, there is a commitment to improving its transparency	This commitment includes: continuously stepping up the level of its information disclosure to the International Aid Transparency Initiative(IATI). In 2015, Korea became a member of IATI to boost aid effectiveness. KOICA launched the Integrated ODA Information System in an effort to promote information disclosure for ensuring aid transparency. To manage data more effectively, KOICA reflected the reporting items with criteria based	Became a member of IATI in 2015	http://www.koica.go.kr/english/koica/Trans/index.html

			on both OECD DAC and IATI in the system. Also, it enables us to publish more accurate and timely data to the public. KOICA has been operating an official website that shows statistics on its ODA activities both in Korean and English. KOICA's updated website provides the public with a user-friendly service that allows the user to easily access various types of data regarding KOICA's activities. Moreover, KOICA expects to increase the cooperation with various domestic and foreign partners through this service.		
Italy, MAE	Very poor	I did not find much information, though Italy recently passed a Freedom of Information Act.		Passed in 2016	http://www.foia4italy.it/en/news/italy-approves-freedom-of-information-act/
Japan, MOFA	Very poor	There is an Active Provision of Information to the Public	MOFA has committed itself to appropriate information provision through various media, such as newspapers,	Active Provision of Information	http://www.mofa.go.jp/policy/other/bluebook/2017/html/chapter4/c040301.html

Donor	ATI Index Rating	Information Disclosure Policy	Summary of policy	Adoption Date of policy	URL to Policy
		MOFA blue book and an Information Disclosure and Public Relations section in Japan's Official Development Assistance White Paper 2006.	television and the Internet in order to gain the understanding and support of Japanese nationals for Japan's foreign policy. Specific measures to provide information concerning ODA and create opportunities for Japanese citizens to come into contact with ODA activities include the issuance of government publications such as the ODA White Paper and the Diplomatic Blue Book.	to the Public: 2015. Information Disclosure: 2006.	http://www.mofa.go.jp/policy/oda/white/2006/ODA2006/html/honpen/hp202050204.htm
France, MINEFI	Very poor	Could not find a policy			
China, MOFCOM	Very poor	There is a "Regulations of the People's Republic of China on the Disclosure of Government Information" policy	Since the enforcement of the "Regulations of the People's Republic of China on the Disclosure of Government Information", MOFCOM has been disclosed government information in an all-around and timely manner in accordance with the regulations and has achieved initial effect. By the end of	2008	http://english.mofcom.gov.cn/article/newsrelease/significantnews/200904/20090406146961.shtml

			2008, a total of 1,692 items of government information from 2003 onwards are available in the government information column on MOFCOM website, and 52 applications on government information disclosure were handled. MOFCOM is committed to enforce the "Regulations of the People's Republic of China on the Disclosure of Government Information," and to actively promote the disclosure of government information.		
UAE	Very poor	Could not find a policy			
World Bank, MIGA	n/a	Yes there is a Access to Information Policy.	There is a presumption in favor of disclosure with respect to the information described in this Policy, absent a compelling reason not to disclose such information. There is a list of exceptions included in the policy as well as		https://www.miga.org/documents/Access_Information_Policy.pdf

Donor	ATI Index Rating	Information Disclosure Policy	Summary of policy	Adoption Date of policy	URL to Policy
			a list of information that is routinely made available. There is a process for requesting information included in the policy.		
World Bank, IBRD	n/a	Yes, there is the The World Bank Policy on Access to Information and The World Bank Policyon Disclosure of Information	The World Bank Policy on Access to Information: Underlying the policy is the principle that the World Bank (namely the International Bank for Reconstruction and Development and the International Development Association) will disclose any information in its possession that is not on its list of exceptions. The policy also outlines a clear process for making information publicly available and provides a right to appeal if information-seekers believe they were improperly or unreasonably denied access to information or there is a public interest case to override an exception that restricts access to certain information.	World Bank Policy on Access to Information: adopted on July 1, 2010. The URL links to a document that reflects revisions made on June 30, 2015	http://pubdocs.worldbank.org/en/393051435850102801/World-Bank-Policy-on-Access-to-Information-V2.pdf

			Based on five principles: Maximizing access to information; Setting out a clear list of exceptions; Safeguarding the deliberative process; Providing clear procedures for making information available; and Recognizing requesters' right to an appeals process.		
DANIDA	n/a	There is a commitment to transparency	Danida is committed to transparent development cooperation. Although Danida is one of the most transparent donors, we are continuously striving to improve the public's access to data from programmes and projects. There is a programmes and projects database.	Open Aid website launched in 2013	http://um.dk/en/danida-en/about-danida/Danida-transparency/http://openaid.um.dk/en/
Asian Infrastructure Investment Bank	n/a	In draft form	The AIIB is currently developing its information disclosure policy. As of January 2018, the policy was released for public discussion.		https://www.aiib.org/en/policies-strategies/operational-policies/public-consultation/.content/_download/draft_policy_on_public_information.pdf

CHAPTER 8

The Making of Global Public Authorities: The Role of IFIs in Setting International Labor Standards

*Yifeng Chen**

Abstract

Through liberal interpretations of their mandates, international financial institutions (IFIs) have been able to constantly redefine their own roles. The activities of IFIs have for a long time moved beyond purely financial matters. In seeking popular legitimacy, during the past decades, IFIs have embarked on a governance vocation and reinvented themselves as actors of global governance. In this way, IFIs increasingly absorb Labor standards into their operational policies. The inclusion of Labor standards into the 2016 Environmental and Social Framework of the World Bank serves as a recent example. This chapter examines the role and limitations of IFIs in setting and enforcing Labor standards. Engagement with Labor issues also presents enormous knowledge management and institutional challenges to IFIs. This brings further cultural, ideological and institutional changes to IFIs. In conclusion, the potential of IFIs transforming into public authorities of global environmental and social justice deserves close scrutiny.

1 Introduction

The attitude of international financial institutions (IFIs) towards Labor protection in general was rather passive and at best ambivalent before the 2000s. Labor protection was not conceived as integral to the IFIs policies. The case of structural adjustment projects is a highly illustrative example, where the mplementation of privatization, marketization and deregulation has led to large scale lay-offs and deterioration of social protection, notoriously in the post-communist reforms of eastern European countries. Empirical studies have shown that the structural adjustment projects enforced by the IFIs in

* Associate Professor of International Law, Peking University Law School. Email: yifeng.chen@pku.edu.cn.

general have led to less protection of economic and social rights, particularly the worker' rights in borrowing countries.[1]

Such a passive approach has its constitutional and philosophical reasons. Constitutionally, most IFIs are barred by their constituent documents from intervening in domestic affairs of member states, and Labor issues are considered a domestic matter par excellence. When the World Bank adopted the comprehensive development framework and added a governance perspective to economic development in the 1990s,[2] Labor protection was left out of the governance dimension on purpose. Labor issues were too domestic and too costly to interfere with. Philosophically, Labor was rendered as an element of production and measured in terms of cost and rigidity in traditional developmental economics. Many restructuring projects funded by IFIs compelled the recipient states to deregulate Labor markets so as to bolster economic development. Labor regulation does not easily fit with the neo-liberal economic doctrines of most IFIs.

However, the past two decades witnessed a changing attitude of IFIs and their growing engagement with Labor protection. The incorporation of Labor protection into the work of IFIs has been a fairly recent phenomenon. The change of position is largely a response to the growing external pressure wrought on IFIs. Public criticism against IFIs on the adverse social impact of their work intensified in the late 1980s. The neo-liberal prescriptions of IFIs met with questions from the borrowing countries and were increasingly challenged among scholars. The pressure from the trade unions in large shareholders, such as the American Federation of Labor—Congress of Industrial Organization (AFL-CIO),[3] also plays an influential role in pressing for the policy changes of the World Bank and the International Monetary Fund (IMF).

1 See M. Rodwan Abouharb & David Cingranelli, *Human Rights and Structural Adjustment* (Cambridge University Press 2007).

2 The Comprehensive Development Framework was advocated by the then World Bank President James Wolfensohn, referring to an inclusive, holistic approach to development that links the social, environmental, governance aspects of development to its economic and financial elements. See James Wolfensohn, "New Directions and New Partnerships, Address to the Board of Governors at the Annual Meetings of the World Bank and the International Monetary Fund (10 October 1995)" in World Bank, *Voices for the World's Poor: Selected Speeches of the World Bank President James D. Wolfensohn, 1995–2005* (World Bank 2005), pp. 28–40.

3 The AFL-CIO has repeatedly requested the World Bank and IMF to commit to international Labor standards. See, for examples, AFL-CIO, "Executive Council Statement on Asian Financial Crisis" (29 January 1998) <https://aflcio.org/about/leadership/statements/asian-financial-crisis> accessed 6 May 2018; AFL-CIO, "Executive Council Statement on Equitable, Democratic, Sustainable Development" (18 February 2000) <https://aflcio.org/about/leadership/statements/equitable-democratic-sustainable-development> accessed 6 May 2018.

After the 2000s, Labor protection started to enter into the forefront of the work of IFIS.

The transformation of IFIS' Labor policy is largely facilitated and aided by the fundamental Labor rights movement advocated by the International Labour Organization (ILO). The ILO has experienced a bitter institutional transformation in a quest for relevance in the post-Cold War world order.[4] Until the late 1990s, the ILO has successfully reinvigorated its international foothold by formulating and advocating a set of fundamental Labor rights,[5] embodied in the Declaration on Fundamental Principles and Rights at Work adopted on 18 June 1998. The declaration, for the first time, formally pronounced a list of Labor rights characterized by fundamentals, i.e., freedom of association and collective bargaining, prohibition of forced Labor, prohibition of child Labor, and non-discrimination in respect of employment and occupation.[6] Equally important, the 1998 Declaration pronounced that such fundamental Labor rights emanate from the fact of states being members of the ILO.

With the adoption of the 1998 Declaration and its follow-up, the ILO embarked upon fundamental Labor rights advocacy. This includes two strategies. One front is the campaign with the member states for universal ratification of ILO fundamental Labor conventions, by far a recognizable success if measured by the steady growth in the number of treaty ratifications. On the other front, the ILO initiated dialogues on the possible integration of Labor standards with IFIS whose work has a significant Labor ramification.[7] A growing international recognition of fundamental Labor rights was observed in the late 1990s and the

4 For a useful reference, see ILO, "Report of the Director-General, Defending Values, Promoting Change: Social Justice in a Globalized Economy: An ILO Agenda" (Geneva: International Labor Office 1994).

5 The notion of fundamental Labor rights is much debated in scholarship. For a critical appraisal, see Philip Alston, "'Core Labor Standards' and the Transformation of the International Labor Rights Regime" (2004) 15 *European Journal of International Law* 457, pp. 457–521.

6 The core Labor rights enshrined in the Declaration are embodied in and endorsed by eight ILO fundamental conventions, chronologically, the Forced Labor Convention, adopted 28 June 1930 (No.29); the Freedom of Association and Protection of the Right to Organize Convention, adopted 9 July 1948 (No.87); the Right to Organize and Collective Bargaining Convention, adopted 1 July 1949 (No.98); the Equal Remuneration Convention, adopted 29 June 1951 (No.100); the Abolition of Forced Labor Convention, adopted 25 June 1957 (No.105); the Discrimination (Employment and Occupation) Convention, adopted 25 June 1958 (No.111); the Minimum Age Convention, adopted 26 June 1973 (No.138); and the Worst Forms of Child Labor Convention, adopted 17 June 1999 (No.182).

7 The ILO tried to initiate with the institutional dialogue with the World Bank and the IMF as early as late 1980s. As part of its efforts, The ILO, in cooperation with other parts of the UN system and the Bretton Woods institutions, organized a High-level Meeting on Employment and Structural Adjustment in November 1987, yielding to no concrete result.

beginning of the new millennium. The inter-agency cooperation between the ILO and IFIs, despite their continued difference of approaches to Labor, was further deepened after the 2008 economic crisis.[8]

The entry of Labor standards into the work of IFIs has important implications for Labor governance at global level and for the function and identity of IFIs as well. The incorporation of Labor standards into the policy documents of IFIs may contribute to the development of a set of autonomous IFI Labor standards. These standards are transnational in nature. Their enactment and enforcement are largely self-standing. They are useful supplements, as well as strong competitors, to the international Labor conventions and to the existing procedures and mechanisms of enforcement. They open new paths of global Labor governance. Meanwhile, increasing engagement with Labor protection and other social policy is also quietly transforming the philosophy, culture and structure of IFIs. In committing to environmental protection and social justice, the IFIs have moved away from their role of financial instrumentality and are reconfiguring themselves into public authorities of global governance. Such a reconceptualization brings new intellectual tools and normative frameworks to interpret and regulate the role of IFIs in global governance.

This chapter offers a comprehensive evaluation of the IFIs' engagement with Labor standards. It aims to examine the paths, mechanisms and limits of how IFIs may set and enforce Labor standards in a transnational context. It provides an overview of the history and status quo of IFIs' adoption of Labor standards in Section 2. The richness and diversity of approaches among IFIs are highlighted. Exploration of the substantive content of IFI Labor standards from a comparative perspective follows in Section 3. Controversies surrounding relevant Labor standards are discussed in detail. In Section 4, the relationship of the IFI Labor standards to the ILO standards is analyzed from a normative perspective, and is also reviewed in light of politics between the ILO and IFIs. Section 5 sketches out several challenges that IFIs face in incorporating Labor standards. The tension persists between an economic perspective and a rights-based approach to Labor. The chapter concludes, in Section 6, with some philosophical reflections on the evolving role of IFIs in global governance.

---

8 The Summit of G20 at London in April 2009 requested the ILO to assess Labor impact of the actions taken and advise on further measures. See G20 Leaders' Statement, "The Global Plan for Recovery and Reform" (2 April 2009) <https://www.treasury.gov/resource-center/international/g7-g20/Documents/London%20April%202009%20Leaders%20final-communique.pdf> accessed 6 May 2018.

2 Labor Standards in Social Policies of IFIs: An Evolutionary Trajectory

The incorporation of Labor protection into the work of IFIs is a fairly recent phenomenon. This was pioneered by a modest reference to the core Labor standards in the social protection strategy of the Asian Development Bank (ADB) in 2001. The ADB committed to ensure that its procurement of goods and services, contractors, subcontractors and consultants was in compliance with core labor standards.[9] Taking that as a starting point, the ADB and ILO embarked upon various forms of cooperation thereafter, and the ILO was invited to provide assistance and advice to the work of ADB, at both policy and project levels.[10] Yet, the actual impact of Labor policy on the work of the ADB should not be overstated. Not only the actual enforcement of Labor rights across the ADB projects remains limited and soft, but also the Labor protection in the ADB is confined to a passive Labor policy to promote the operational efficiency of Labor markets.

A full recognition of Labor standards had to wait until the adoption of the Performance Standards on Social & Environmental Sustainability by the International Finance Corporation (IFC) in 2006.[11] Labor and working conditions are featured as a self-standing performance standard. This was the first time a significant IFI had given its full endorsement to the Labor standards in an operational policy. The IFC Labor standards are characterized by the following features, *inter alia*: an express reference to the ILO fundamental Labor conventions, a comprehensive recognition of all core Labor rights, a due emphasis on the occupational health, and an extended protection to contracted workers and workers in supply chains. The IFC Labor standards were further elaborated in the revised Performance Standards of 2012.[12]

---

9 ADB, "Social Protection Strategy" (2001) <https://www.adb.org/sites/default/files/institutional-document/32100/social-protection.pdf> accessed 6 May 2018, pp. 15–6.

10 A comprehensive cooperation agreement was signed between the ILO and ADB. In addition, the ILO and ADB also agree on reciprocal representations on each other's annual meeting, as well as a regular senior consultation meeting on a yearly basis. See Memorandum of Understanding between the Asian Development Bank and the International Labour Organization (9 May 2002) <https://www.adb.org/sites/default/files/institutional-document/33511/files/mou-ilo.pdf> accessed 6 May 2018.

11 IFC, "Performance Standards on Social & Environmental Sustainability" (30 April 2006) <https://www.ifc.org/wps/wcm/connect/608f3a804942f69aaa86fe4f5ddda76e/SustainabilityPolicy.pdf?MOD=AJPERES> accessed 6 May 2018.

12 IFC, "Performance Standards on Social & Environmental Sustainability" (1 January 2012) <https://www.ifc.org/wps/wcm/connect/115482804a0255db96fbffd1a5d13d27/PS_English_2012_Full-Document.pdf?MOD=AJPERES> accessed 6 May 2018.

The successful incorporation of Labor standards by the IFC is largely attributable to the fact that the IFC engages exclusively in private sectors. Those potential clients who gain access to the IFC are usually those economically better-off, administratively well-organized companies. These IFC policy requirements are often in alignment with existing corporate policies on social responsibility and their implementation does not raise insurmountable difficulties from the perspective of a company. Moreover, in essence the Labor policy of the IFC usually goes little beyond requiring the companies to comply with the existing national laws where they operate. The scenario would get much more complicated when an IFI which engages principally in public lending tries to extend its policy to Labor issues.

The example set by the IFC was quickly followed by the European Bank for Reconstruction and Development (EBRD) in 2008 and the European Investment Bank (EIB) in 2009.[13] The EBRD adopted its first environmental policy in 1991.[14] A renewed version of the Environmental and Social Policy was adopted in 2008 where Labor and working conditions were inserted as a separate standard.[15] The EBRD acknowledges its due diligence obligation not to finance projects in contravention of the host country's international legal obligations on environmental protection and human rights. In the 2008 policy, the EBRD emphasized the importance of respect for the freedom of association and right to collective bargaining, which was non-existent in its previous policy statement. Like the IFC, it fully endorses all ILO core Labor standards. Notably the EBRD also paid heed to the law and practice of the European Union on non-discrimination and retrenchment.

The EIB adopted in 2009 the Environmental and Social Principles and Standards and expressly acknowledged the ILO core Labor standards.[16] The EIB policy applies to both public sector and private sector, albeit that the ensuing obligations of clients in different sectors do differ in nature.[17] In its 2013 Environmental and Social Handbook, the EIB further extended its recognition to

13 The EBRD expressly acknowledged that its policy review is partly driven by the adoption of performance standards by the IFC in 2006. See EBRD, "Sustainability Report" (2008), p. 42.

14 It is to be noticed that in the previous version of Environmental Policy of 2003, the EBRD had already addressed "worker protection issues" including occupational health and safety, harmful child Labor, forced Labor and discriminatory practices. See EBRD, "Environmental Policy" (2003) <http://www.ebrd.com/downloads/research/policies/policy.pdf> accessed 6 May 2018.

15 EBRD, "Environmental and Social Policy" (12 November 2008) <http://ebrd.com/downloads/research/policies/2008policy.pdf> accessed 6 May 2018.

16 EIB, *Environmental and Social Handbook* (2013), pp. 18–19.

17 *Ibid*, p. 15.

the UN Guiding Principles on Business and Human Rights.[18] Another feature of the EIB policy is its emphatic protection for migrant workers to whom employers are required to accord fair and non-discriminatory treatment.[19] Moreover, the EIB also instituted an independent Labor audit system. Where the EIB considers the project as involving a high risk of Labor violations or such wrongful activities having occurred, the EIB may require its borrowing clients to carry out a Labor audit by commissioning an independent third party.[20] As the EIB has constantly sought to align itself with the policies of the European Union on sustainability and accountability, its Labor and social policy is broad and proactive.

The precedents set by the IFC, the EBRD and the EIB were inspiring and encouraged other IFIs. Since then, there is a growing acceptance of Labor standards among IFIs. Of course, many other IFIs have refrained from instituting a Labor policy so far, the International Monetary Fund (IMF) and the International Fund of Agricultural Development (IFAD) being prominent examples.

For those IFIs that incorporate Labor standards, there are roughly two categories. In some cases, a comprehensive framework for Labor protection has been pursued. For example, in 2013 the African Development Bank (AfDB) Group[21] adopted its Integrated Safeguards System.[22] Its policy on Labor protection is also comprehensive and is close to that of the IFC and of the EBRD. Another high profile case was the adoption by the World Bank of its Environmental and Social Framework in 2016 after several years' of consultation and debates. In those cases, Labor protection is developed as an elaborate, self-standing standard. Substantive Labor rights, coverage of workers, management of Labor relations and grievance mechanisms are established.

In some other cases, a succinct version of an environmental and social policy is enacted with a brief reference to Labor standards. The examples could include the Sustainability Policy of the Nordic Investment Bank (NIB) adopted on 1 September 2011, where the NIB required its clients to respect

18 *Ibid*, p. 70.

19 *Ibid*, p. 73.

20 *Ibid*, p. 76.

21 The African Development Bank Group includes African Development Bank (AfDB) and African Development Fund (AfDF).

22 African Development Bank Group, "Integrated Safeguards System: Policy Statement and Operational Safeguards" (2013) <https://www.afdb.org/fileadmin/uploads/afdb/Documents/Policy-Documents/December_2013_-_AfDB%E2%80%99S_Integrated_Safeguards_System__-_Policy_Statement_and_Operational_Safeguards.pdf> accessed 6 May 2018.

the four core Labor rights and to provide for safe and healthy working conditions.[23] The Black Sea Trade and Development Bank (BSTDB) also upgraded its Environmental and Social Policy in 2013 and openly committed to "respect for human rights in a working environment," as embodied in the ILO core Labor standards.[24] In 2016 the New Development Bank (NDB) adopted its Environmental and Social Framework which sets occupational health and safety at the center of Labor protection.[25] And in the same year, the Asian Infrastructure Investment Bank (AIIB) approved its Environmental and Social Framework and prescribed Labor standards for both public and private sectors. In addition, projects involving use of forced Labor or child Labor are expressly listed on AIIB's list of exclusions from financing.[26]

The heterogeneity and richness of IFIs in their approaches to Labor protection are to be emphasized. Firstly, the level of Labor protection is uneven between different IFIs. While some IFIs are capable of enforcing a comprehensive framework of Labor standards, some afford only a limited scheme of protection. Some limit applicable Labor standards to the four core Labor standards plus safe working conditions, and some also cover other categories of Labor standards such as wages and rest, migrant workers, and others. Some institutions extend protection from direct workers to contracted workers and supply chain workers, yet many others limit their protection to workers directly engaged by borrowers.

Secondly, the mechanisms of enforcement are diverse. Labor standards could be enforced through a variety of means and procedures, including prior plans or commitments of the borrower, a project's on-site grievance mechanism, independent Labor inspection, or an IFI's complaint mechanism. In some cases, projects or clients engaging in serious Labor violations are listed as exclusions from eligibility for financing.

Thirdly, institutionalization of Labor standards within IFIs varies in terms of degree and means. The majority consider Labor protection as an essential

23 NIB, "Sustainability Policies and Guidelines" (21 March 2012) <https://www.nib.int/filebank/56-Sustainability_Policy_Guidelines-2012.pdf> accessed 6 May 2018.

24 See BSTDB, "Environmental and Social Policy" (1 January 2014) <https://www.bstdb.org/about-us/how-we-operate/Environmental_and_Social_Policy.pdf> accessed 6 May 2018.

25 NDB, "Environmental and Social Framework" (11 March 2016) <https://www.ndb.int/wp-content/themes/ndb/pdf/ndb-environment-social-framework-20160330.pdf> accessed 6 May 2018.

26 AIIB, "Environmental and Social Framework" (February 2016) <https://www.aiib.org/en/policies-strategies/_download/environment-framework/20160226043633542.pdf> accessed 6 May 2018.

element of sustainability,[27] while some takes a no-harm approach and Labor matters are treated in their safeguards policies,[28] and still others have lifted Labor protection up to one of their institutional core values as in the case of the World Bank.[29] The difference of approaches is not just a matter of institutional willingness or awareness of Labor protection but may also reflect varying institutional philosophies on Labor.

In the course of gradual absorption of Labor standards by IFIs, the ILO has played an indispensable role in the dissemination of knowledge and expertise about Labor standards. For example, the ADB has engaged in close cooperation with the ILO. A testimony to such cooperation was the joint publication of a handbook on core Labor standards in 2006.[30] The EBRD also actively resorted to the ILO expertise when designing its Labor standards. In 2006, a thematic meeting on Labor issue was hosted by the ILO where the EBRD staff met with representatives from trade unions, employers and ILO experts.[31] Another prominent example can be found in the formulation of the Environmental and Social Framework of the World Bank. The World Bank has organized three Labor expert meetings respectively in Jakarta (2013), London (2015) and Washington (2015).[32] In all meetings, the ILO representatives were present.

Inter-agency learning is an important factor accounting for the spread of Labor standards. The Multilateral Finance Institutions Working Group on Environment (MFI-WGE) was initiated in 1990s and serves as a useful platform for senior managers of IFIs to discuss and coordinate policies towards

27 The EBRD is a good example in this regard. See EBRD, "Environmental and Social Policy" (12 November 2008).

28 This is the case of the African Development Bank Group's Integrated Safeguards System.

29 World Bank, "Review and Update of the World Bank's Safeguard Policies: The Proposed Environmental and Social Framework, Background Paper" (2 September 2014), p. 1.

30 ADB & ILO, *Core Labor Standards Handbook* (Manila 2006).

31 See EBRD, "Sustainability Report" (2006), p. 11.

32 See World Bank, "World Bank's Safeguard Policies Review and Update, Expert Focus Group on the Emerging Area, Labor and Occupational Health and Safety" (Indonesia 23 March 2013) <https://consultations.worldbank.org/Data/hub/files/meetings/Safeguards_Focus_Group_Labor_Indonesia_Summary_Final.pdf> assessed 6 May 2018; World Bank, "World Bank's Safeguard Policies Review and Update, Labor expert group" (London 21 January 2015) <https://consultations.worldbank.org/Data/hub/files/consultation-template/review-and-update-world-bank-safeguard-policies/en/meetings/safeguards_london_focus_group_meeting_jan_21.pdf> assessed 6 May 2018; World Bank, "Meeting of Labor Experts on the Second Draft of the World Bank's Environmental and Social Standard 2: Labor and Working Conditions (ESS 2)" (Washington DC 18 September 2015) <https://consultations.worldbank.org/Data/hub/files/consultation-template/review-and-update-world-bank-safeguard-policies/en/meetings/ess2_meeting_report_0915.pdf> assessed 6 May 2018.

environmental and social issues. As increasingly social issues are included in the safeguards policy, this working group has been recently renamed as Multilateral Finance Institutions Working Group on Environmental and Social Standards (MFI-WGESS). This working group is rather informal but has been instrumental for institutional learning on environmental and social standards. For example, the African Development Bank expressly acknowledged that its earlier drafts of safeguards policies "have been reviewed by the IFC, World Bank, Asian Development Bank and other members of the MFI Working Group on the Environment (MFI-WGE)."[33] The World Bank also expressly acknowledged that its Labor standards are "derived from provisions of other MDBS."[34]

3 The Rise of Transnational Labor Standards of IFIS: Content and Controversies

As the engagement with Labor standards by IFIs grows, there emerges a recognizable body of Labor standards that are formulated, applied and enforced in a transnational context. While Labor standards are traditionally considered a rather state-centered matter, clearly states are no longer the only *loci* where Labor standards are debated and enacted, nor are states the only actors.[35] On the contrary, Labor standards are increasingly visible in free trade agreements, investment arrangements and in the policy documents of the IFIs. Such a body of Labor standards is prominently transnational by nature. Not only does its formulation occur outside states, so too does its enforcement. Exactly by recognizing and enforcing Labor standards in a transnational space, the IFIs play an increasingly relevant and appreciated role.

The IFI Labor standards are formulated in policy documents of IFIs, usually approved by the boards of executive directors. As an institutional policy and internal regulation, they address primarily the staff of IFIs. The IFI Labor standards do not automatically bind the member states or companies. Strictly speaking, the application of the IFI Labor standards is project-specific. The scope of application is not based upon the principle of *personam* jurisdiction, but instead upon the principle of *in rem* jurisdiction. The Labor standards can

33 See the statement in the "Acknowledgement of the African Development Bank Group, Integrated Safeguards System: Policy Statement and Operational Safeguards" (2013).

34 World Bank, "World Bank Safeguard Policies Review and Update, Proposed Environmental and Social Framework: Background Paper" (2 September 2014), p. 11.

35 The same is true with the ILO. The role of the ILO in formulating hard international Labor standards is declining in recent years.

only be extended to its borrowers through, and to the extent of, project loans and grants.

The choice of the term "transnational" is a purposeful decision here to highlight the operational feature of the IFI Labor standards.[36] The IFI Labor standards do not belong to the formal corpus of international Labor standards, a term traditionally associated with ILO conventions and recommendations. The IFI Labor standards are not "international" in origin. In a project-specific manner, the IFI Labor standards are transmitted to and enforced by borrowers, be they public or private. Through project loans, a transnational space is constructed and maintained, and various actors and norms interact within the space with the IFI sitting at the center. Such a transnational space is built upon the capabilies and resources of the IFIs. And the IFI Labor standards are part of the normative edifice of the transitional space.

3.1 *Content of IFI Labor Standards*

The body of IFI Labor standards is not monolithic, but rather amorphous. It is not a single set of uniform Labor standards, but an aggregation of various sets of independent Labor standards practiced by different IFIs. To group all those standards under the label of IFI Labor standards risks reduction and oversimplification of the richness, diversity and nuance of the IFIs in practicing Labor standards. Some IFIs have incorporated a comprehensive scheme of Labor standards, equal to a mini Labor code.[37] Some may just include general principles in their policy documents.[38]

Yet, a comparative survey shows that a hard core of IFI Labor standards does exist, which is comprised of the ILO fundamental Labor rights, also called core Labor standards. Freedom of association and collective bargaining, prohibition of forced Labor, prohibition of child Labor and non-discrimination are solidly established as the foundation of the IFI Labor standards. However, even as the core Labor standards are widely accepted, their exact contents are in no way uniform or identical. The levels of commitment and strengths of enforcement hinge upon every institution's own philosophy, tradition and capacity.

Another essential aspect of the IFI Labor standards involves safe working conditions. This is the least politically sensitive and morally uncontested part of Labor standards. It is among the first cluster of Labor standards received by

36 For a genealogical account on the use of the concept in the literature of international law and international relations, see Christer Jönsson, "Capturing the Transnational: A Conceptual History" in Jonas Tallberg & Christer Jönsson (eds), *Democracy Beyond the Nation State? Transnational Actors and Global Governance* (Palgrave Macmillan 2010), pp. 22–44.

37 See for example the World Bank and the EBRD.

38 See for the examples of NIB, NDB and AIIB.

the IFIs. Occupational health and safety was already mentioned in the EBRD Environmental Policy of 2003.[39] The World Bank's relevant standards have their origin in its early Environmental Health and Safety Guidelines (EHSG). The World Bank's current standards on occupational health and safety are extensive. They require, among others things, identification of potential hazards, preventive and protective measures, preparedness and responses to emergency and effective remedies for occupational injuries, deaths, disability and disease. The right of workers to refuse to work in hazardous working environments is also reaffirmed in the World Bank Environmental and Social Framework.[40]

Of course, core Labor standards and safe working conditions are not exclusive items of recognized IFI Labor standards. Other standards may involve workers' rights related to hours of work, wages, overtime, compensation and benefits,[41] social security,[42] and the protection of migrant workers.[43] The IFIs enjoy considerable discretions to elaborate their own policy preferences and priorities.

3.2 *The Reach of IFI Labor Standards: Applicable Scope*

To whom are the IFI Labor standards to be applied? What is the scope of protected workers? What are possible jurisdictional linkages? What is the criterion to set the borderline of the IFI Labor standards? A determination on the applicable scope often involves considerations of economic, legal and political factors.

The jurisdictional linkage for the IFIs is financing projects, involving IFI resources. Then the question is whether all persons working on the project or for the project are subject to protection. It is indisputable that those workers the borrowers or clients directly contracted for the implementation of the project are subject to the protection of IFI Labor standards. These workers are called "direct workers." This reflects typically a perspective that treats the borrowers as actual employers and the legal linkage could be established on the basis of employment contracts. Yet, this usually consists of only a small portion of the total Labor force that works on a project. In the first draft of its Environmental and Social Framework, the World Bank limited the applicability of Labor standards to those project workers directly employed by the borrowers. This received critical comments from workers' organization as this formalistic

39 See EBRD, "Environmental Policy" (2003), p. 3, footnote 1.

40 World Bank, "Environmental and Social Framework" (2016), pp. 57–58.

41 *Ibid*, p. 54.

42 See EBRD, "Environmental and Social Policy" (2008), p. 23.

43 See EIB, *Environmental and Social Handbook* (2013), p. 70.

approach would confine the protection of workers to an extremely limited scope.[44] It is a legitimate concern that the responsibility of a borrower could be easily circumvented through outsourcing and by use of agency workers.

Very often, many workers working on the project are engaged by a third party to perform certain functions for the project, known as "contracted workers." Many IFIs expressly extend their Labor standards to the protection of contracted workers. These workers are not directly contracted as employees of the borrowers. Nevertheless a jurisdictional linkage might be established on the basis that their work effectively contributes to the implementation of the project. Such a contribution test sometimes risks an unwarranted expansion of the applicable scope to an undesirable extent. Theoretically, a project may involve thousands of contracts with third parties for procurement of different services. This is the logic of division of Labor and specialization in modern society. Obviously, not all workers, even those who might come to perform services on site, can be necessarily qualified as contracted workers. Then the question arises where the line is to be drawn to distinguish those workers subject to protection and those that are not.

It seems that the test of "core functions" has been widely accepted. The EBRD has limited the scope of contacted workers to those who "performs work directly related to the core functions of the project."[45] An identical definition has been used by the World Bank.[46] The IFC employs the term "core business processes," and yet its actual meaning is the same as "core functions" in practice. As the World Bank provides, "'core functions' of a project constitute those production and/or service processes essential for a specific project activity without which the project cannot continue."[47] This means that only those workers who are essential to the operation of a business or a project are qualified as contracted workers. And the responsibility of the borrowers to Labor protection would not extend to an unknown boundary. In practice, what are the core functions and who are serving the core function remains a highly debatable question. However, efforts seem to be invested towards achieving a reasonable and balanced approach.

As for the contracted workers, they would normally enjoy the same level of protection as offered to direct workers. Moreover, additional efforts may be

44 ITUC/Global Unions, "Major Weaknesses in World Bank's Draft Labor Standards Safeguards" (22 July 2014), p. 4; "French Non-paper on the Bank's Safeguards Review" (April 2015); "German Comments on the World Bank Safeguards Review" (April 2015); "United States Comments on World Bank Safeguards Review – Phase 2" (26 March 2015).

45 EBRD, "Environmental and Social Policy" (2008), p. 25.

46 World Bank, "Environmental and Social Framework" (2016), p. 52.

47 *Ibid.*

demanded from borrowers. This could include, for example, making reasonable efforts in choosing legitimate and reliable third parties, monitoring third parties' performances in Labor protection and ensuring the availability of grievance mechanism for contracted workers.[48]

Probably the most controversial case is whether the Labor standards should reach to the "workers of supply chains." To address the Labor situation in supply chains is largely borrowed from the model of corporate social responsibility. The linkage for IFI Labor standards could only be explained by measuring the market influence the IFIs and their borrowers are capable of exercising as a business partner. It was the IFC which for the first time requested its clients to address Labor situations in supply chains in its performance standards of 2006. The IFC limited the responsibility of its clients to inquiring of its suppliers of Labor-intensive industries about child Labor and forced Labor.[49] The same provision was followed by the EBRD in 2008. Then in 2012, the IFC extended its regulation of supply chain workers to cover workplace safety. Meanwhile, a limitation was added to cover primary supply chains only.[50] The obligation of the borrowers in dealing with the Labor abuse of the supply chain is comparatively soft. It is widely acknowledged that "the ability of the client to fully address these risks will depend upon the client's level of management control or influence over its primary suppliers."[51] Therefore, the borrowers may require the primary supplier to take appropriate steps to remedy child Labor, forced Labor, or unsafe working conditions, or, in case of need, switch business to responsible suppliers.

The subjection of the supply chain to the IFI Labor standards may have its rationale for the private sector, as it could take advantage of the corporate social responsibility model. Yet it is highly questionable whether it is appropriate or feasible to mechanically transpose the system to sovereign lending. Firstly, in the case of sovereign loans it is essential to stress the sovereign nature of the borrowers in terms of responsibility to Labor protection. It is neither desirable nor productive to reduce the sovereign nature of the borrowers to their market role. The borrowers may address child Labor, forced Labor and safe working conditions through legislative, administrative and judicial means. From the perspective of a sovereign, domestic suppliers are of no difference to other legal subjects who are obliged to abide by relevant domestic laws. Secondly, in

48 See World Bank, "Environmental and Social Framework" (2016), p. 58; also IFC, "Performance Standards on Social & Environmental Sustainability" (2012), p. 5.

49 See IFC, "Performance Standards on Social & Environmental Sustainability" (2006), p. 10.

50 See IFC, "Performance Standards on Social & Environmental Sustainability" (2012), p. 6.

51 *Ibid.* An almost identical expression can be found in the World Bank, "Environmental and Social Framework" (2016), p. 60.

relation to workers of supply chains, the IFI Labor standards normally impose upon the borrowers with relatively soft obligations, such as due diligences, inquiry, and switching to new suppliers in case of persistent violations. Those provisions completely ignore the sovereign nature of the borrowers. In cases of child Labor and forced Labor, a responsible sovereign should prosecute the suppliers according to its national laws, and not substitute its legal duties with business decisions. Therefore, the current regime as it stands may function to weaken the protection for workers rather than strengthen it. Last but not least, as pointed out by China and India during the consultation on the World Bank's Environmental and Social Framework, many suppliers are from abroad and it is extremely difficult for the borrowers to monitor the actual Labor conditions of foreign suppliers.[52]

Sovereign states and private sector corporations as clients of the IFIs are fundamentally different in some regards. To apply a corporate social responsibility model to public lending could be counter-productive to Labor protection. The application of Labor standards to workers of supply chains in the public sector would require reconsideration.

3.3 *Politics of Labor Standards: The Freedom of Association as an Example*

Even though the core Labor standards receive broad endorsement, their substance and actual enforcement exhibit profound differences in practice. For example, it is noticed that different countries have very different approaches to the workers' right of unionization. There were, and probably still are, hesitations among the IFIs to include the freedom of association and collective bargaining, which is considered a highly political and sensitive issue in borrowing countries. Even for those rights of a seemingly less political nature,

52 The opinion of the Chinese government is expressed in a World Bank consultation meeting in China, see "Review and Update of the World Bank's Environmental and Social Safeguard Policies, Phase 3, Feedback Summary: Consultative Meeting with Provincial Governments" (Kunming 29 October 2015) <https://consultations.worldbank.org/Data/hub/files/consultation-template/review-and-update-world-bank-safeguard-policies/en/meetings/final_feedback_summary_for_phase_3_consultation_with_chinese_provincial_governments_and_pmos_in_yunnan_october_29.pdf> assessed 6 May 2018. The position of the Indian government can be found at the "Review and Update of the World Bank's Environmental and Social Safeguard Policies," Phase 3, Feedback Summary: Consultative Meeting with Indian Governmental Officials (New Delhi 5–6 November 2015) <http://consultations.worldbank.org/Data/hub/files/consultation-template/review-and-update-world-bank-safeguard-policies/en/meetings/final_feedback_summary_for_phase_3_consultation_with_indian_ministries_state_governments_and_pias_november_5-6.pdf> assessed 6 May 2018.

such as the prohibition of child Labor, the matter may also be received with divergent attitudes in different cultures.

The freedom of association is probably the most politically sensitive right of workers. For many countries, the freedom of association lies at the heart of Labor protection. And the freedom of association is deeply embedded in a liberal political tradition. Labor protection through institutionalized unionization of Labor has functioned in a highly effective manner in countries like Sweden and Finland.[53] Yet, in some other countries, the right to organize is not purely a matter of Labor protection and its exercise is restricted by law or in practice.[54] This may include prior approval or registration for the formation of trade unions, and other forms of restrictions. The difference of positions towards the right to organize among states is also demonstrated by the fact that a number of countries have not ratified the Freedom of Association and Protection of the Right to Organize Convention (No. 87) or the Right to Organize and Collective Bargaining Convention (No. 98). Out of the eight ILO fundamental conventions, both conventions have received the least number of ratifications.[55]

The initial attitude of IFIs towards the freedom of association has also been very cautious. The Labor rights tackled by IFIs used to have a limited spectrum with a special focus on safe working conditions and prohibition of child or forced Labor. An explicit reference to freedom of association was often absent. As observed by Francis Maupin, the former legal counsel of the ILO, "freedom of association and collective bargaining continue to be regarded as civil rights which [World] Bank activities might facilitate, but it still believes that it is not in its mandate to actively promote them, and even less so where they might interfere with economic performance."[56] This is partly due to the economic

53 See for example Reinhold Fahlbeck & Bernard Johann Mulder, *Labor and Employment Law in Sweden* (Juristförlaget 2009), pp. 16–18.

54 See the observations of the ILO in its global report on the freedom of association, in ILO, "Freedom of Association in Practice: Lessons Learned, Global Report under the follow-up to the ILO Declaration on Fundamental Principles and Rights at Work" (International Labor Conference, 97th Session, 2008), p. 11.

55 By the end of March 2018, 154 countries have ratified the ILO Convention No.87, see <http://ilo.org/dyn/normlex/en/f?p=NORMLEXPUB:11300:0::NO:11300:P11300_INSTRUMENT_ID:312232:NO> assessed 6 May 2018, and 165 countries have ratified ILO Convention No.98, <http://ilo.org/dyn/normlex/en/f?p=NORMLEXPUB:11300:0::NO:11300:P11300_INSTRUMENT_ID:312243:NO> assessed 6 May 2018. These numbers are much lower than other 6 ILO fundamental conventions. In Contrast, the Worst Forms of Child Labor Convention (No.182) has received 181 ratifications by far.

56 Francis Maupain, *The Future of the International Labour Organization in the Global Economy* (Hart Publishing 2013), p. 78.

perspective of seeing trade unions negatively as free riders.[57] Moreover, many developing countries where the IFIs operate hold a conservative position towards freedom of association, and those IFIs engaging with public sectors are barred from interfering into the political affairs of the borrowing sovereigns. This was still the case when the World Bank proposed its first draft of Environmental and Social Framework in 2014. In its standard on Labor and working conditions, the World Bank refrained from mentioning the freedom of association among its objectives. Instead, the World Bank took a deferential attitude to the borrowing country. It expressly limited its support to the freedom of association only if the national laws of the borrowing country recognize it.[58]

This cautious approach of the World Bank met with fierce criticisms from Labor NGOs and experts, the ILO and developed countries.[59] The main arguments are summarized as follows. First of all, all core Labor standards are indivisible and as a whole they constitute the floor of protection for workers. There is no reason to segregate the freedom of association from other standards. Secondly, freedom of association and collective bargaining are political rights by nature, and so are other core Labor standards. Freedom of association cannot be justifiably excluded on the grounds of its political nature. Thirdly, the silence of the World Bank might be construed to be permissive of suppressive or retaliatory measures against workers seeking to exercise freedom of association.[60] Fourthly, the obligation to promote core Labor standards arises from states' membership in the ILO.[61] As such, neither the World Bank nor the states should refuse to implement freedom of association on the basis of national laws.[62]

---

57 It used to be the mainstream opinion of the World Bank, see Hannah Murphy, "The World Bank and Core Labor Standards: Between Flexibility and Regulation" (2014) 21 *Review of International Political Economy* 399, p.405, p.417.

58 World Bank, "Environmental and Social Framework: Setting Standards for Sustainable Development, First Draft for Consultation" (30 July 2014) <https://consultations.worldbank.org/Data/hub/files/consultation-template/review-and-update-world-bank-safeguard-policies/en/phases/first_draft_framework_july_30_2014.pdf> assessed 6 May 2018, pp. 36–37.

59 See World Bank, "Safeguard Policies' Review Consultations: Nordic Baltic Position as of February 23, 2015" <http://consultations.worldbank.org/Data/hub/files/nordic_baltic_comments_of_27_feb_2015.pdf> assessed 6 May 2018.

60 ITUC/Global Unions, "Major Weaknesses in World Bank's Draft Labor Standards Safeguards" (22 July 2014), pp. 2–3.

61 ILO, "Declaration on Fundamental Principles and Rights at Work and its Follow-up," adopted by the International Labor Conference at its Eighty-sixth Session (Geneva 18 June 1998).

62 ITUC/Global Unions, "Major Weaknesses in World Bank's Draft Labor Standards Safeguards" (22 July 2014), pp. 2–3.

The World Bank quickly yielded to this pressure after a first round of consultation. The Bank switched to the opposite position in the second draft of the Environmental and Social Framework and provided an unqualified support to the freedom of association as part of its Labor policy. Such a radical change of position generated much concern among developing countries. The primary concern was the absolute nature of the World Bank statement. It is suggested by countries like China that the exercise of freedom of association and collective bargaining should be in accordance with national laws of borrowing countries.[63] Some also suggest that the arrangement concerning the freedom of association and collective bargaining should be specified so as not to cause frustration to project implementation.[64] In response, the World Bank decided to qualify its "support to principles of freedom of association and collective bargaining of project workers in a manner consistent with national law."[65] This formula entered the final text of the World Bank's Environmental and Social Policy in 2016.[66]

3.4 *Feasibility of an Alternative Mechanism*

A highly relevant issue is concerned with the permissibility of the so called "alternative mechanism." To put it simply, in cases where the national laws of the borrowing countries arbitrarily prohibits or restricts the freedom of association, should workers be allowed to develop other means of solidarity as a remedy? In its second draft, the World Bank openly recognized the feasibility, as well as the lawfulness, of the alternative mechanisms autonomously

63 For the opinions of China, see "Review and Update of the World Bank's Environmental and Social Safeguard Policies, Phase 3, Feedback Summary: Consultative Meeting with Provincial Governments" (Kunming 29 October 2015) <https://consultations.worldbank.org/Data/hub/files/consultation-template/review-and-update-world-bank-safeguard-policies/en/meetings/final_feedback_summary_for_phase_3_consultation_with_chinese_provincial_governments_and_pmos_in_yunnan_october_29.pdf> assessed 6 May 2018.

64 World Bank, "Comments/Observations of the Government of Bangladesh on the World Bank's Environmental and Social Safeguard Framework and other Related Documents" (January 2016), <http://consultations.worldbank.org/Data/hub/files/comments_from_govt_of_bangladesh_on_essf-01_12_15.pdf> assessed 6 May 2018, p. 4.

65 World Bank, "Summary of Phase 3 Consultations and Bank Management Responses," p. 22.

66 The qualification of "in a manner consistent with national law" was harshly criticized by the ILO for the reason that a formula as such "undercuts the universal principles adhered to by the ILO's 187 member states and jeopardizes the purpose of having such an objective." See ILO, "Statement on the World Bank Environmental and Social Policy" (8 August 2016) <http://www.ilo.org/global/about-the-ilo/newsroom/statements-and-speeches/WCMS_508328/lang--en/index.htm> assessed 6 May 2018.

developed by workers. “Where national law restricts workers’ organizations, the project will not restrict workers from developing alternative mechanisms to express their grievances and protect their rights regarding working conditions and terms of employment.”[67] The final text of 2016 further imposed an obligation of non-retaliation on the borrowing country. “The Borrower will not discriminate or retaliate against project workers who participate, or seek to participate, in such workers’ organizations and collective bargaining or alternative mechanisms.”[68]

The meaning of the term “alternative mechanism” mentioned above is rather obscure and elusive. The World Bank offers no indication as to what possible remedial measures it actually refers to. Judging from the content, this paragraph is almost identical to the relevant words in the Labor standards of the IFC and most likely was transplanted from there. The IFC’s explanations in its guidance notes shed some light on the alternative mechanism. Two scenarios are conceived. In the case of an absolute prohibition of forming trade unions, the clients of the IFC are requested to give formal recognition to worker committees and have dialogue with the workers’ representatives. Or alternatively, when in some cases the national laws are silent on the matter, the clients are encouraged to give recognition to workers’ organizations and engage collective bargaining with them.[69] In other words, the alternative mechanism in the Labor standards of the IFC requires no more than a private recognition and enforcement of relevant Labor standards to the extent that is permissible under national laws.

However, to transpose the notion of an alternative mechanism from the IFC which engages exclusively with the private sector, to the World Bank which, to the contrary, deals exclusively with sovereign loans could be profoundly misleading and bring frustration. The clients of the World Bank are sovereign states. By requiring borrowing countries not to “seek to influence or control these alternative mechanisms,” and not to retaliate against the workers who participated in workers’ organization, the World Bank mistakenly mixes the states’ role as public institutions with private employers. In other words, the World Bank is asking the borrowing countries to give exemption to the workers

67 Moreover, “the Borrower should not seek to influence or control these alternative mechanisms.” World Bank, “Environmental and Social Framework” (2016), p. 53.

68 *Ibid*, p. 55.

69 IFC, “Guidance Notes: Performance Standards on Social & Environmental Sustainability” (31 July 2007) <http://www.ifc.org/wps/wcm/connect/topics_ext_content/ifc_external_corporate_site/ifc+sustainability/our+approach/risk+management/performance+standards/environmental+and+social+performance+standards+and+guidance+notes> assessed 6 May 2018, pp. 41–42.

who might have breached domestic laws by organizing or participating in the workers' organization.

The inclusion of the alternative mechanism received critical repercussions from developing countries. For example, Chinese officials were of the opinion that the alternative mechanism "will be considered only where the national law allows such mechanism."[70] Bangladesh and others were very much concerned about undesirable conflict with the World Bank standards and national laws if the alternative mechanism were to be put into practice.[71]

The key to the debate is whether the alternative mechanism is within or outside of the ambit of national law.

The World Bank has yet to define the precise concept of alternative mechanism for its own Labor policy. It is, however, very clear that, if the World Bank were to give any meaningful interpretations to the alternative mechanism, it would have to interpret the concept fundamentally differently from that of the IFC. Foremost, it should not overlook the sovereign nature of the borrowers. It should also recall that the Labor standards applicable to the public and private sectors may not be identical. It may be desirable for those IFIs engaging with both public and private sectors to take a dualistic approach to Labor protection.

4 The Nature of IFI Labor Standards: Their Relationship to the ILO Standards

An interesting aspect of the IFI Labor standards is their relationship with the ILO standards. More specifically, when the IFI Labor standards give concrete

70 See "Review and Update of the World Bank's Environmental and Social Safeguard Policies, Phase 3, Feedback Summary: Consultative Meeting with Chinese Governmental Officials" (Beijing 27 October 2015) <http://consultations.worldbank.org/Data/hub/files/consultation-template/review-and-update-world-bank-safeguard-policies/en/meetings/final_feedback_summary_for_phase_3_consultation_with_chinese_central_government_and_institutions_in_beijing_october_27.pdf> assessed 6 May 2018.

71 See "Comments/Observations of the Government of Bangladesh on the World Bank's Environmental and Social Safeguard Framework and other Related Documents" (January 2016) <http://consultations.worldbank.org/Data/hub/files/comments_from_govt_of_bangladesh_on_essf-01_12_15.pdf> assessed 6 May 2018, pp. 4–5; also "Brief of Statement Made by Mr. Subhash Chandra Garg, Executive Director for Bangladesh, Bhutan, India and Sri Lanka, at the Committee on Development Effectiveness on 24 June and 1 July, 2015 on ESF" <https://consultations.worldbank.org/Data/hub/files/consultation-template/review-and-update-world-bank-safeguard-policies/en/materials/final_statement_by_ed_subhash_garg_eds12_on_esf.pdf> assessed 6 May 2018.

expressions to the core Labor standards, should the reference be made to the ILO fundamental Labor conventions and its Declaration on Fundamental Principles and Rights at Work of 1998, or should the IFI Labor standards simply embody the substance of the core Labor standards without resorting to specific ILO documents?

The practice of IFIs in this regard has been diverse. Those IFIs that adopt a comprehensive scheme of Labor standards tend to make a full reference to the ILO fundamental Labor conventions. This is the case for the IFC's Performance Standards of 2006. The IFC expressly acknowledges that its Labor standards "have been in part guided by a number of international conventions negotiated through the International Labour Organization (ILO) and the United Nations (UN)." A further reference to all eight ILO fundamental Labor conventions was detailed in a footnote.[72] The same applies more or less to the EBRD's Environmental and Social Policy of 2008, and to the AfDB Group's Integrated Safeguards System of 2013. Some other IFIs with a relevant succinct policy document may avoid explicit reference to the ILO conventions, as in the case of the NIB's Sustainability Guidelines of 2012. Yet, one may also make a brief reference to the ILO Conventions as in the case of the BSTDB's Environmental and Social Policy of 2014. Another way of looking at the matter is by examining the portfolios and activities of the IFIs. Those IFIs engaged more, or exclusively, with the private sector are more inclined to refer to the ILO Conventions. On the contrary, those engaged more with the public sector are more cautious in referring to the ILO Conventions.

To give reference to the ILO standards or not is not just a matter of formality or theoretical interest. Rather, this will largely affect the normative operation of the IFI Labor standards, as well as their foundational authority. Are the IFI Labor standards simply to be understood as no more than a transposed expression of established ILO Labor standards, or rather, does their authority derive from the IFIs themselves and as such constitute a set of Labor standards *sui generis*? And if there should arise differences of opinions of certain Labor standards, would the IFIs have to resort to the ILO Conventions and relevant jurisprudence to search for a correct interpretation, or would the IFIs be entitled to develop their own institutional standards and jurisprudence?

When the World Bank drafted its Labor standards, a number of Western countries requested the World Bank to link its Labor standards to the ILO

72 IFC, "Performance Standards on Environmental and Social Sustainability" (1 January 2012), Performance Standard 2 Labor and Working Conditions, para. 2.

Conventions.[73] The US urged the Bank to incorporate reference to the ILO Declaration on the Fundamental Principles and Rights at Work.[74] The ILO also actively lobbied for the inclusion of the ILO Conventions. An obvious advantage of reference to the ILO Conventions is that the very content of IFI Labor standards has a reliable source. To borrow the ILO standards could avoid reopening many debates that were already concluded at the time of drafting ILO Conventions. At the end, since the IFIs are not specialized in Labor protection, it may be desirable to heed the knowledge and expertise of the ILO. Moreover, as the ILO standards are internationally recognized standards, it may also be conducive to a uniform application of Labor standards.

Yet, the proposal of incorporating the ILO Conventions in the World Bank social policies was viewed with much vigilance among developing countries. The major concern is that this might amount to a de facto imposition of ILO Conventions and bypass the ratification procedures.[75] In other words, the ILO fundamental Labor conventions may be enforced through World Bank policies against a borrowing country even if the country has not acceded to all the ILO fundamental Conventions. The traditional ILO approach to the promotion of Labor standards relies upon voluntary ratification of Labor conventions by states. And to ratify a treaty or not is always an essential feature of the sovereign prerogative. However, if the ILO Conventions are referred to in the Labor standards of the IFIs, the sovereign borrowers are obliged to implement those Labor standards in the role of clients irrespective of their non-ratification. World Bank Labor standards would be equivalent to a coerced application of ILO Conventions. It is therefore in this consultation that China suggested the Bank confine itself to reference to general principles, but not the ILO Conventions.[76]

---

73 See for an example, "Review and Update of the World Bank's Environmental and Social Safeguard Policies, Phase 2, Feedback Summary: Consultative Meeting with Consultation with Government Officials from Belgium and the Netherlands" (Brussels 10 November 2014) <https://consultations.worldbank.org/Data/hub/files/consultation-template/review-and-update-world-bank-safeguard-policies/en/meetings/safeguard_review_phase_2_consultations_2014_-_feedback_summary_brussels_government_and_multilaterals_meeting_november_10.pdf> assessed 6 May 2018.

74 "United States Comments on World Bank Safeguards Review–Phase 2" (26 March 2015) <https://consultations.worldbank.org/Data/hub/files/2015-3-26_usg_comments_on_draft_wb_esf_final.pdf> assessed 6 May 2018.

75 For example, the ADB considers the core Labor standards as automatically applicable. "Internationally recognized labor standards, when ratified, are also part of the legislative framework of a DMC. With regard to the Core Labor Standards, no explicit ratification is needed for them to be part of the legislative framework of a country." See ADB, "Social Protection Strategy" (2001).

76 "Review and Update of the World Bank's Environmental and Social Safeguard Policies, Phase 3, Feedback Summary: Consultative Meeting with Chinese Governmental

Yet, there is another important aspect to the matter. It would not only have normative relevance on operation of the IFI Labor standards, but also has a strong implication for the relationship between the IFIs and the ILO. It is in the interest of the ILO to develop a body of ILO-centered Labor standards at the global level. A reference to the ILO and its work would naturally reinforce the authority of the ILO in Labor matters. To a certain extent, a strengthened role of the ILO is also in the interest of the international community in general.[77] The emergence of autonomous Labor standards outside the ILO system could possibly divert and compete with the ILO and its standards-setting authority. It is useful to recall an internal observation by an ILO official in 1994 that the ILO faces the challenges of "competing organizations," "competing standards" and ultimately, "competing visions."[78]

Seen in this light, one may gain a better appreciation of the institutional rivalry between the World Bank and the ILO. The World Bank in its Environmental and Social Framework decided against direct reference to any ILO instruments.[79] In explaining its decision, the World Bank made it very clear that it is exactly the autonomy of the Labor standards and of the Bank that animates such a political decision. "It is Management's view that the requirement for both World Bank and Borrower to comply with the ES [Environmental and Social] Framework should be self-standing, and should not require reference to external sources to make this judgment."[80] The ILO was profoundly

Officials" (Beijing 27 October 2015) <http://consultations.worldbank.org/Data/hub/files/consultation-template/review-and-update-world-bank-safeguard-policies/en/meetings/final_feedback_summary_for_phase_3_consultation_with_chinese_central_government_and_institutions_in_beijing_october_27.pdf> assessed 6 May 2018.

77 For example, the 1996 Ministerial Conference of the WTO in Singapore, as a tentative conclusion to the trade and Labor debate within in the WTO, expressly supports the leading role of ILO as "the competent body to set and deal with" core Labor standards. See WTO, "Singapore Ministerial Declaration" (13 December 1996) <https://www.wto.org/english/thewto_e/minist_e/min96_e/wtodec_e.htm> assessed 6 May 2018.

78 Lee Swepston, "The Future of ILO Standards" (1994) 117(9) *Monthly Labor Review* 16, pp. 16–23.

79 The attitude of the World Bank towards external institutions has been consistently conservative. A known example is World Bank's explicit rejection of the binding force of the resolution of the United Nations (UN) Security Council acting under the Chapter VII of the UN Charter.

80 World Bank, "World Bank Safeguard Policies Review and Update: Summary of Phase 2 Consultations and Bank Management Responses" (July 2015) <https://consultations.worldbank.org/Data/hub/files/consultation-template/review-and-update-world-bank-safeguard-policies/en/phases/clean_summary_of_phase_2_consultations_and_bank_management_reponses_final_draft_for_consultation_july_1_2015.pdf> assessed 6 May 2018.

disappointed by this. Immediately after the World Bank published its Environmental and Social Framework, the ILO publicly pronounced its dissatisfaction. It stated that "from the outset the ILO expressed concern with Bank Management's decision to exclude direct references to ILO core Labor conventions from the ESF [Environmental and Social Framework]."[81]

The case of the World Bank makes a good example that highlights the autonomous status of the IFI Labor standards. The legal validity of such Labor standards does not depend on the ILO Conventions or other normative documents. Nor is the substance of the Labor standards defined or constrained by the ILO conventions. The IFI Labor standards constitute a set of independent, self-contained Labor standards with distinct sources, procedures and mechanisms, in parallel to traditional concept of international Labor law centered on and formulated by the ILO. These Labor standards do strengthen the Labor protection at global and transnational levels, but they are beyond the terrain of ILO standards. In this sense, even though the substance of the IFI Labor standards might be identical to those in the ILO standards, they are capable of supplementing, or even competing with, the ILO standards. They are not at all simply a repetition of existing standards.

The difference between the World Bank and the ILO is not concerned with actual Labor standards, but about who is entitled to prescribe Labor protection in an increasingly globalized world. While the authority of the ILO is highly acknowledged, the World Bank has refused to concede the ILO a monopolized say on Labor standards. Putting it differently, the ILO does not have higher authority than the World Bank in speaking to Labor standards. It can be expected that close cooperation between the World Bank and the ILO will increase and grow steadily in the future. Meanwhile, with assistance from the ILO, the World Bank is likely to develop its own expertise and knowledge in Labor protection in connection with its own Labor policy and project implementation.

5 Problems and Challenges

5.1 *Philosophical: Tension between a Neoliberal Perspective and a Rights-based Approach*

The foremost challenge for IFIs to incorporate Labor standards is not only institutional, but also intellectual and philosophical. The most difficult part is

81 ILO, "Statement on the World Bank Environmental and Social Policy" (8 August 2016) <http://www.ilo.org/global/about-the-ilo/newsroom/statements-and-speeches/WCMS_508328/lang--en/index.htm> assessed 6 May 2018.

how to integrate Labor protection into the mainstream economic theories of IFIs. Typically, an economic perspective treats Labor as a factor of production and is usually in favour of flexibility of Labor markets and deregulation of social protection.

The controversies surrounding the World Bank publication "Doing Business" is an illustrative example of the embedded neoliberal economic thoughts of the IFIs.[82] "Doing Business" is a flagship publication of the World Bank launched in 2004, aiming to measure the business environment across the world with quantitative indicators. In its early years, the "Employing Workers" indicator largely measured rigidity of hiring and firing workers and their employment conditions. Its underpinning philosophy is that rigid Labor regulation leads to unemployment in formal sectors, and ultimately reduction in productivity growth.[83] Accordingly, the more regulatory and protective a country's Labor regulations are, the lower ranking it receives.[84] And the recommended reform measures include, among others, introduction of part-time and fixed-term employment contracts, and reduction of the minimum wage for young workers.[85]

This provoked fierce protests from the ILO, trade unions and Labor law scholars in general.[86] The ILO criticized the methodological flaws of the Employing Workers indicators and expressed the concern that the ranking system would "discourage countries from ratifying and abiding by international Labor Conventions and Recommendations."[87] The international trade unions are profoundly concerned with the fundamentally bias against Labor regulation of the Employing Workers indicators. They condemned in particular the fact that the World Bank, in using the indicators, was eliminating workers' protection.[88] In response, the World Bank conceded a more balanced approach to Labor protection, committed to a better alignment with the ILO core Labor

---

82 For the ongoing controversy regarding the publication, see Hannah Murphy, "The World Bank and Core Labor Standards: Between Flexibility and Regulation" (2014) 21 *Review of International Political Economy* 399.

83 See World Bank, "Doing Business in 2004," p. 29.

84 On the politics of knowledge behind the ranking and a case study of the Doing Business Indicators, see Kevin E. Davis, Benedict Kingsbury & Sally Engle Merry, "Indicators as a Technology of Global Governance," (2012) 46 *Law and Society Review* 71, pp. 71–104.

85 See World Bank, "Doing Business in 2004," p. 30.

86 See Yaraslau Kryvoi, "The World Bank and the ILO: Two Visions of Employment Regulation" in Roger Blanpain & Claire Grant (eds), *Fixed-term Employment Contracts: A Comparative Study* (Wolters Kluwer 2009), pp. 47–59.

87 See International Labor Office, "The United Nations and Reform: Developments in the Multilateral System, World Bank Doing Business Report: The Employing Workers Indicator" (November 2007) GB.300/4/1.

88 ITUC/Global Unions, "The IFIs' Use of Doing Business to Eliminate Workers' Protection: Analysis of Doing Business 2008 and New Country Evidence" (Washington 2007) <https://www.ituc-csi.org/IMG/pdf/doing_business.pdf> assessed 6 May 2018.

standards,[89] and subsequently broadened the spectrum of measurement to include protective elements such as job quality. As of 2011, "Doing Business" has removed Labor regulation from the measuring criteria of ranking. Instead Labor regulation is included in the publication only as a referential annex.

The difference between a neoliberal approach and a rights-based approach is indeed structural. Another telling example is the attitude of the IFIs towards trade unions. The trade unions are considered to be free riders in the view of the World Bank.[90] The International Monetary Fund is reported to hold the same opinion.[91] In essence, trade unions are difficult to analyze in economic terms of efficiency and productivity. In the 2017 evaluation of the IMF on its social policy, the IMF staff was reported to have felt that the IMF and ILO staffs "did not speak the same language."[92]

To fully integrate Labor protection in the work of IFIs would require a paradigmatic change in economic thinking to reconceptualize Labor as an inherent good. Labor is approached not as purely a factor of production in economic terms, but also as one of the very foundational values upon which economic activities are based. In other words, the IFIs have to embed Labor protection into their economic work as an essential part of their foundational philosophy, i.e., what are the elements of a sound economy and where the boundary of economic activities lies.[93] This practically would mean to modify or even rewrite the philosophy of the mainstream economic theory, which is a formidable task.

5.2 *Constitutional: The Contestable Intra Vires Basis*

The intervention of IFIs in Labor regulation calls for the question of constitutionality of their policies. Policies and actions of IFIs, especially those to which member states have a strong stake, have to be grounded solidly on an *intra*

---

89 See World Bank, "Doing Business 2010," pp. 22–23; World Bank, "Doing Business 2011," p. 94.

90 See Hannah Murphy, "The World Bank and Core Labor Standards: Between Flexibility and Regulation" (2014) 21 *Review of International Political Economy* 399, p. 405, p. 417.

91 See Franz Christian Ebert, "International Financial Institutions' Approaches to Labor Law: The Case of the International Monetary Fund," in Adelle Blackett & Anne Trebilcock (eds), *Research Handbook on Transnational Labor Law* (Edward Elgar 2015), pp. 124–137.

92 IMF, "The IMF and Social Protection: 2017 Evaluation Report," p. 30.

93 For example, the integration of environmental protection in the policy of the World Bank is greatly facilitated by the publication of "Development and the Environment" in 1992, which "presented environmental issues in a language that economists (inside and outside the Bank) could understand." See Robert Wade, "Greening the Bank: The Struggle over the Environment, 1970–1995" in Devesh Kapur, John P. Levis & Richard Webb (eds), *The World Bank: Its First Half Century, Volume 2: Perspectives* (Brookings Institution Press 1997), pp. 712–713.

vires basis, enumerated or implied, from the constitutional documents of IFIs. Otherwise, *ultra vires* acts of an international organization may be politically challenged by dissenting member states, but may also incur institutional responsibility under international law.[94]

Most constitutions of IFIs do not expressly provide for constitutional mandates for engagement with Labor issues or environmental and social policies in general. With few exceptions,[95] IFIs are often charged with a seemingly neutral, purely financial role. An expansive interpretation of their mandate would still stop short of direct engagement on Labor policy. A good example to the point can be seen from information revealed in the 2017 evaluation of the IMF on its social policy. According to the report, the initiative of social protection was skeptically received among IMF staff and its relevance to the mandate of the IMF was questioned.[96] Similarly, internal skepticism also arose when the World Bank first introduced its environmental policy in 1970s.[97]

Moreover, many IFIs have a non-intervention clause in their constitutions. For example, the World Bank is required not to consider "political or other non-economic influences or considerations" in its decision-making.[98] In the same vein, the IFC is prohibited from interfering in the political affairs of any member, and can only weigh economic considerations in their operations.[99] The same principle applies almost identically also to ADB and AIIB.[100] The principle of non-intervention is particularly relevant in the case of Labor regulation, a matter so deeply considered as domestic. And any intervention by IFIs would require compelling justifications and solid constitutional grounds.

Consequently, IFIs have developed their social policies in a very pragmatic manner. The engagement of IFIs with Labor protection is built around the

94 See "Draft Articles on the Responsibility of International Organizations, with Commentary," in *United Nations International Law Commission Report on Work of Its Sixty-third Session* (26 April to 3 June and 4 July to 12 August 2011) UN Doc. A/66/10, pp.54–172.

95 Among others, the EBRD is a known exception for its mandate to "foster the transition towards open market-oriented economies and to promote private and entrepreneurial initiative in the Central and Eastern European countries." See Agreement Establishing the European Bank for Reconstruction and Development art 1.

96 IMF, "The IMF and Social Protection: 2017 Evaluation Report," p. 30.

97 See Robert Wade, "Greening the Bank: The Struggle over the Environment, 1970–1995" in Devesh Kapur, John P. Levis & Richard Webb (eds), *The World Bank: Its First Half Century, Volume 2: Perspectives* (Brookings Institution Press 1997), pp. 626–627.

98 Articles of Agreement of the International Bank for Reconstruction and Development art 3.05(b).

99 Articles of Agreement of the International Financial Corporation art 3.9.

100 Articles of Agreement of the Asian Development Bank art 36(2); Articles of Agreement of the Asian Infrastructure Investment Bank art 31(2).

concept of sustainability.[101] In some cases, this has been done without an enumerated constitutional basis—environmental and social sustainability is considered an implied element to the notion of sound economy. The IFC justifies its environmental and social policy based upon the linkage between a sustainable private sector development and poverty reduction.[102] The World Bank emphasizes the relevance of social development and inclusion to the World Bank Group's corporate goals of ending extreme poverty and promoting shared prosperity, and further justifies its engagement in light of its support to the realization of human rights. On the contrary, the AIIB is fortunate to be equipped with an enumerated competence to make bank policies to address environmental and social dimensions.[103] The EBRD tries to anchor its social policies on the constitutional commitment to promote "environmentally sound and sustainable development."[104] EIB highlights its nature of being a funding institution of European Union and seeks to align its environmental and social policy with those of the European Union.[105] A general observation is that, with few exceptions, the constitutional ground for IFIs to engage in Labor policy remains weak and contestable.

Therefore, the IFIs' Labor regulation started with technical and morally uncontested fields, typically, safe working conditions and prohibition of use of forced Labor. The IFI Labor standards quickly expanded to an extensive list. The environmental and social policy is usually built upon the so-called "do no harm" approach. Such a "do no harm" approach was expressly acknowledged by the IFC in 2006 when explaining the very purpose of its environmental and social policy.[106] The *raison d'être* is to prevent and remedy the undesirable external effects of international financing. This presents the image of IFIs' social

---

101 One also observes that, with the introduction of Labor policy, IFIs started to rename their instruments of safeguards policy to be sustainability policy, or environmental and social policy, indicative of a paradigmatic shift of approaches. For an excellent exposition on the topic in the context of the IFC, see Christopher Wright, "From 'Safeguards' to 'Sustainability': The Evolution of Environmental Discourse inside the International Financial Corporation" in Diane Stone & Christopher Wright, *The World Bank and Governance: A Decade of Reform and Reaction* (Routledge 2007), pp. 67–87.

102 IFC, "Policy on Social & Environmental Sustainability" (30 April 2006), p. 1.

103 "The Bank shall ensure that each of its operations complies with the Bank's operational and financial policies, including without limitation, policies addressing environmental and social impacts." Articles of Agreement of the Asian Infrastructure Investment Bank, art 13(4).

104 Agreement Establishing the European Bank for Reconstruction and Development, art 2.1 (vii).

105 EIB, "Environmental and Social Policy" (2009), p. 5.

106 IFC, "Policy on Social & Environmental Sustainability" (30 April 2006), p. 2.

policies as an unavoidable necessity. Ten years later, however, the World Bank pronounced a more ambitious position and vowed to "go beyond" the "do no harm" approach. While it remains unclear what this means in practice, one may reasonably speculate that the World Bank could be more dedicated to intrusive social policies. This bold assertion might bring the constitutionality, as well as the legitimacy, of Labor and other social policies back to the forefront of debate.

5.3 *Institutional: Building Knowledge and Capacity*

Even if it seems fashionable for IFIs to commit to Labor standards, to actualize and realize them in specific projects remains a formidable task for IFIs. Global governance is largely about governance through expertise and knowledge.[107] IFIs are also in urgent need to accumulate knowledge about Labor regulation in assessing project risks and also in monitoring project implementation on site. The World Bank in its Social Protection and Labor (SPL) Strategy 2012–22 "highlights the central importance of appropriate knowledge in SPL practice, especially through engendering a global South-South conversation about what works and how in SPL."[108]

IFIs have been increasing their investment in acquiring expertise and knowledge about Labor. For example, it was reported that in 2005 the EBRD "ran a series of training workshops on Labor issues" with 125 attendants at the bank's headquarters.[109] And in 2007 the EBRD organized a two-day training course on Labor issue for its whole staff of the Environment and Sustainability Department.[110] The World Bank also started to recruit Labor experts to assist its work in Labor protection. A separate Labor department was set up as well. Inter-agency collaboration between IFIs and the ILO could be expected to intensify in the forthcoming years.

The incorporation of Labor protection is in a way reshaping and reconstituting the IFIs, intellectually and institutionally. Ultimately, if IFIs seriously uphold environmental and social sustainability as their core values, this may even contribute to a quiet change of the institutional culture within IFIs.

---

107 For an interesting study on the World Bank's environmental policy from a knowledge/power perspective, see Michael Goldman, *Imperial Nature: The World Bank and Struggles for Social Justice in the Age of Globalization* (Yale University Press 2005).

108 World Bank, "Social Protection and Labor Strategy 2012–22: Resilience, Equity, and Opportunity" <http://siteresources.worldbank.org/SOCIALPROTECTION/Resources/280558-1274453001167/7089867-1279223745454/7253917-1291314603217/SPL_Strategy_2012-22_FINAL.pdf> assessed 6 May 2018, p. 11.

109 See EBRD, "Sustainability Report 2005," p. 18.

110 See EBRD, "Sustainability Report 2007," p. 47.

5.4 *Operational: Division between Public and Private Sectors*

Difference between public and private sectors remains an important factor that is underappreciated in the formulation and implementation of Labor standards. Sovereign states and private corporations are fundamentally different in term of legal nature, capabilities, influences, resources and available measures. To require a private company to implement IFI Labor standards is usually no more than asking the private company to abide by national laws. It is in most cases "a law-abiding requirement." On the contrary, to require sovereign states to abide by IFI Labor standards may amount to imposition of a set of international Labor standards on states, in essence "a law-changing requirement."

Although the World Bank policy requirement strictly speaking is project-specific, the implementation of relevant Labor standards may also have broad implications for domestic Labor standards in general. It is observed by David Freestone, a former chief counsel and the head of Environment and International Law Group at the World Bank, that in the fields of environmental and social policies, "many borrowing countries have internalized the broad principles of these procedures and incorporated them into national law."[111] In other words, in the case of sovereign loans, the enforcement of IFI Labor standards may compel legal reform and policy change of a sovereign state.

There is a real risk for a sovereign state to take, i.e., to acquire a loan would have to be traded for higher Labor standards. It could be a burden both for the borrowing countries and for the lending institutions. It is natural that IFIs engaging with the public sector experience much resistance from their borrowers. Many IFIs have been very cautious on the issue whether and how far the Labor standards should be prescribed.

It might be desirable for those IFIs working with both public and private sectors to apply different standards to different kinds of clients. Noticeably, the AIIB has adopted a dualistic approach to Labor standards. In addition to those general standards, the AIIB sets a specific provision addressing the "labor management relationships in private sector projects." The private projects are requested to develop a sound Labor management system consistent with national law including timely payment, adequate rest, fair treatment and non-discrimination, compliance with national law relating to workers' organizations and collective bargaining, and an accessible grievance mechanism.[112] The practice of the AIIB serves as a good example of how a dualistic approach can function.

---

111 David Freestone, *The World Bank and Sustainable Development: Legal Essays* (Martinus Nijhoff Publishers 2013), p. 49.

112 AIIB, "Environmental and Social Framework" (2016), p. 36.

6 Conclusions: The Rise of Global Public Authorities

The issue of Labor protection has become a prominent social and political issue in a globalized era. Labor protection is no longer monopolized by sovereign states within their territory. Increasingly Labor standards are addressed in a transnational context. The engagement of the IFIs in Labor protection is a visible example. Labor standards are recognized and enforced in policy documents of IFIs. In the globalization era, Labor issues have become such a pertinent and universal issue that they permeate various sections of international politics. Labor protection becomes a language of empowerment capable of generating legitimacy for action. This makes it possible for international actors to participate in global Labor governance, directly or indirectly, proactively or responsively.

As IFIs increasingly turn from a fiscal perspective on development to a governance approach to development, IFIs are moving away from their purely financial nature. Instead, by focusing on environmental protection and social justice, IFIs are turning into actors of public authority that are capable of enacting and enforcing their own institutional values, principles and standards. Increased engagement with Labor protection and other social policy is transforming the institutional nature of those IFIs into public authorities of global governance.

When IFIs set and enforce Labor standards *vis-à-vis* their clients, be they sovereigns or private entities, IFIs recognizably entertain a considerable degree of power and influence. These Labor standards are implemented against all clients indiscriminately on a project-specific basis, yet capable of general influences and constraints on the preferences and decisions of clients. Of course, one may say that states and companies are free to decide whether to take loans from IFIs or not. Yet loans from IFIs in the modern world are extremely scarce resources, and access to IFI loans in most cases is a privilege. This is particularly true for development loans and grants from IFIs. Once a loan agreement is concluded, the borrowers are obliged to implement the Labor standards of IFIs in the financed projects. In a way, financial loans are powerful instruments of leverage for IFIs to globalize Labor standards.

The notion of public authority here is defined in a functionalistic logic.[113] As long as an institution engages in defining public interest and providing public good in the political dimension of a society, irrespective of whether the

113 For a useful discussion on what is the political, see Chris Thornhill, "Public Law and the Emergence of the Political" in Cormac Mac Amhlaigh (et. al), *After Public Law* (Oxford University Press 2013), pp. 25–55.

authority is based upon a legal mandate in its constituent document, the institution may be understood to be exercising public authority. The public authority of IFIs derives from the very fact that the IFIs are dealing with public matters in international society. As globalization deepens, environment, indigenous people, Labor, and other social issues increasingly transcend national borders and become global concerns. Authorities are continuously generated by the actual regulatory exercise over these public matters.[114]

This approach to public authority is different from a formalistic approach to ascertaining the public nature of an institution. According to the prevalent opinion,[115] the publicness of IFIs can be traced back to the legal foundations of their establishment. If an international organization is established at intergovernmental level, then its contribution to public goods and its public nature is presumed. Global regulatory institutions are often treated as "public entities" *per se*.[116] The delegation of powers from states confers an original legitimacy to IFIs. Yet, an intergovernmental organization could also be perfectly a private institution among the constituent parties. One may think of the International Tin Council that bankrupted in London and raised a series of law suits against it.[117] The nature of an international organization being public or private very much depends on what it does and in whose interests it acts. As long as it is capable of, and is actually embarking upon, the creation and regulation of public goods, an international institution exercises public authority.

IFIs' involvement in regulating social issues can be seen in light of institutional evolution, as most of those matters are not expressly enumerated as their institutional mandates. The regulatory authority often comes as implied powers and relies on innovative interpretations of the constituent documents. This brings doubt as to the constitutionality of IFIs' engagement in Labor and social policies. However, such constitutional weakness in reality is often compensated by functional effectiveness of the institution, by the acquiescence of

114 It is similarly observed by a scholar of public law in the domestic context that "all governing bodies now claim their authority not from some original conferral of jurisdiction but from their ability effectively to discharge public (i.e., social) tasks." Martin Loughlin, *Foundations of Public Law* (Oxford University Press 2010), p. 462.

115 Some tend to take a formalistic approach by looking at the legal basis of an institution. See Armin von Bogdandy, Philipp Dann & Matthias Goldmann, "Developing the Publicness of Public International Law: Towards a Legal Framework for Global Governance Activities" (2008) 9 *German Law Journal* 1375, pp. 1383–1384.

116 See Benedict Kingsbury, "International Law as Inter-Public Law" in Henry R. Richardson & Melissa S. Williams (eds), *NOMOS XLIX: Moral Universalism and Pluralism* (New York University Press 2009), p. 169.

117 See *Maclaine Watson & Co. Ltd v International Tin Council* [1989], 26 October 1989, United Kingdom House of Lords, 81 International Law Reports 670.

the regulated and of international society at large, and, at times, by the support of dominant actors within the institution.

The characterization of IFIs as public authorities carries with it four noticeable implications. First of all, the IFIs, when exercising public authority, are to be bound by a set of principles of public laws, both procedural and substantive. The principles such as reasoned decisions, public participation, transparency, rationality, proportionality are all relevant.[118] And as such, these principles are to be found beyond the constituent documents of an international institution. They might have to be drawn from general principles of law or from comparative citations to domestic public laws.[119] Secondly, accountability regimes are to be developed for IFIs in relation to their exercise of public authority. Such accountability regimes would grant access to wronged individuals to challenge the activities of IFIs in Labor and social policy. Of course, such accountability regimes could be more diverse than those in domestic arenas. Institutional arrangements such as Ombudsman, or the Inspection Panel in case of the World Bank, are good examples. Thirdly, the changing self-perception of IFIs may bring a conscious adaptation of institutional culture, language, structure, and style of how power is exercised, as well as perceived institutional legitimacy,[120] further accelerating an institutional transformation into public authorities. Increasingly, the IFIs absorb social justice as their institutional values and rationales. Last of all, but not least in implications, IFIs can construct and expand public spheres for debating and deliberating public goods at the global level. Through engaging Labor and other social policies, IFIs will thereby contribute to the developing and shaping of a global public.

118 See Benedict Kingsbury, Nico Krisch & Richard B. Stewart, "The Emergence of Global Administrative Law" (2005) 68 *Law and Contemporary Problems* 15.

119 See Armin von Bogdandy, "General Principles of International Public Authority: Sketching a Research Field" (2008) 9 *German Law Journal* 1909.

120 For a useful examination of the remodeling effect the environmental policy had on the IFC, see Christopher Wright, "From 'Safeguards' to 'Sustainability': The Evolution of Environmental Discourse inside the International Financial Corporation" in Diane Stone & Christopher Wright, T*he World Bank and Governance: A Decade of Reform and Reaction* (Routledge 2007), pp. 67–87.

CHAPTER 9

The World Bank's Sanctions System: Using Debarment to Combat Fraud and Corruption in International Development

*Pascale Hélène Dubois**, *J. David Fielder***, *Robert Delonis****, *Frank Fariello***** *and Kathleen Peters******

Abstract

This chapter presents the main features of the World Bank Group's sanctions system and considers its contribution to global efforts to promote good governance. It first introduces the basic features of the World Bank Group's sanctions system, an administrative law system that has evolved since its inception in 1996. The chapter then briefly reviews the history of that evolution and considers where the system stands today. The chapter also considers the broader international context in which the system was established and continues to operate and concludes by examining some of the lessons learned over the course of the system's 20-year evolution.

* Pascale Hélène Dubois, Vice President, World Bank Group Integrity Vice Presidency, pdubois@worldbank.org.

** J. David Fielder, Manager, World Bank Group Integrity Vice Presidency, jfielder@worldbank.org.

*** Robert Delonis, Senior Litigation Specialist, World Bank Group Integrity Vice Presidency, rdelonis@worldbank.org.

**** Frank Fariello, Lead Counsel, World Bank Legal Vice Presidency, ffariello@worldbank.org.

***** Kathleen Peters, Senior Legal Consultant, World Bank Group Integrity Vice Presidency, kpeters1@worldbank.org.

The authors wish to thank Sheherezade C. Malik, Consultant, World Bank Legal Vice Presidency; Corinne Champilou, Legal Analyst, World Bank Group Integrity Vice Presidency; Lisa Miller, Integrity Compliance Officer, World Bank Group Integrity Vice Presidency; and Arjun Ponnambalam, Senior Consultant, World Bank Group Integrity Vice Presidency, for their invaluable assistance and contributions in the preparation of this article.

 | DOI:10.1163/9789004408326_010

1 A Short History of Anti-corruption Developments in The International Context

The World Bank Group's (WBG)[1] sanctions system grew out of its operational procurement framework, and its evolution has been shaped by the broader international fight against corruption. It would seem now intuitively obvious that the ability to exclude corrupt actors from WBG-financed development activities would be a logical, and perhaps essential, measure to ensure the proper use of WBG funds. But the sanctions system was not an original, or even early, part of the WBG's fiduciary toolkit.

The Articles of Agreement establishing the International Bank for Reconstruction and Development (IBRD)—which, together with the International Development Association, is referred to as the "World Bank" (Bank)—date from 1945, when the Bank was created under the Bretton Woods Agreement to help rebuild Europe after the Second World War.[2] The WBG sanctions system, on the other hand, dates only from 1996, nearly 50 years later.[3]

What brought about this change in approach? In part, the establishment of the sanctions system was a reaction to contemporaneous changes in anti-corruption laws, norms and practices at the national level. The first legal instrument to support this change, the US Foreign Corrupt Practices Act (FCPA), had been enacted some 20 years prior, in 1977.[4] But it was not until the 1990s and 2000s that the FCPA began to be robustly enforced.[5] Early enforcement

1 The WBG consists of the International Bank for Reconstruction and Development (IBRD), International Development Association (IDA), International Finance Corporation (IFC) and Multilateral Investment Guarantee Agency (MIGA). The International Centre for the Settlement of Investment Disputes (ICSID) is also a part of the WBG, but its operations are not covered by the sanctions system.

2 International Bank for Reconstruction and Development Articles of Agreement (IBRD Articles of Agreement) (as amended effective 27 June 2012) arts I & IX, s 3.

3 World Bank, "World Bank Sanctions Regime: An Overview" <http://siteresources.worldbank.org/EXTOFFEVASUS/Resources/Overview-SecM2010-0543.pdf> accessed 19 April 2018; see Dick Thornburgh, Ronald Gainer & Cuyler Walker, "Report Concerning the Debarment Processes of the World Bank" (14 August 2002) ("Thornburgh Report") 10–12.

4 Foreign Corrupt Practices Act of 1977 (as amended 15 U.S.C. ss. 78dd-1, *et seq*).

5 See Stanford Law School, "Foreign Corrupt Practices Act Clearinghouse, A Collaboration with Sullivan & Cromwell LLP: DOJ and SEC Enforcement Actions" <http://fcpa.stanford.edu/statistics-analytics.html> accessed 17 January 2018 (providing a chart of the FCPA's enforcement history from 1977 to the present); see also Tov Krever, "Curbing Corruption? The Efficacy of the Foreign Corrupt Practices Act" (2007) 33 NC J Intl L & Com Reg 83, 93 (stating that in its first two decades, FCPA enforcement was "sporadic" at best and confined to high profile cases); Russell Gold & David Crawford, "US, Other Nations Step Up Bribery Battle" *Wall Street Journal* (New York, 12 September 2008) B1 (noting that the FCPA's early years were

efforts were tempered by the US Department of Justice's (DOJ) concerns that strong enforcement of the Act could potentially harm US relations with its allies.[6] Since the early 2000s, acknowledging that corruption "is a hugely destabilizing force," the DOJ has moved toward more vigorous FCPA enforcement, and has increased the severity of the penalties imposed for violations.[7] Since the mid-2000s, enforcement by the US Securities and Exchange Commission (SEC) has also become more muscular, with the creation of a specialized unit within its Enforcement Division that investigates potential FCPA violations.[8]

A change in attitude on the part of firms, governments and public opinion helped accelerate a move towards the criminalization of foreign bribery. Before this change, it had been generally accepted—indeed often expected—for firms to pay bribes to secure public contracts abroad. In fact, in many countries bribes were a tax-deductible business expense.[9]

In 1996, the Member States of the Organization of American States (OAS) adopted the Inter-American Convention Against Corruption, which was the first international anti-corruption convention.[10] The following year, the Organization for Economic Cooperation and Development (OECD) concluded the landmark Convention on Combating Bribery of Foreign Public Officials in International Business Transactions, commonly known as the "OECD Anti-Bribery Convention."[11] The OECD Anti-Bribery Convention advanced

---

characterized by "long periods of little activity and few prosecutions," experiencing a drastic increase in activity since the early 2000s).

6 W.L. Larson, "Effective Enforcement of the Foreign Corrupt Practices Act" (1980) 32 Stan L Rev 561, n 1.

7 "Mendelsohn Says Criminal Bribery Prosecutions Doubled in 2007" (16 September 2008) 22 Corporate Crime Reporter 36(1) <www.corporatecrimereporter.com/mendelsohn091608.htm> accessed 18 January 2018; see Gold & Crawford (n 5).

8 Steven R. Peikin, "Reflections on the Past, Present, and Future of the SEC's Enforcement of the Foreign Corrupt Practices Act" (*US Securities and Exchange Commission*, 9 November 2017) <www.sec.gov/news/speech/speech-peikin-2017-11-09#_ednref6> accessed 18 January 2018 (noting that since the unit's creation, the SEC has initiated 106 FCPA-related actions against 101 entities and 38 individuals).

9 See Martine Milliet-Einbinder, "Writing Off Tax Deductibility" (*OECD Observer*, April 2000), <http://oecdobserver.org/news/archivestory.php/aid/245/Writing_off_tax_deductibility_html> accessed 18 January 2018 (noting that in the late 1990s, in countries such as Australia, Austria, Belgium, France, Germany, Luxembourg, The Netherlands, Portugal, New Zealand and Switzerland, bribes to foreign public officials were considered tax-deductible expenses, sometimes with the caveat that the recipient's identity be disclosed).

10 Organization of American States, Inter-American Convention Against Corruption (B-58) (adopted at the third plenary session of Member States, 29 March 1996).

11 Organization for Economic Cooperation and Development, Convention on Combating Bribery of Foreign Public Officials in International Business Transactions (OECD

international anti-corruption enforcement across regions and now has 43 States Parties across all parts of the world.[12]

The 1990s also saw more open recognition and discussion of corruption's harm to development outcomes—in economic literature and beyond.[13] This emerging consensus helped prompt the 1993 foundation of Transparency International by Peter Eigen, a former Bank staff member.[14] It also helped international financial institutions (IFIs) to understand that corruption is more than just a minor "transaction cost," or a political issue that they were prohibited from tackling.[15] The now-famous speech by WBG President James

---

Anti-Bribery Convention) (adopted by the Negotiating Conference 21 November 1997, opened for signature 17 December 1997).

12 Ibid; OECD, "OECD Anti-Bribery Convention Ratification Status as of May 2017" <www.oecd.org/daf/anti-bribery/WGBRatificationStatus.pdf> accessed 17 January 2018.

13 See, for example, World Bank Group, "World Development Report 1997: The State in a Changing World" (1997) 99–109; Cheryl Gray & Daniel Kaufmann, "Corruption and Development" (March 1998) Finance & Development 7. More recently, the World Bank's entire 2017 World Development Report was dedicated to governance issues. World Bank Group, "World Development Report 2017: Governance and the Law" (2017).

14 Transparency International, "FAQs on Transparency International: Why Was Transparency International Founded? & How Was Transparency International Founded?" <www.transparency.org/whoweare/organisation/faqs_on_transparency_international/9> accessed 17 January 2018.

15 The IBRD's Articles of Agreement prohibit it from interfering in the "political affairs of any [of its] member[s]," and from being "influenced in [its] decisions by the political character of a member." IBRD Articles of Agreement (n 2) art IV, s 10. Further, the articles require the Bank's loan proceeds to be used "without regard to political or other non-economic influences or considerations." ibid art III, s 5(b). This "political prohibition" has dictated the Bank's policy considerations and the way it conducts its operations. While the Bank was to avoid "complex political considerations," as it developed "the operational experience 'to deal with a large number of governance and institutional issues which have direct relevance to its development mandate, ... and corruption had become a major issue of development policy, the Bank could take action in relation to the fight against corruption.'" Hassane Cissé, "Should the Political Prohibition in Charters of International Financial Institutions Be Revisited? A Case of the World Bank" in Hassane Cissé, Daniel D. Bradlow & Benedict Kingsbury (eds), *International Financial Institutions and Global Legal Governance* (3 World Bank L Rev 59, 78–79, 2012) (quoting Ibrahim F.I. Shihata, "Corruption: A General Review with an Emphasis on the Role of the World Bank" (1997) 15 Dick J Intl L 451, 475–476). Further, the fiduciary duty of multilateral development banks (MDBs), such as the World Bank, to their stakeholders to ensure proper use of stakeholder funds "underlies sanctions, which operate as a key disincentive against the misuse of MDB funds." Stephen S. Zimmermann & Frank A. Fariello, Jr., "Coordinating the Fight against Fraud and Corruption: Agreement on Cross-Debarment among Multilateral Development Banks" in Cissé, Bradlow & Kingsbury (n 15) 189–190.

Wolfensohn in 1996, in which he described corruption as a cancer,[16] was a landmark in this change in IFIs' approach to corruption.

There have been numerous other milestones in the 20 years since. In 2005, the United Nations (UN) Convention Against Corruption (UNCAC) entered into force.[17] UNCAC has perhaps been the most far-reaching international anti-corruption convention, as it requires its 183 States Parties to, among other things, pass domestic legislation criminalizing the bribery of foreign public officials and the officials of public international organizations.[18]

Following the OECD Anti-Bribery Convention and UNCAC, and accelerating in recent years, many countries passed new or strengthened anti-corruption laws. These include the 1999 Canadian Corruption of Foreign Public Officials Act,[19] the 2010 United Kingdom Bribery Act,[20] China's 2011 and 2015 anti-bribery amendments to its Criminal Law,[21] India's 2013 Lokpal and Lokayuktas Act to combat corruption,[22] the 2014 Brazil Clean Company Act[23] and France's 2016 Law on Transparency, the Fight Against Corruption and Modernization of Economic Life, commonly called the "Sapin II" Act.[24]

Other important milestones were not driven by governments or international organizations. For example, the Panama Papers, and the more recent Paradise Papers, were disclosed and analyzed by the International Consortium of Investigative Journalists, and have helped to put a global spotlight on the links between illicit financial flows and corruption.[25] The corruption and

16 James Wolfensohn, "People and Development" (Address to the Board of Governors at the Annual Meetings of the World Bank and the International Monetary Fund, 1 October 1996) <http://documents.worldbank.org/curated/en/135801467993234363/pdf/99712-WP-Box393210B-PUBLIC-1996-10-01-People-and-Development.pdf> accessed 18 January 2018.

17 United Nations Convention Against Corruption (UNCAC), UNGA Res 58/4 (adopted 31 October 2003, entered into force 15 December 2005).

18 Ibid art 16; UNODC, "UNCAC Signature and Ratification Status" <www.unodc.org/unodc/en/corruption/ratification-status.html> accessed 17 January 2018.

19 Corruption of Foreign Public Officials Act, S.C. 1998, c 34.

20 2010 United Kingdom Bribery Act c.23.

21 Criminal Law of the People's Republic of China, pt 2, Ch VIII (Crimes of Embezzlement and Bribery) (adopted at the Second Session of the Fifth National People's Congress on 1 July 1979, amended 25 February 2011); and Criminal Law of the People's Republic of China Amendment 9 (promulgated 29 Aug. 2015).

22 The Lokpal and Lokayuktas Act (2013) No 1 of 2014, India Code (rev 29 July 2016).

23 Law No 12.846 (1 August 2013). The Act took effect in January 2014, and thus is commonly referred to as a 2014 statute.

24 Law No 2016-1691 (9 December 2016).

25 International Consortium of Investigative Journalists (ICIJ), "The Panama Papers" <https://panamapapers.icij.org/> accessed 17 January 2018; ICIJ, "The Paradise Papers" <www.icij.org/investigations/paradise-papers/> accessed 17 January 2018.

money laundering issues raised by these disclosures have been taken up by international policy-making bodies, such as the Financial Action Task Force[26] and the G20 Anti-Corruption Working Group,[27] which are exerting an increasing influence on this global agenda.

The WBG's anti-corruption work matured alongside these international developments and alongside the partners who lead them. Diagnostic work, institutional capacity building and global initiatives are at the forefront of the Bank's anti-corruption efforts. The Bank's diagnostic work includes an array of analytical tools to measure corruption nationally and globally. The Worldwide Governance Indicators permit cross-country comparisons regarding corruption and governance indicators and provide data on specific issues, such as the frequency of bribe payments and the complexity of regulatory environments.[28] Nationally, the Bank analyzes corruption risks for particular sectors and performs survey-based diagnostic work.[29] The Bank also identifies and works to address corruption risks at the country and project levels, through tools like Country Policy and Institutional Assessments (CPIAs), the Systematic Operations Risk-Rating Tool (SORT) and Anti-Corruption Action Plans.[30]

The Bank's institutional-capacity-building work involves support for client countries in the creation, reform and development of institutions such as domestic anti-corruption agencies, laws and regulatory systems, including in corruption-affected areas like procurement and customs.[31] Further, in 2007 the WBG and the United Nations Office on Drugs and Crime (UNODC) jointly formed the Stolen Asset Recovery Initiative (StAR), "to end safe havens for corrupt funds" by working with developing countries "to prevent the laundering of

26 Financial Action Task Force, "Who We Are" <www.fatf-gafi.org/about/> accessed 17 January 2018.

27 G20 Argentina 2018, "Work Streams: Anti-Corruption" <www.g20.org/en/g20-argentina/thematic-areas/anti-corruption> accessed 17 January 2018.

28 World Bank, "Worldwide Governance Indicators: Control of Corruption" <http://info.worldbank.org/governance/wgi/#doc> accessed 5 February 2018.

29 Ibid.

30 See World Bank, "Fast Track Brief: The World Bank's Country Policy and Institutional Assessment—An Evaluation" (30 June 2009); World Bank, "DataBank: Worldwide Governance Indicators" <info.worldbank.org/governance/wgi/#doc> accessed 5 February 2018; World Bank, "Guidance Note: Systematic Operations Risk-Rating Tool (SORT)" (25 June 2014) <pubdocs.worldbank.org/en/972311473706061935/SORTGuidanceNote2014.pdf> accessed 5 February 2018; World Bank Group, "Transparency, Good Governance and Anti-Corruption Mechanisms" <http://ppp.worldbank.org/public-private-partnership/overview/practical-tools/good-governance-anticorruption#anticorruption> accessed 5 February 2018.

31 See, for example, World Bank, "Combating Corruption" (26 September 2017) <www.worldbank.org/en/topic/governance/brief/anti-corruption> accessed 5 February 2018.

the proceeds of corruption and to facilitate more systematic and timely return of stolen assets."[32] The WBG's global initiatives draw on international partnerships, notably through civil society engagement and transparency movements, to implement anti-corruption programs.[33] Examples include the Extractive Industries Transparency Initiative (EITI), the Construction Sector Transparency Initiative (CoST) and Open Contracting.[34]

Other multilateral and regional development banks have been key partners in this journey[35]—in line with the 2006 Joint International Financial Institution Anti-Corruption Task Force (IFI Task Force), in which involved multilateral development banks (MDBs) agreed to harmonize their approaches to combatting corruption.[36] As a result, their investigative and sanctions systems all share many core elements, among the most important of which includes harmonizing the definitions for the then four sanctionable practices (i.e., "corrupt," "fraudulent," "coercive" and "collusive" practices):[37]

---

32 World Bank & UNODC, "Stolen Asset Recovery Initiative (StAR)" <https://star.worldbank.org/star/> accessed 19 January 2018.

33 See World Bank, "Combating Corruption" (n 31).

34 Extractive Industries Transparency Initiative, "The Global Standard for the Good Governance of Oil, Gas and Mineral Resources" <www.eiti.org> accessed 5 February 2018; Construction Sector Transparency Initiative, "Home" <www.constructiontransparency.org/home> accessed 5 February 2018; Open Contracting Partnership, "About" <www.open-contracting.org/about/> accessed 5 February 2018.

35 The International Monetary Fund (IMF) was also engaged in this initiative, noting that though it encourages and supports anti-corruption efforts in both project lending and dealings with private entities, "[u]nlike the other member institutions, the IMF does not engage in project lending or lending to the private sector. It maintains procedures tailored to the circumstances of the IMF to deal with potential issues of staff misconduct and safeguard the use of Fund resources." "International Financial Institutions Anti Corruption Task Force, Uniform Framework for Preventing and Combating Fraud and Corruption" (IFI Task Force) (September 2006) 1.

36 Ibid. In addition to the WBG, the IFIs involved in this IFI Task Force were the African Development Bank, the Asian Development Bank, the European Bank for Reconstruction and Development, the Inter-American Development Bank, the European Investment Bank and the IMF.

37 See Zimmermann & Fariello (n 15) 191 (noting that each MDB established its own "integrity" office to investigate corruption allegations, created its own adjudicative mechanism to assess the merits of these allegations and ultimately settled on debarment as the most likely sanction to be imposed). Eventually, an automatic cross-debarment regime was also agreed upon to improve the deterrent effect of sanctions by individual MDBs and to compound the effects of a public debarment on an entity by foreclosing the possibility of that entity being awarded contracts with other MDBs. ibid 196–198. Further, for a more in-depth discussion on the Bank's sanctions process and the impact of general legal principles on this sanctions system, see Pascale Hélène Dubois & Aileen Elizabeth Nowlan,

- The Asian Development Bank (ADB), which passed its first Anticorruption Policy in 1998,[38] has an Office of Anti-Corruption and Integrity (OAI) that receives allegations of fraud and corruption by ADB staff or in ABD-financed projects.[39] OAI then reviews these complaints to ensure that they meet the requirements to proceed with a full-fledged investigation.[40] The investigative process varies depending upon whether the subject is a staff member or a third party (for example, consultants, bidders, contractors or suppliers). For staff-member allegations, OAI reports its findings to the Budget, Personnel and Management Systems Department, which reviews OAI's report and conducts administrative proceedings when appropriate.[41] For allegations involving third parties, investigative subjects may submit responses to allegations to the Integrity Oversight Committee (IOC).[42] The IOC then determines the credibility of the responses and decides whether to impose any remedial actions or sanctions.[43] Sanctions may be appealed to the Sanctions Appeals Committee.[44] In addition to conducting investigations, OAI also engages in project procurement-related reviews, advises on integrity due diligence to minimize risks in its private sector projects and disseminates information on its anti-corruption policy.[45]
- The Inter-American Development Bank (IADB) approved its first sanctions framework in 2001.[46] Its current Sanctions System consists of investigation and adjudication phases.[47] The Office of Institutional Integrity (OII), an

"Global Administrative Law and the Legitimacy of Sanctions Regimes in International Law" (2010) 36 Yale J Intl L 15.

38 Asian Development Bank (ADB), Office of the Auditor General, "Annual Report on the Major Activities of the Anticorruption Unit 2003" (January 2004) pt 1, para 1.

39 ADB, "Office of Anti-Corruption and Integrity" <www.adb.org/site/integrity/overview> accessed 19 January 2018.

40 ADB, "Anti-Corruption and Integrity: Investigations" <www.adb.org/site/integrity/investigations> accessed 19 January 2018.

41 ADB, "Process for Dealing with Allegations of Integrity Violations by ADB Staff" <www.adb.org/sites/default/files/page/161290/process-for-dealing-with-allegations-adb-staff.pdf> accessed 19 January 2018.

42 ADB, "Process for Dealing with Allegations of Integrity Violations Involving Bidders, Consultants, Contractors, Suppliers, or Other Third Parties in ADB-Related Activities" <www.adb.org/sites/default/files/page/161290/process-for-dealing-with-allegations-external-parties.pdf> accessed 19 January 2018.

43 Ibid.

44 Ibid.

45 ADB, "Office of Anti-Corruption and Integrity" (n 39).

46 Inter-American Development Bank (IDB), "IDB Sanctions System" <https://www.iadb.org/en/about-us/idb-sanctions-system%2C8619.html> accessed 22 January 2018.

47 Ibid.

independent advisory office, investigates allegations of prohibited practices.[48] If OII concludes that a prohibited practice has occurred, a two-step adjudication process commences, with a Sanctions Officer issuing a determination that can be appealed to a Sanctions Committee.[49] Specifically, if the Sanctions Officer determines that the subject engaged in a prohibited practice, it notifies the subject of the commencement of sanctions proceedings and gives the subject an opportunity to respond.[50] The Sanctions Officer then evaluates the sufficiency of all the evidence and issues a "determination" of whether sanctions are appropriate.[51] The Sanctions Officer's determination can be appealed to the Sanctions Committee, which independently reviews the evidence and is not bound by the Sanctions Officer's decision.[52]

- The European Bank for Reconstruction and Development's (EBRD) investigative work dates back to the early 2000s.[53] It presently has an Office of the Chief Compliance Officer (OCCO) that investigates allegations of fraud, corruption and other misconduct by EBRD staff or under EBRD-financed projects.[54] If misconduct is discovered under an EBRD-financed project, EBRD also follows a two-tier enforcement process involving an Enforcement Commissioner (first tier) and an Enforcement Committee (second tier) to decide and impose the appropriate sanction.[55]
- The European Investment Bank's (EIB's) Anti-Fraud Policy and related Investigation Procedures, published in 2013 and based upon the IFI Task Force's Uniform Framework, sets forth EIB's policy in preventing and deterring corruption, fraud, collusion, coercion, obstruction, money laundering and terrorist financing (jointly, Prohibited Conduct).[56] At present, the EIB

48 Ibid.

49 Ibid.

50 Ibid.

51 Ibid.

52 Ibid.

53 Specifically, its Office of the Chief Compliance Officer (OCCO) has investigated staff misconduct since 2002 and misconduct under EBRD-financed procurements since 2005. European Bank for Reconstruction and Development (EBRD), "EBRD Anti-Corruption Report" (November 2006) 17 & 19.

54 EBRD, "Integrity and Compliance" <www.ebrd.com/integrity-and-compliance.html> accessed 18 January 2018.

55 EBRD, "Enforcement Policy and Procedures" POL/2017/01 (4 October 2017) s III.

56 European Investment Bank (EIB), "Policy on Preventing and Deterring Prohibited Conduct in European Investment Bank Activities" ("EIB Anti-Fraud Policy") (17 September 2013). For a predecessor policy, see EIB, "EIB Guidelines on Fighting Corruption, Fraud, Money Laundering and the Financing of Terrorism" (2 May 2006).

Inspectorate General has a Fraud Investigations Division (IG/IN) that investigates Prohibited Conduct in EIB-financed projects and activities.[57] IG/IN also conducts proactive integrity reviews, training and awareness-raising activities and integrity policy work,[58] and cooperates closely with the European Anti-Fraud Office (OLAF).[59] EIB also recently adopted an Exclusions Policy under which it can debar firms that engaged in Prohibited Conduct.[60]

- The African Development Bank (AfDB) Office of Integrity and Anti-Corruption (PIAC, formerly called IACD) was founded in 2006,[61] and aims to deter, prevent and investigate sanctionable practices or staff misconduct affecting the AfDB.[62] PIAC's Investigations Division conducts administrative fact-finding inquiries into allegations of misconduct and refers findings of misconduct involving AfDB staff to the AfDB President for action.[63] Sanctionable practices occurring under AfDB-financed projects are addressed through an independent, two-tier decision-making system involving an Independent Sanctions Commissioner and Sanctions Appeals Board.[64] In addition to its Investigations Division, PIAC also has an Integrity and Prevention Division that holds trainings, conducts outreach and develops due diligence and risk assessment tools.[65]
- Most recently, the Asian Infrastructure Investment Bank (AIIB) has appointed Investigations Officers (reporting to the Managing Director of the Compliance, Effectiveness and Integrity Unit) to investigate suspected Prohibited Practices (as defined by AIIB).[66] If a party has engaged in a Prohibited Practice, AIIB utilizes a two-tier sanctions system, involving a Sanctions

57 EIB, "Investigating Prohibited Conduct" <www.eib.org/about/accountability/anti-fraud/index.htm> accessed 18 January 2018.

58 Ibid.

59 "EIB Anti-Fraud Policy" (n 56) 2, s II.

60 EIB, "Exclusion Policy" (19 February 2018).

61 African Development Bank (AfDB), Integrity and Anti-Corruption Department, "Integrity and Anti-Corruption Progress Report 2009–2010" (2011) 14; AfDB, "Integrity and Anti-Corruption" <www.afdb.org/en/about-us/organisational-structure/integrity-and-anti-corruption/> accessed 17 January 2018.

62 AfDB, "Integrity and Anti-Corruption."

63 Ibid.

64 AfDB, "Integrity and Anti-Corruption: Sanctions" <www.afdb.org/en/about-us/organisational-structure/integrity-and-anti-corruption/sanctions/> accessed 17 January 2018.

65 AfDB, "Integrity and Anti-Corruption: Divisions" <www.afdb.org/en/about-us/organisational-structure/integrity-and-anti-corruption/divisions/> accessed 17 January 2018.

66 Asian Infrastructure Investment Bank, "Policy on Prohibited Practices" (8 December 2016) 5, s 3.4.

Officer and Sanctions Panel, to impose an appropriate sanction.[67] The AIIB also follows the cross-debarment decisions of other MDBs.[68]

The International Monetary Fund (IMF) has recently raised the profile of its anti-corruption efforts. As recently as September 2017, Christine Lagarde, the IMF's Managing Director, reinforced the IMF's commitment to tackling corruption, noting that "[t]he Board agreed that [member countries] would benefit from an increase in granular policy advice, and a candid, even-handed assessment of the economic impact of corruption."[69] Guided by its understanding that "systemic corruption can undermine prospects for delivering sustainable and inclusive growth," in the same year, the IMF published a report detailing its anti-corruption efforts in its economic reviews and IMF-supported programs in its member countries.[70]

These institutional developments have been accompanied by a sea change in popular attitudes, especially among young people. According to a 2017 World Economic Forum youth survey, the two subjects of greatest concern for young people today are climate change and corruption.[71] They no longer wearily accept corruption as an inevitable part of life in many countries, as their parents once did.

In parallel, this period has seen an international movement towards incentivizing "clean business practices" in the private sector, as reflected in the use of compliance programs and monitors in US Department of Justice Deferred or Non-Prosecution Agreements.[72] The WBG sanctions system has itself contributed to the wider adoption of "private sector integrity compliance" frameworks through its use of debarments with conditional release and conditional non-debarments, both of which require sanctioned firms to enhance their compliance programs.[73]

---

67 Ibid 6–12, ss IV–VII.

68 Ibid 17–18, s XII.

69 Christine Lagarde, IMF Managing Director, "Addressing Corruption with Clarity" (Brookings Institution, Washington, DC, 18 September 2017) <https://www.imf.org/en/News/Articles/2017/09/18/sp091817-addressing-corruption-with-clarity> accessed 26 January 2018.

70 IMF, "IMF Policy Paper: The Role of the Fund in Governance Issues—Review of the Guidance Note—Preliminary Considerations" (August 2017).

71 World Economic Forum, "Global Shapers Survey" (2017) 15 <www.shaperssurvey2017.org/static/data/WEF_GSC_Annual_Survey_2017.pdf> accessed 22 January 2018.

72 The first official guidance regarding the use of such monitors was issued in 2008. Memorandum from Craig Morford, Acting Attorney General, to Heads of Department Components, United States Attorneys, re: Selection and Use of Monitors in Deferred Prosecution Agreements and Non-Prosecution Agreements with Corporations (7 March 2008).

73 World Bank, "Bank Procedure: Sanctions Proceedings and Settlements in Bank Financed Projects" ("World Bank Sanctions Procedures") (issued 28 June 2016) s III(A)(9.01)(b) &

2 The WBG Sanctions System: An Introduction

Although often referred to with the shorthand "fraud and corruption," the WBG sanctions five distinct forms of misconduct: fraud, corruption, collusion, coercion and obstruction of a WBG Integrity Vice Presidency (INT) investigation.[74] In 2006, the WBG revised its definitions of fraudulent, corrupt, collusive and coercive practices to clarify and harmonize them with the definitions used by the AfDB, ADB, EBRD, EIB and IADB.[75]

The WBG's sanctions system is designed both to protect the integrity of WBG development projects and to deter future wrongdoing, while at the same time incentivizing the remediation and rehabilitation of sanctioned entities.[76] Among other measures, the sanctions system provides for the suspension and debarment of firms and individuals found to have engaged in sanctionable practices when competing for, or executing, Bank-financed contracts.

The sanctions system finds its legal basis in the Bank's "fiduciary duty" to take appropriate measures to ensure that its funds—the WBG committed more than USD61 billion in loans, grants, equity investments and guarantees in 2017[77]—are used for their intended purposes, with due attention to considerations of economy and efficiency.[78] This duty is set out in the Bank's Articles of Agreement.

Further, the sanctions system flows naturally from the Bank's role as a development institution. Fraud and corruption, and the poor governance they both symptomize and help perpetuate, harm development at the national and project levels. At the national level, corruption acts as a drag on investment and economic growth. A recent IMF research paper estimated that bribery alone could cost between USD1.5 and 2 trillion annually, or roughly two percent of global GDP; and observed that corruption adversely affects financial stability, public and private investment, human capital formation, total factor

(d); World Bank Group Integrity Vice Presidency, "2016 Annual Update" (2016) (INT, "2016 Annual Update"); World Bank Group Integrity Vice Presidency, "2017 Annual Update" (2017) (INT, "2017 Annual Update") 29–30. For a further discussion of the pro-competitive objectives of the WBG sanctions system, see Bart Stevens & Robert Delonis, "Leveling the Playing Field: A Race to the Top" (2013) 5 World Bank L Rev 399.

74 "World Bank Sanctions Procedures" (n 73) s II(r).

75 IFI Task Force (n 35) 1; Anne-Marie Leroy & Frank Fariello, "World Bank Study: The World Bank Group Sanctions Process and Its Recent Reforms" (2012) 11.

76 World Bank Group, "WBG Policy: Sanctions for Fraud and Corruption" (issued 13 June 2016) s III(A); see Leroy & Fariello (n 75) (articulating the early history of the World Bank Sanctions System and the relevant reforms that have since followed).

77 World Bank, "Annual Report" (2017) 3 (regarding WBG fiscal year 2017).

78 IBRD Articles of Agreement (n 2) art III, s (5)(b).

productivity, taxation and revenue collection (and thus government spending) and more.[79] At the project level, INT investigations have found corruption schemes that involved millions of dollars in project funds; corruption schemes hidden by false reports of project progress; and bribes funded by false, inflated invoices.[80] All of this wastage of project funds directly harms the development impact of these projects.

The WBG sanctions system was the first of its kind among international organizations and it has evolved significantly since its inception in 1996. The development of the WBG's sanctions system reflects a continued dedication to the core pillars of good governance, including transparency, stakeholder participation, the rule of law and accountability, coupled with a focus on providing an effective and efficient sanctions system to ensure that the institution's funds are used for their intended purposes.

Under its original configuration, decisions to investigate an allegation, and to pursue an administrative sanctions case, involved members of the Bank's legal department (including the General Counsel), senior Bank audit and procurement officials and a Managing Director.[81] An internal Sanctions Committee heard every case, regardless of whether it was contested, and was comprised of still more of the Bank's senior-most staff: two Managing Directors, the General Counsel and two Vice Presidents.[82] The final sanctioning decision was made by the President of the Bank, based upon the Sanctions Committee's recommendation.[83]

Between this system's creation in 1996 and its review in 2002, only 18 cases were concluded, resulting in the debarment of 74 entities.[84] With time, the sanctions system evolved to respond to the operational and due process considerations prompted by this initial incarnation.

In 2007, following the issuance of a seminal report of recommendations by former US Attorney General and UN Under-Secretary General Dick Thornburgh,[85] the system was reconfigured as a more formal two-tiered process, which is detailed below. The introduction of a two-tier system was driven

79 IMF, "IMF Staff Discussion Note, Corruption: Costs and Mitigating Strategies" (SDN/16/05, 2016) 5–11.
80 World Bank Group Integrity Vice Presidency, "Annual Update Fiscal Year 2015" (2015) 5–8; INT, "2016 Annual Update" (n 73) 7–8.
81 "Thornburgh Report" (n 3) 13–14.
82 Ibid 14–15.
83 Ibid 19.
84 Ibid 20.
85 Ibid.

by an operational need to expedite case resolutions,[86] and to address risks arising during case pendency, while also enhancing due process. Among other things, the Bank understood that the decision to publicly list sanctioned entities and individuals could significantly impact those parties. The two-tiered process sought to continue to ensure that every sanctions decision was based on sufficient evidence and subject to independent adjudication, while also allowing for expeditious resolution of uncontested cases.

3 The Investigative Process

Typically, a sanctions case starts with an allegation of one or more of the five sanctionable practices.

The Bank's Anti-Corruption Guidelines,[87] which are incorporated in legal agreements with borrowing countries, and the Bank's Procurement Regulations[88] and related bidding documents[89] all reference the Bank's definitions of sanctionable practices, as well as the consequences of engaging in them.[90] INT applies these definitions in its work, using those stated in the relevant procurement or contract documents, or else those stated in the underlying legal agreements for the project.[91]

86 For a detailed discussion on the reasons that led to the creation of a two-tiered sanctions system, see the Thornburgh Report (n 3). The Report noted, for example, that problems such as the spike in caseload and their complexity, the increasingly dilatory and aggressive tactics displayed by respondents and the average length of time between case referral and final disposition would make it difficult for the Bank to adjudicate matters that presented credible evidence of corrupt behavior. It reasoned that a two-tiered system would permit the Bank to dispose of certain cases without necessitating a full hearing before the Sanctions Committee and would allow for the temporary suspension of actors from eligibility. ibid 35–36.

87 World Bank, "Bank Directive: Guidelines on Preventing Fraud and Corruption in Projects Financed by IBRD Loans and IDA Credits and Grants" (rev 1 July 2016).

88 World Bank, "Procurement Regulations for IPF Borrowers, Procurement in Investment Project Financing, Goods, Works, Non-Consulting and Consulting Services" (rev November 2017) 11 & 69–71 (Annex IV).

89 See, e.g., World Bank, "Standard Procurement Document, Request for Bids—Goods (Two Envelope Bidding Process)" (October 2017) 8, Instruction to Bidders 3.1.

90 The Bank sanctions system does not, however, require prior notice in order to have jurisdiction over a party. World Bank Group Legal Vice Presidency, "Advisory Opinion on Certain Issues Arising in Connection with Recent Sanctions Cases, No. 2010/1" (15 November 2010) 7–8.

91 Ibid 9–10.

INT, which is responsible for investigating allegations of sanctionable practices in WBG-financed projects, assesses every allegation that it receives. Complaints that fall outside of INT's jurisdiction are referred to other areas of the WBG, as appropriate.

INT decides whether to launch a full investigation by applying a set of case selection criteria, which include the status of the project and contract at issue, and the risk to the project (for example, the amount of funds involved). If INT elects not to investigate a case, INT works, where appropriate, with WBG operational staff to address the issues raised through other corrective measures, such as taking procurement or project support actions.

In conducting its investigations, INT is guided by the *International Financial Institutions' Principles and Guidelines for Investigations*.[92] If, after investigation, INT believes it has uncovered sufficient evidence that a firm or individual has engaged in one or more sanctionable practices, it provides the firm or individual with that evidence and provides an opportunity to respond. In doing so, INT investigations apply a "more likely than not" standard of proof.[93] If INT finds their explanation insufficient, INT may commence formal proceedings against the firm or individual by submitting a "Statement of Accusations and Evidence" to the Bank's Suspension and Debarment Officer (the SDO)[94] or, if the case relates to IFC or MIGA, to the relevant Evaluation Officer.[95] This is the first tier of the WBG's two-tiered adjudicative sanctions process.

92 IFI Task Force (n 35) attachments 4–8.

93 INT, 2017 Annual Update (n 73), p. 24.

94 "World Bank Sanctions Procedures" (n 73) s III(A)(3.01). INT also can file a Request for Temporary Suspension in cases where INT's investigation is ongoing, but INT already believes it has sufficient evidence to conclude that, more likely than not, a party has engaged in a sanctionable practice. If OSD agrees that the evidence presented supports the finding of a sanctionable practice and that the alleged sanctionable practice would warrant a minimum debarment period of two years if it had been included in a Statement of Accusations and Evidence, it can temporarily suspend the Respondent for up to one year, during which INT must continue and complete its investigation. Thereafter, INT must either file a full Statement of Accusations and Evidence against the Respondent, or the temporary suspension expires. ibid s III(A)(2).

95 For more information on the sanctions procedures for IFC and MIGA, see International Financial Corporation, "Sanctionable Practices: Overview Sanctions Process" <www.ifc.org/wps/wcm/connect/Topics_Ext_Content/IFC_External_Corporate_Site/AC_Home/Sanctionable_Practices/> accessed 19 January 2018 and World Bank, "MIGA Sanctions Procedures" <www.miga.org/Documents/MIGA-Sanctions-Procedures1.pdf> accessed 19 January 2018, respectively.

4 The Sanctions Process

The SDO is tasked with evaluating whether INT's allegations, as presented, are supported by "sufficient evidence,"[96] meaning that it is "more likely than not" that the alleged misconduct occurred.[97]

If the SDO determines that there is insufficient evidence to support one or more of the accusations, the case is referred back to INT for the removal of the unsupported accusation(s) or, at INT's discretion, for further investigation.[98]

In cases where the SDO determines that there is sufficient evidence for each of the accusations presented, the SDO issues a "Notice of Sanctions Proceedings" (Notice) to the accused firm(s) or individual(s)—called the "Respondent"—giving the Respondent the opportunity to review and respond to the case against it. In this Notice, the SDO also recommends a sanction, which is imposed if the Respondent chooses not to contest the case.[99]

The appropriate sanction is determined by considering aggravating and mitigating factors that are set out in the Bank's Sanctioning Guidelines.[100] Aggravating factors include the severity of the misconduct, the harm caused, interference with INT's investigation and a history of adjudicated misconduct. Mitigating factors include the Respondent's minor role in the misconduct, evidence of voluntary corrective action and cooperation with the investigation.[101]

Any Respondent that the SDO recommends debarring for six months or more is "temporarily suspended."[102] This means that, from the moment the Notice is issued, that Respondent is no longer eligible to be awarded new Bank-financed contracts or otherwise participate in new Bank-financed activities.[103] This is done to protect Bank-financed operations pending the outcome of sanctions proceedings. It also removes incentives to prolong sanctions proceedings. Information about temporary suspensions is made available to WBG staff and member country counterparts, but is not made public.

Respondents are then afforded a series of opportunities to contest the accusations and/or the recommended sanction. First, within 30 days of receiving

---

96 "World Bank Sanctions Procedures" (n 73) s II(u).

97 Ibid s III(A)(8.02)(b)(i).

98 World Bank, "The World Bank Office of Suspension and Debarment Report on Functions, Data and Lessons Learned 2007–2015" (2nd edn, 2015) ("OSD Report 2007–2015") 12.

99 "World Bank Sanctions Procedures" (n 73) s III(A)(4).

100 Ibid s III(A)(9.02).

101 Ibid s III(A)(9.02)(e).

102 Ibid s III(A)(4.02)(a).

103 Temporary suspension has the same effect as debarment, which is discussed further below.

a Notice of Sanctions Proceedings, a Respondent may submit a written explanation to the SDO. This explanation may present arguments and evidence why the case should be withdrawn, or the recommended sanction revised. The SDO issues a formal, written review of all explanations.[104]

If the SDO does not withdraw the case, the Respondent may contest it before the second tier of the sanctions process, the WBG Sanctions Board, by submitting a Response, which is due within 90 days of receipt of a Notice of Sanctions Proceedings.[105] The Sanctions Board has seven members, all external to the WBG, supported by a permanent Secretariat. Under its statute, the Sanctions Board is charged with reviewing and taking decisions in sanctions cases fairly, impartially, diligently, independently from any other entity and solely on the merits of the case.[106]

If a Respondent does not contest the case to the Sanctions Board, the SDO imposes its recommended sanction, and issues a Notice of Uncontested Sanctions Proceedings, which is posted on the Bank's public website.[107] Historically, about two-thirds of Respondents have chosen not to contest their cases to the Sanctions Board.[108]

If a Respondent submits a Response to the Sanctions Board, INT, in turn, may also submit a Reply within 30 days after receipt of the Response.[109] The Sanctions Board then reviews the case on a *de novo* basis, and is not bound by the SDO's findings or recommended sanction(s). The Sanctions Board may hold a hearing at the request of INT, the Respondent or the Sanctions Board Chair. The Sanctions Board then issues a written, fully-reasoned decision resolving the case, which is posted on the Bank's public website.[110] Sanctions Board decisions are final, with no opportunity for further appeal.[111]

---

104 "World Bank Sanctions Procedures" (n 73) ss III(A)(2.02–2.04), III(A)(4.02).

105 Ibid s III(A)(5.01)(a).

106 World Bank Group, "WBG Policy: Statute of the Sanctions Board" ("Statute of the Sanctions Board") (issued 18 October 2016) ss III(A)(1) & III(B)(1)–(5).

107 World Bank, "Suspension and Debarment Officer Determinations in Uncontested Proceedings" <web.worldbank.org/WBSITE/EXTERNAL/EXTABOUTUS/ORGANIZATION/ORGUNITS/EXTOFFEVASUS/0,,contentMDK:22911816~menuPK:7926949~pagePK:64168445~piPK:64168309~theSitePK:3601046,00.html> accessed 22 January 2018.

108 "OSD Report 2007–2015" (n 96) 10.

109 "World Bank Sanctions Procedures" (n 73) s III(A)(5.01)(b).

110 ibid ss III(A)(8.01), III(A)(10.01); see World Bank, "Sanctions Board Decisions" <web.worldbank.org/WBSITE/EXTERNAL/EXTABOUTUS/ORGANIZATION/ORGUNITS/EXTOFFEVASUS/0,,contentMDK:23059612~pagePK:64168445~piPK:64168309~theSitePK:3601046,00.html> accessed 19 January 2018.

111 "World Bank Sanctions Procedures" (n 73) s III(A)(8.03). The Sanctions Board has, however, ruled that it will consider requests for reconsideration of its decisions in narrowly

5 Overview of Potential Sanctions and Integrity Compliance Conditions

There are five potential sanctions: debarment, debarment with conditional release, conditional non-debarment, restitution and reprimand:

- Debarment renders an entity ineligible, either indefinitely or for a stated period, to be awarded or benefit from a new Bank-financed contract, be a nominated sub-contractor or supplier in a Bank-financed contract, receive the proceeds of Bank financing or otherwise participate in the preparation or implementation of a Bank-financed project. Such ineligibility also applies to IFC, MIGA and Bank Guarantee and Carbon Finance projects.[112] Debarment is only prospective and does not result in the cancellation of contracts under execution, although it can prevent contract amendments or extensions if they are viewed as constituting new or additional work.
- Debarment with conditional release has the same effect as fixed-term debarment, but ends only if the entity fulfills stated remedial, preventive or other conditions for release from sanction.[113]
- Conditional non-debarment permits an entity to retain its eligibility to participate in Bank-financed projects and activities, and seek and receive Bank-financed contracts, but only if it fulfills specified remedial and preventive conditions.[114]
- Restitution requires the entity to make financial or other restitution to the affected WBG Borrower or some other entity.[115]
- A Reprimand comes in the form of a letter admonishing the entity for its misconduct.[116]

The default or "baseline" sanction is debarment with conditional release. This sanction, along with conditional non-debarment, provides an opportunity for a sanctioned entity to work with the WBG's Integrity Compliance Office (ICO). Under these conditions, an entity will be released and therefore exit from debarment only after having met the conditions specified in the relevant sanctioning document. In most cases involving firms, the integrity compliance conditions to be met include requiring the firm to demonstrate that it has implemented an integrity compliance program that is consistent with

---

defined and exceptional circumstances. See, for example, Sanctions Board Decision No 107 (11 January 2018) 2 para 4.

112 "World Bank Sanctions Procedures" (n 73) s III(A)(9.01)(c).

113 Ibid s III(A)(9.01)(d).

114 Ibid s III(A)(9.01)(b).

115 Ibid s III(A)(9.01)(e).

116 Ibid s III(A)(9.01)(a).

the principles set out in the WBG's public Integrity Compliance Guidelines.[117] The WBG Integrity Compliance Officer evaluates and ultimately determines whether entities have fulfilled the conditions for their release from sanction.[118]

Integrity compliance is taking on a more prominent and more preventive role in the sanctions process. Like other development organizations, the WBG is increasingly leveraging private finance and private sector engagement to meet the sustainable development goals. A greater private sector role presents a new set of risks—and opportunities—in the Bank's fiduciary work.

In that regard, the ICO is increasingly seeking opportunities, such as through workshops, for the WBG to promote the voluntary adoption of integrity compliance principles and programs among private sector entities simply as a good business practice rather than only in response to a WBG sanction. Such an expansion of the WBG's integrity compliance work, beyond sanctions, could further augment preventive measures aimed at enhancing the proper use of funds in WBG-financed projects. The ICO also is leveraging the experience of previously sanctioned firms. For example, the ICO has developed a mentoring program whereby firms that have been released from sanction after meeting their integrity compliance conditions are paired with currently sanctioned firms to provide guidance and feedback on the sanctioned firms' integrity compliance program enhancement efforts.[119] In addition, released firms more broadly tend to publicly promote integrity compliance because they want to ensure that there is a level playing field that disfavors corrupt actors and rewards their integrity compliance program effort and investment.

6 Negotiated Resoluction Agreements

Negotiated Resolution Agreements (NRAs or Settlements) incentivize proactive remediation by firms (what some would call "consideration for cooperation") and provide a streamlined alternative to the contested adjudication of sanctions cases. A Settlement provides for the resolution of an investigation or sanctions case through a mutually agreed settlement between the Respondent and INT. A Settlement may be entered into at any point prior to or during sanctions proceedings, until the SDO issues a Notice of Uncontested Sanctions

117 World Bank, "Summary of World Bank Group Integrity Compliance Guidelines" <http://siteresources.worldbank.org/INTDOII/Resources/IntegrityComplianceGuidelines_2_1_11web.pdf> accessed 19 January 2018.

118 "World Bank Sanctions Procedures" (n 73) s III(A)(9.03)(d).

119 INT, "2017 Annual Update" (n 73) 20–21.

Proceedings, or the Sanctions Board issues a decision.[120] INT provides all Respondents with an opportunity to resolve their case through a Settlement.

INT negotiates a draft Settlement with the Respondent. The negotiated Settlement is cleared by the Bank's General Counsel for legal adequacy, and then submitted to the SDO to confirm that: (i) the Respondent entered into the Settlement freely, fully informed of its terms and without any form of duress; and (ii) the Settlement's terms do not manifestly violate the Bank's Sanctions Procedures or Sanctioning Guidelines.[121]

Respondents benefit from Settlements because they provide for certainty of outcome and provide for a lesser sanction than if the case were contested, as Settlements include mitigating credit for cooperation and admission of wrongdoing.[122] The Bank benefits from the Respondent's commitments to cooperate with INT, provide INT with information that INT can use in other cases and either implement or improve its integrity compliance program. Both sides gain clear procedural benefits from the abbreviated process: A Settlement permits a speedier resolution of matters and requires a smaller investment of resources.

7 Lessons Learned

From the experience of implementing the WBG's sanctions system, in particular the two-tiered system as it has existed since it began to operate in 2007, seven lessons can be drawn.[123]

The first lesson is that independence is crucial for due process. The measure of a truly independent sanctions system is the ability to investigate, adjudicate and sanction without internal or external interference—in other words, to resist pressure to either investigate or sanction where there is insufficient evidence, or to not investigate or sanction when a party is high-profile or powerful.

A second lesson is the importance of transparency in procedures, as well as case outcomes and the reasons for them. There are always limits to the

120 "World Bank Sanctions Procedures" (n 73) s III(B)(2).

121 See World Bank, "World Bank Group Settlements: How Negotiated Resolution Agreements Fit Within the World Bank Group's Sanctions System" <http://siteresources.worldbank.org/INTDOII/Resources/NoteOnSettlement Process.pdf> accessed 20 January 2018.

122 World Bank, "World Bank Group Sanctioning Guidelines" (1 January 2011) <http://siteresources.worldbank.org/EXTOFFEVASUS/Resources/WorldBankSanctioningGuidelines.pdf> accessed 19 January 2018.

123 See "OSD Report 2007–2015" (n 97) 18–19.

disclosure of information; some information needs to be kept confidential—for instance the identity of confidential witnesses. However, experience and common sense tell us that meaningful public disclosure can help to confer legitimacy on the system and promote its deterrent effect. In the WBG's system, the full text of Sanctions Board decisions,[124] as well as reports on OSD decisions in uncontested cases,[125] are posted online. The full text of the legal framework for the system is also publicly available,[126] as are annual reports, information notes and advisory opinions.[127]

A third lesson is the importance of written procedures. These include carefully drafted policies; clear terms of reference setting out the roles and responsibilities of all the actors in the system; written internal procedures; and documented decision-making. Generating these procedures well in advance, before a live matter presents itself, is something the Bank has found very useful. Internal processes are important. Documenting one's thinking and thought process that lead to decisions helps ensure equal treatment of all Respondents. Documentation promotes internal discipline and quality and allows an examination of decisions over time.

A fourth lesson is to create appropriate vehicles for resolving new policy issues, which arise inevitably in any system. When they do arise, it is crucial to know in advance who the decision maker will be for vetting and resolving them. At the Bank, this role is played by the Sanctions Advisory Committee.[128]

A fifth lesson is the importance of having a range of appropriate options and tools for proportionate case outcomes. As outlined in this article, the WBG has a range of sanctions outcomes available, as well as a range of process options, including settlements, uncontested cases and contested cases. These tools

124 World Bank, "Sanctions Board Decisions" <http://web.worldbank.org/WBSITE/EXTERNAL/EXTABOUTUS/ORGANIZATION/ORGUNITS/EXTOFFEVASUS/0,,contentMDK:23059612~pagePK:64168445~piPK:64168309~theSitePK:3601046,00.html> accessed 19 January 2018.

125 "Suspension and Debarment Officer Determinations in Uncontested Proceedings" (n 106).

126 See World Bank, "Procedures and Other Key Documents" <http://web.worldbank.org/WBSITE/EXTERNAL/EXTABOUTUS/ORGANIZATION/ORGUNITS/EXTOFFEVASUS/0,,contentMDK:21299248~menuPK:3726884~pagePK:64168445~piPK:64168309~theSitePK:3601046,00.html> accessed 22 January 2018.

127 See World Bank, "Publications" <http://www.worldbank.org/en/about/unit/integrity-vice-presidency/publications> accessed 22 January 2018.

128 See World Bank, "Bank Directive: Sanctions for Fraud and Corruption in Bank-Financed Projects" (effective 1 July 2016) <http://siteresources.worldbank.org/EXTOFFEVASUS/Resources/3601045-1377105390925/Directive_Bank_Directive_Sanctions_for_Fraud_and_Corruption_in_Bank_Financed_Projects(6.28.2016).pdf> accessed 21 January 2018.

were developed with an emphasis on the simplification of procedures and on remediation and prevention. They also provide the flexibility required to identify and apply sanctions that best "fit" the sanctionable conduct at issue.[129]

A sixth lesson is that data matters. All international organizations now understand the importance of data and data analytics. IFIs may be able to attain significant preventive gains by comparing known fraud and corruption risk patterns against present and future project designs, mining e-procurement tender data for red flags of collusion among bidders or utilizing due diligence information to identify shell companies or entities known to be corruption risks.

A seventh and final lesson relates to the importance of measuring timelines. These aid accountability both within the system and with external entities. They also are vital for ensuring—and tracking—the efficiency of all the sanctions actors. A good case management system is essential. What gets measured gets done. Both INT and OSD provide extensive, public data on investigation and sanction case types, progress and outcomes, as well as preventive and integrity compliance activities.[130]

129 "World Bank Sanctions Procedures" (n 73) s III(A)(9.02).

130 See, for example, INT, "2017 Annual Update" (n 73) 23–35; "OSD Report 2007–2015" (n 96).

PART 4

2017 AIIB Law Lecture

CHAPTER 10

The Necessity of Cooperation between International Organizations

*Miguel de Serpa Soares**

October 20, 2017

Excellencies,
Ladies and Gentlemen,

It is a pleasure to join you today for the inaugural AIIB law lecture. Let us hope this is one of many such events in the years to come.

I congratulate you on this initiative. Being together here today can only be of benefit to us all. I look forward to our discussions.

I wish to speak during my lecture to an issue that is of importance to each and every one of us, individually, as well as to the institutions and organizations that we serve. That is the necessity of cooperation between international organizations.

Let us begin this story like all good stories: in the middle. From there we can see where we have been and speculate as to where we might be going.

We live, I think it is fair to say, in an age of international organization. I have chosen that latter word carefully.

International organization consists not only of international organizations, properly so-called, and here we might specify "intergovernmental organizations" established pursuant to an international agreement, but also organization more broadly. International organization is the organization of international life.

If we were to use the term as it is commonly understood, as opposed to how it might be limited by strict definition—such that it might apply beyond the sphere of cooperation between States—then we could also include within the broad category of international organization other aspects of cooperation between individuals and entities sitting in one place, and other individuals and entities sitting somewhere else, half-way across the world.

* United Nations Under-Secretary-General for Legal Affairs and United Nations Legal Counsel.

We might think of trade unions or of multinational or transnational corporations; we might think of international courts—not only of the criminal kind, but also those addressing trade and investment disputes. We could think of uniform rules on navigation and telecommunications. We could think of international film festivals or the Olympic games.

We could even think, without trying too hard, of what a former member of the United Nations Office of Legal Affairs, Mr. Oscar Schachter, once referred to as the "invisible college" of international lawyers, "dispersed throughout the world...dedicated to a common intellectual enterprise."

With that context, let us unpack, for a few minutes, what I mean when I say necessity. Later I will speak to what I mean when I refer to cooperation.

Under the heading of necessity, we could ask why such international organization, formal and informal, visible and invisible, exists.

No one person has the answer to that question. And I would not presume to be the world's expert on the subject.

Sitting as we are in the People's Republic of China, we might recall the quote from Confucius that "real knowledge is to know the extent of one's ignorance."

There are things we might know, and there are many more things that we do not. Engaging the unknown and seeking to further our knowledge is difficult, but vital.

Under that guidance, let me say a few words about why we might consider international organization to be necessary.

First, I think it is fair to say that international organization exists because it serves an essential purpose.

The challenges we face and the aims we try to achieve—these cannot be addressed without bringing people together in specific ways.

International organization does that. It takes people from here, and there, with this objective and that objective, with this capacity and that capacity, and puts them in a situation where they can work together to achieve mutual goals. It collects resources—financial, human and material—and coordinates them for the benefit of all.

It is clear that climate change, development, threats to security, among others, do not stop at borders. They traverse them. They are everywhere. They affect us all.

The 2030 Agenda for Sustainable Development and the Sustainable Development Goals and related targets are not for one country, or another; they are for the entire planet and everyone—indeed everything—in it.

As the General Assembly noted at its adoption of the 2030 Agenda, it "is a plan of action for people, planet, prosperity" and "[a]ll countries and all stakeholders, acting in collaborative partnership, will implement" it.

Clearly this requires some organizational principles, some stitching together of the various threads.

But that is not all. I would like to make a point that goes beyond the usual: international problems, therefore international solutions.

International organization has reached a much more complex level. It is much more calibrated and specialized.

I realize I am addressing a room today that might have forgotten more about economics than I will ever know, but let me borrow from the economic field.

Each specialty, each organization, indeed each actor, that comprises this lively form of international organization of which we are all a part brings a certain comparative advantage.

In order to team these various actors, to maximize the efficiencies that each of them have to achieve the greatest impact, we must recognize the strengths that each brings to the table and look for ways to connect.

The form of international organization differs, necessarily, based what we are trying to connect and for what purpose.

The United Nations, with its broad principles and purposes, enshrined in the Charter, and its three pillars: peace and security, development and human rights—is going to be structured differently, will have different attributes, than an intergovernmental organization with a more specialized mandate.

Its membership might be different; its chief administrative officer and international civilian staff might be empowered to take different kinds of decisions. There are different mandates, and various contexts in which they are implemented.

The United Nations has also been around now for some time. At seventy years young, it has far outlasted its predecessor, the League of Nations.

This comes with certain benefits. The United Nations provides a tremendous platform and, collectively, we can rely on an extensive body of experience and practice.

It also comes with challenges. The Organization must continue to adapt from the vision of 1945 to meet today's demands.

This involves shifts in form and functions, as well as in mandates. The big, punctuating, changes are rare—the United Nations is a large bureaucracy and practices have developed over time; its Member States also have many political aims.

This makes for an active organization but also one that evolves—evolutions, not necessarily revolutions—to address the needs of all of its Member States. It also tends to create a diverse organization, with many pieces, all going in particular directions.

This can be seen in the recent address by the Secretary-General to the high-level session of the General Assembly, in which he identified seven threats and tests.

These ranged from the nuclear threat, to terrorism, to unresolved conflicts, to climate change, to inequality, to cybersecurity, to human mobility.

The work of the Organization is far-reaching. These threats and tests are daunting. We cannot address them without working together, and, perhaps more importantly, understanding each other.

They will take all of our skills and all of our attention. As the Secretary-General noted, "we must act as one, because only together, as united nations, can we fulfill the promise of the Charter and advance human dignity for all".

I cannot speak in great detail about the particular objectives of the Asian Infrastructure Investment Bank or, for that matter, of other international financial institutions. But I can appreciate the ambition of what they are trying to achieve, and I can see where synergies between our organizations may exist.

We can all realize the value of mobilizing the financial resources that the world possesses—which are many—and directing them toward the common good, in a way that reduces inequality and enhances opportunity.

Infrastructure is imperative. In a real and practical way, it brings the world together. It improves connectivity, it makes getting from here to there—both literally and figuratively—easier. It creates larger freedom.

By the terms of its Articles of Agreement, the mandate of the Asian Infrastructure Investment Bank includes fostering sustainable economic development and improving infrastructure connectivity in Asia, as well as promoting regional cooperation and partnership in addressing development challenges.

It seeks, in particular, to utilize its resources, to projects and programs that will contribute most effectively to the harmonious economic growth of the region as a whole, with special regard to the needs of less developed members of the region.

It is in this context that we might appreciate the immense potential of the Belt and Road Initiative, which has established close cooperation with a large number of multilateral development banks, including the AIIB.

While the Belt and Road Initiative is different than the 2030 Agenda, both have sustainable development as their overarching objective. Both strive to create opportunities. Both aim to deepen connectivity in infrastructure, trade, finance, policies and, perhaps most important of all, among peoples.

It is crucial to strengthen the links between the Initiative and the Sustainable Development Goals. They can reinforce one another in order to achieve true sustainable development.

In turn, this highlights the value in connecting the work of the Asian Infrastructure Investment Bank, the majority of whose Membership are along the Belt and Road, and the work of the United Nations.

If we can boil it down, the essence of necessity with respect to cooperation between international organizations is this:

> We have mutual aims and different strengths. In order to achieve those mutual aims, we must capitalize on our strengths. An increase in specialization means we must bring more actors into the fold. We must be inclusive, not limited. We must be organized effectively so that we can raise our collective efforts.

Now, I promised that I would explain cooperation, and to its aspects to which I refer in this context.

Let me digress for a moment.

I have been speaking in lofty terms and you might be forgiven for mistaking me for a politician, but let me assure you, I am a lawyer, through and through.

As Legal Counsel for the United Nations, I am charged with creating the structures that enable Organization to function. My tools are memoranda, agreements and opinions. I am measured by the advice I provide and the arrangements I reach on behalf of the Organization.

When they are at their best, international lawyers, those members of the "invisible college," are the architects of the international system.

Handed a vision—for instance, sustainable development—we give it a form.

We develop the principles to bring it to fruition. We sharpen those principles in practice. We ensure those principles can sustain external shocks. We link the work of the United Nations to the work of others so that we may become a stronger force.

The United Nations System that emerged out of the aftermath of World War II is not something esoteric. It is a series of international agreements, beginning with the Charter of the United Nations.

The Charter provides, in its Article 53, that the Security Council shall, where appropriate, utilize such regional arrangements or agencies for enforcement action under its authority. The use of such capacities requires legal arrangements.

Article 57 of the Charter provides that the various specialized agencies, established by intergovernmental agreement and having wide international responsibilities, as defined in their basic instruments, in economic, social, cultural, educational, health, and related fields, shall be brought into relationship with the United Nations.

Article 63 of the Charter empowers the Economic and Social Council to enter into such agreements, defining the terms on which the agency concerned shall be brought into relationship with the United Nations. Such agreements are also subject to approval by the General Assembly, consisting of all 193 Member States.

So-called "related" organizations, such as the International Atomic Energy Agency, the World Trade Organization, the Preparatory Commission for the Comprehensive Nuclear-Test-Ban Treaty Organization, the Organization for the Prohibition of Chemical Weapons and the International Organization for Migration, have also been brought into a relationship with the United Nations and comprise a part of the United Nations System.

Each Member organization of the United Nations System has entered into a legal agreement to become so. Each is held to the commitments that it has made.

Those agreements would not have proven as effective and durable as they have been absent the hard work and expertise of international lawyers.

Therefore, when I speak of cooperation in this context, it is not something abstract. It is the nuts and bolts of legal work. It is the process of negotiating and agreeing to cooperative arrangements between and among international organizations.

Such arrangements may take different forms. I noted that the AIIB Charter also requires the Bank to complement, rather than compete with, other development organizations and a number of cooperation agreements have been concluded for such purposes. I can speak only to the practice of the United Nations in this regard, but this may be illustrative of the work in other international organizations as well.

The arrangements that the United Nations reaches with other international organizations occur along a spectrum depending on the extent of the cooperation and the obligations each organization is prepared to undertake.

I mentioned relationship agreements. These might be considered the most formal kind of agreements. The most recent is that which was concluded with the International Organization for Migration in 2016.

This relationship agreement defines the terms on which the United Nations and the International Organization for Migration shall be brought into relationship with each other in order to strengthen their cooperation and enhance their ability to fulfil their respective mandates in the interests of migrants and their Member States.

It provides, among other things, that the two organizations will "cooperate closely within their respective mandates and to consult on matters of mutual interest and concern."

By the terms of the agreement, the International Organization for Migration will participate in the United Nations System Chief Executives Board for Coordination and its subsidiary bodies.

The agreement also provides for reciprocal representation, as well as measures for information sharing, administrative cooperation and personnel exchanges, among other matters.

The International Organization for Migration is a key contributor in many places where the United Nations deploys operations, including its peacekeeping forces.

Peacekeeping is a central United Nations activity; it is also one of the Organization's most complex and challenging tasks.

In carrying out its peacekeeping functions, the Organization relies on contributions from Member States, as well as other international organizations.

The Secretary-General is seeking, in this context, to forge closer partnerships with key regional organizations such as the African Union, the European Union, the League of Arab States and the Organization of Islamic Cooperation.

He recently concluded a "Joint United Nations-African Union Framework for Enhanced Partnership in Peace and Security," which establishes the following principles, among others:

- Both organizations note the primary role of the Security Council in the maintenance of international peace and security, as well as the essential role of regional arrangements, as also provided for in the Charter;
- Both organizations recognize that the attainment of peace is critical to the achievement of development goals, to which both Organizations are committed;
- In addressing conflict, the organizations will strive, wherever possible, to reach a common understanding of the problems and, through consultative decision-making, develop a collaborative approach and seek to achieve "maximum convergence";
- This will he guided by the principles of mutual respect and, here is that term again, comparative advantage.

The Joint Framework is not a binding agreement; but it does provide clarity in objectives as well as roles and functions. It is hoped that it will serve as a useful guide for continuous cooperation between the two organizations in this most demanding of areas.

The United Nations continues to strengthen and modernize its peacekeeping forces. This sometimes requires us to work alongside and in partnership with other security actors in the theatre of operations.

In such situations, we must be clear on the legal arrangements. This is important for coordination. It also delineates the responsibility of each organization under international law for its acts and omissions.

The approach of the United Nations is to seek, where possible, to conclude formal arrangements, such as exchanges of letters, with organizations with which it is conducting joint or parallel operations. This is to avoid situations of uncertainty.

Such arrangements have occurred with the European Union forces that operated in Chad, the African Union forces that operate in Somalia—and they may soon occur with respect to the deployment of a G5 Sahel Force in Mali, which will operate alongside the United Nations force there.

These arrangements set forth the role and responsibility of each organization and also, importantly, establish that each force will be under separate command and control and operate under its own rules of engagement.

The arrangements also address claims. The standard clause is that each party will handle claims that may be made arising out of acts of its personnel, and that each party would hold the other harmless in respect of such claims.

The parties also renounce the possibility of bringing claims against each other, with the exception of claims concerning loss or damage resulting from the gross negligence or willful misconduct or the other party or its personnel.

Peace and security is of course not the only area where cooperation and clear legal arrangements to that effect are important.

I mentioned earlier the shared goal of the United Nations and the Asian Infrastructure Investment Bank with respect to sustainable development, enshrined in the 2030 Agenda and the AIIB Charter, respectively.

Like many other organizations, including multilateral development banks, the United Nations, represented by the Department of Economic and Social Affairs, recently also entered into a Memorandum of Understanding with the People's Republic of China, to establish a framework of cooperation to promote the implementation of the 2030 Agenda by supporting the Belt and Road Initiative in areas of common interest.

The cooperation envisioned under the Memorandum of Understanding aims to promote and support international cooperation in the pursuit of sustainable development in all countries, including through the Belt and Road Initiative in accordance with the mandates, priorities and comparative advantages of the United Nations and the People's Republic of China.

I trust that this Memorandum, and the cooperative steps that it envisions, will also contribute to bringing the United Nations and the Asian Infrastructure Investment Bank closer together, noting that most countries along the Belt and Road have joined the Bank and they all have endorsed the 2030 Agenda.

Aside from peace and security and development, there are other technical arrangements between international organizations that also come to mind.

For instance, the United Nations has established a Security Management System that aims to ensure the safety and security of its personnel in various parts of the world.

Various organizations not already a part of the United Nations System, for instance the Asian Development Bank, have entered into a Memorandum of Understanding with the United Nations to participate in the Security Management System.

In all, more than 50 international organizations comprise the membership of the United Nations Security Management System.

These arrangements provide an important basis upon which the safety and security of such personnel can be assured in difficult and insecure environments.

Finally, we might consider more informal arrangements. These could be written or they may evolve through practice.

In the spirit of the "invisible college," my office arranges, each year, for meetings of the legal advisers of the specialized agencies, as well as the separately-administered agencies, funds and programmes and the United Nations field legal offices, specifically its peacekeeping and special political missions. Some of you may have participated in such events over the years, including, of course, Mr Gerard Sanders, who had served as General Counsel at IFAD, a UN specialized agency, before he joined the AIIB.

At these meetings, we do not necessarily discuss formal legal arrangements. Rather, we share experiences and consider issues of mutual concern.

There is something special that emerges when we are able to sit together in an informal setting. Lawyers share a specialized language. We are able to communicate and understand each other. I expect that that spirit is also captured here today.

Excellencies,
Ladies and Gentlemen,

I hope that you have found these remarks illustrative of the necessity of cooperation between international organizations.

This is a matter that will continue to demand our attention and our hard work as lawyers and as international civil servants.

If you will allow me, let us return, in conclusion, to Confucius once again. You will forgive me. But I find his comments and quotations to be very insightful.

The quotation that I will turn to now is the following:

> The man who moves a mountain begins by carrying away small stones.

When I read this quotation, I think of the mountains, the challenges that we all have. There are those that we might face alone; but, as I have tried to demonstrate, there are many more that we face together.

When we consider our mountains, there are some that require an ascent, while others might be tunneled. Still others might be brought low with force.

In order to be effective, we might face each challenge not by thinking of its totality, of its sheer size, but of the series of measures, day in and day out, that might allow us to begin, step by step, stone by stone, to move it.

If we commit to such a process; if we commit to working together—then we might find, over the course of time, that we have made that mountain a little less impassable.

Such is my hope; and I trust it is yours as well. Thank you.

PART 5

2017 AIIB Legal Conference Report

CHAPTER 11

AIIB Legal Conference Report

*Christopher Smith**

1 Introduction

On October 17 and 18, the Asian Infrastructure Investment Bank (AIIB) held its inaugural Legal Conference. The 2017 Legal Conference was convened as part of AIIB's inaugural Legal Week (October 16–21), organized under the initiative of AIIB's Office of General Counsel. The Legal Week was organized around four events: (i) the Legal Conference; (ii) the inaugural AIIB Law Lecture; (iii) a meeting of Chief Legal Officers of Asia-based international financial institutions (IFIs); and (iv) a series of internal trainings for AIIB staff.

The Legal Conference brought together nearly 100 eminent legal practitioners and academics. Four panel discussions were held on the following topics: (i) the governance role of multilateral shareholders; (ii) institutional design and effective governance; (iii) external dimensions and a governance mandate; and (iv) governance and the rule of administrative law. Following the panel discussions, the Legal Conference convened a plenary session on good governance and modern IFIs, and the President of AIIB, Jin Liqun, delivered closing remarks.

At the close of the Legal Conference, Miguel de Serpa Soares, the United Nations Under-Secretary-General for Legal Affairs and United Nations Legal Counsel, delivered the inaugural AIIB Law Lecture, entitled "The Necessity of Cooperation between International Organizations." The Legal Week continued with a meeting of Chief Legal Officers of Asia-based IFIs, chaired by AIIB's General Counsel, Gerard Sanders, with opening remarks from President Jin and participation of legal chiefs of the Asian Development Bank, the Credit Guarantee & Investment Facility, the ECO Trade and Development Bank, the Eurasian Development Bank, the Green Climate Fund and the International Investment Bank. The Legal Week closed with a series of internal trainings for AIIB staff on a variety of legal topics pertinent to AIIB's operations.

This report is intended to provide a summary of the discussions held as part of the Legal Conference.

---

* Senior Counsel, Office of the General Counsel, AIIB.

2 Panel 1: The Governance Role of Multilateral Shareholders

This panel discussed a number of critical matters with respect to the role of Shareholders. The concept of shareholder veto was examined. Veto power is used relatively frequently in some institutions (i.e., the IMF), but not so much in others. The principal application of the shareholder veto is to amend an institution's charter, a step which certain stakeholders, including bondholders of an institution, would not want an institution to take lightly.

It was noted that shareholder representatives also come in certain flavors (governors and directors). Their respective powers are delineated in an institution's charter, but also touch on the following concerns: providing effective leadership of the organization; mobilizing resources; addressing fiduciary concerns for taxpayer money; establishing a conducive domestic legal environment for the institution; promoting the institution domestically; respecting the international character of the institution; maintaining the institution's relationship with other organizations; and, for some shareholders, maximizing resources for their constituencies. These concerns also involve recurring themes, including reputation risk, transparency and the proper balance between politics and economics.

It was pointed out by some panelists that certain international organizations, for example, the Global Climate Fund (GCF) and the Global Fund to Fight AIDS, Tuberculosis and Malaria (Global Fund), do not have shareholders, but rather stakeholders, which contributes to the ambiguous legal status of such organizations. In the case of both the GCF and the Global Fund, since their funding is entirely donor-based, neither organization is active on the capital markets and, as such, do not need to earn the trust of the financial markets. The panel also discussed the weak accountability chain between the board and the institution and the thin line between board oversight and execution.

The question was raised as to what the role of the legal department is in an international organization? Some panel members pointed out that the general counsel needs to gain the trust of her colleagues and must encourage open communications. There was an suggestion that there should be a special code of conduct for lawyers in international organizations, which would deal, in part, with ethical considerations and confidentiality, which was not widely supported. One general counsel emphasized that the role of general counsel is to represent the institution, not the management, and pointed out that boards may not fully appreciate this independence. Another participant underlined that the role of general counsel is frequently to say no to management, providing an example from his own practice where the general counsel discovered a circumstance where management was not entirely candid with the board.

The discussion then moved to the legal personality of international organizations. It was noted that often, the systemic interests of an international organization differ from the interests of certain member states, which can create substantial tension. It can also lead to what one participant described as "magic"–when the international community comes together to accomplish something that an individual member state is not able to do.

The panel exchanged views on the International Law Commission (ILC)'s draft articles on the responsibility of international organizations, in light of several essential aspects, including privileges and immunities, national law and accountability. One participant discussed the International Oil Pollution Compensation Fund (IOPCF) case, where the UK courts imposed a freezing order on the IOPCF despite the organization's privileges and immunities.

Another participant asked whether treaty-based independence is the best form of independence for an international organization and whether other ways to demonstrate independence exist (citing, e.g., the delivery of a legal opinion from the organization's general counsel). One responded that some treaties are more equal than other treaties. Another responded that it is important to understand the domestic mechanisms that underlie the supply of resources to the international organization. For example, callable capital for the IFIs in which the US participates is authorized by the US Congress, but not allocated, and thus is subject to domestic political processes.

Another participant requested the panel to consider distinctions in duties between an international organization's governors and its nominated board of directors. It was noted that governors are often paid by domestic taxpayers, while directors are paid by the institution, and in one instance a director's salary was capped by the country whose constituency he represented. Different views were expressed on the implication of a director's freedom to split her votes and on the functioning of a director of a single-member constituency.

It was noted that the difficulties of enforcing against a sovereign are exacerbated when the sovereign is one of the organization's member states. The ability of an institution to enforce its preferred creditor status against a sovereign, for example, is not as simple as getting a judgment and executing on the judgment. The IFI would need to rely on other (albeit imperfect) tools.

The panel discussed whether it would be good for the international system if membership in international organizations were required. One participant highlighted that countries' participation in IFIs is transactional in nature, and if a country believes that its interests continue to be maintained by membership, then it will remain a member.

3 Panel 2: institutional Design and Effective Governance

A challenge for the AIIB is how to harness its two legitimacies: the input legitimacy (or, political legitimacy) and the output legitimacy (or, quality of work performed by AIIB). AIIB needs to deliver on both of these fronts. It was noted that all IFIs "ride three horses" at the same time: their member states; their own secretariat; and the countries that receive funds.

It was suggested that AIIB can take at least the following five lessons from other organizations regarding the concept of board representation. First, there should be two-way communication between the board and member states. Second, boards should avoid micromanagement. Third, headship selection and accountability and performance review are key to an MDB's political legitimacy. It was noted that now is "not the finest hour" for leadership of international organizations, with many heads being forced to resign due to incompetence, harassment or corruption. One speaker noted that the IMF's decision to establish an annual board review of the managing director is a positive development, but perhaps a little too formal and overly dependent on written statements.

Fourth, and this relates more to the output legitimacy of the bank, is how to collaborate with other, similar organizations in order to avoid duplication and encourage the leveraging of acquired information. Fifth—and again relating to outcome legitimacy—is evaluation. It was noted that organizations often find it very difficult to stomach external, independent evaluation, but it is this type of evaluation that is most effective in picking up on fundamental questions that the public or borrowers are asking.

It was noted that AIIB was set up as an IFI despite the trend towards arguably more novel legal structures, like the GCF. The charters of other IFIs served as the inspiration for AIIB's Articles of Agreement. Even non-resident boards are not so rare anymore. Debate about whether to have a resident or non-resident board goes back to Bretton Woods. It was noted that the most novel provision of the AIIB Board is its ability to establish an oversight mechanism over management, which demonstrates that board residence doesn't necessarily mean oversight. One participant remarked as to how surprised he was that it took the IMF over 40 years to establish such an oversight mechanism and that other MDBs "didn't discover corruption until the mid-1990s." It was also noted that oversight mechanisms in legacy IFIs were grafted onto existing systems and usually in response to a crisis, whereas with the AIIB such mechanism is baked into bank governance and recognized in its Articles of Agreement.

The panel then discussed the force of geopolitics in IFIs, and for those IFIs that raise funds from the capital markets, the importance of backing by credit worthy member countries.

The discussion subsequently moved to what drives effectiveness in the boards of IFIs, drawing comparisons between IFI boards and boards of commercial financial institutions (CFIs). A few drivers of IFI board effectiveness were proposed and examined, including: (i) size of the board; (ii) leadership of the board; (iii) knowledge, skills and experience of the directors; (iv) director diversity; (v) tenure of directors; (vi) personal commitment of the directors; (vii) workload of the board and distribution of workload in the committee structure; (viii) support of the board and (ix) maintenance of the effectiveness of the board.

The following five reforms were examined as a means to enhance IFI board effectiveness: (i) allow board input on board profile; (ii) lengthen board tenures and "throw some institutional sand" in the replacement mechanism used for board members who exit the board before end of tenure; (iii) explicitly disclose levels of participation or absenteeism in board and committee meetings in board self-evaluation exercise; (iv) expand the format for the participation of outsiders and those with no voting rights and (v) institutionalize board evaluation and report key findings in annual reports, including the role of the President as chairman of the board (and not his performance as CEO).

One participant noted the risk of box-ticking when it comes to establishing a corporate governance framework. Box-ticking is prevalent, which is both good and bad. In banks, there is less shareholder pressure; pressure comes more from those in supervisory roles. In order to institutionalize good corporate governance across an organization, an organization needs to pay attention to the tone at the top and also bring directors closer to the organization. Another participant noted that the tone at the top was not the biggest concern; rather it was "the tone deaf at the top" which was more troubling.

It was noted that development is difficult. The system of development lending is "pro cyclical" and "favoritistic," i.e., there are certain favored country-recipients. The challenge and opportunity for a new institution like AIIB is to be counter-cyclical and to locate and lend to "donor orphans."

One participant remarked that it is particularly important for AIIB, as a newcomer, to avoid certain pitfalls, such as board micromanagement. AIIB should delegate authorities to the President, but if AIIB is to do so while also demonstrating to the world that it is a *multilateral* (and not Chinese) institution, then AIIB needs to underscore its multilateralism, both in respect of its relationship with members and the outcome of its work. However, another participant reminded the panel that the more AIIB delegates to management, the stronger its oversight mechanism needs to be.

4 Panel 3: External Dimensions and a Governance Mandate

The discussion moved to the role of IFIs in setting international labor standards. It was noted that since 1990s, the ILO has become a global leader in the setting of international labor standards, recognizing in 1998 a series of eight international labor conventions as fundamental to the protection of the four core labor rights in the Declaration on the Fundamental Principles and Rights. Since 1998, the ILO has actively encouraged other IFIs to adopt labor standards and rights.

The level of commitment to labor standards varies across IFIs, with different levels of coverage and means of enforcement. It was also noted that the protection of labor is a powerful tool that enhances the legitimacy of IFIs.

The discussion shifted to gender diversity on corporate boards in Asia. Studies suggest that gender equality is not just a moral obligation. Gender diversity is the key to avoiding excessive risk-taking; gender diversity on boards also adds value. It was noted that positive results have been achieved in this regard in Europe, although not so much in Asia.

It was noted that quotas work well in promoting gender diversity on boards. In the absence of quotas, the main driver in promoting gender diversity is a change in company culture. The related practice and rules in Europe, the US and Asia were discussed.

The panel examined then what IFIs are doing to promote gender diversity on boards, given their mandate and their role as investors. To improve gender diversity, it was proposed that IFIs need to continue to work with governments and make a strong business case in favor of diversity (for example, it was pointed out that countries with higher levels of gender equality enjoy higher levels of economic growth and companies with more women on their boards have higher economic returns).

It was noted that law plays an important role in achieving effective governance at IFIs. The discussion, consequently, shifted to how the rule of law is maintained at the IMF and the in-house lawyer's role in fostering such rule of law.

IMF plays a firefighter role in that it assists countries facing balance-of-payments crises. It plays a role in good times too, through the promotion of a stable international monetary system. While the IMF's role has undergone changes over the years in response to various crises, the role of legal counsel at the IMF has also changed (including more frequent travel to member countries to help strengthen their respective legal frameworks). Lawyers at the IMF play a critical role in the institution's rule of law, serving in three broad capacities: (i) traditional in-house counsel role, (ii) trusted advisor to member countries and (iii) public policy contributor.

In its in-house role, legal counsel advises the IMF's three decision-making organs on the consistency of their decisions with the institution's Articles of Agreement, rules and regulations.

In its role as trusted advisor, legal counsel advises member countries, largely through the provision of technical assistance. Traditionally, legal technical assistance focused mainly on central banking, bank resolution and tax/budget policy, but the areas in which assistance is given has expanded in recent years. One discussant noted that many private lawyers are also in a position to offer technical assistance and queried whether there is competition between IMF technical assistance and technical assistance provided by private lawyers. In response, one participant expressed her view that the IMF technical assistance program does not compete with private lawyers' ability to provide similar assistance, reminding the panel that the IMF can only provide technical services to governments.

Regarding IFI cooperation with the private sector, more generally, it was noted that the vast majority of EBRD's investments are in the private sector (and it is EBRD's role to encourage more private sector investment); the link, however, between that private sector work, on the one hand, and legal reform work, on the other hand, is not always easily made.

Legal counsel at the IMF also contributes to the design and implementation of international policies. Legal counsel is able to utilize its "institutional memory" in the design of new policies and, as a repository of institutional information, to ensure that management and the IMF's departments think through every issue before a policy is enacted. Two policies, in particular, that the IMF's legal counsel has been involved in relate to de-risking and fintech.

The discussion turned to the key ingredients of being an effective legal counsel in the IFI space. First, legal counsel must be independent, objective and consistent. The legal counsel's main client must be the Articles of Agreement. Second, legal counsel must be problem solvers, not just compliance officers. Third, an effective legal counsel needs to understand where the line is between legal and policy advice. On legal issues, lawyers should have exclusive responsibility. On policy issues, lawyers comprise just one group of personnel providing input. Fourth, legal counsel must be effective communicators and must possess the ability to explain their legal advice to non-lawyers, be they directors, management or economists. It was also highlighted that continuity is key—a lawyer's institutional memory is very helpful in ensuring policy coherence and consistency.

The discussion turned to the IMF's governance structure, which, it was noted, is *sui generis*. It combines the features of a private company with those of an international agency.

One participant asked the panel whether IFIs face limits in the setting of standards, particularly in the labor and gender spheres. One respondent noted there are indeed limitations as standards setting is very political since it ultimately reflects national policy choices. Another respondent added that the EBRD in its legal reform work does not impose a particular approach on how countries implement best practices in setting standards, although she notes that countries are indeed very competitive in setting such standards. IFIs have a role to play in sharing best practices (in part because they are seen as relatively independent), and one strategy IFIs could adopt is to leverage the competitiveness of countries: tell one country what an IFI has done for its neighbor in terms of setting standards, and often this will incentivize the country to think about how it could also meet the standards in question. At the same time, it is important for IFIs to recognize that each country has capacity constraints that may prevent it from adopting standards that other countries are better equipped to handle. It is not necessarily fair to insist that all countries adopt identical standards.

From a labor relations standpoint, one of the most difficult issues facing IFIs is how to get their own houses in order. The IMF, for example, focuses on people management and how to motivate people to work (from a non-compensation perspective). It was noted that the IMF has good rules on paper. More generally, IFI rules on labor should be common sensical and easy to implement and they must have "enforcement teeth." There is a connection between human rights and workers' rights, with one participant noting that the Black Sea Trade and Development Bank stipulates in its social framework that labor protection is a fundamental human right.

One participant raised the topic of "smart governance," akin to the concepts of smart cities and smart infrastructure. How will IFIs be innovators? He noted that there is a feeling AIIB may end up just as another sister of the World Bank, while also recognizing that there is an equal chance AIIB may go in a different direction. The AIIB is a work in progress, but the governance structure will be different—with a focus on greater delegation to management and a membership base distinct from other institutions. AIIB does not have the burden of "long-enshrined rules" that other, more mature institutions must cope with. Another participant noted that IFIs do struggle sometimes with innovation, particularly in the field of technology. Before IFIs can cooperate with their clients on new technologies, such as blockchains, IFIs need to take the time to better understand these advancements themselves.

In the context of standards setting, one participant asked why certain standards, and not others, are used, and how IFIs draw boundaries in such a way that choosing which standards to promote is not seen as arbitrary. In response, another participant suggested that such standards could be found in the international legal obligations of IFIs, which itself would be an interesting topic for a future conference.

5 Panel 4: Governance and the Rule of Administrative Law

The discussion shifted to ways in which IFIs use debarment to combat fraud and corruption. Fighting international, cross-border corruption, in contrast to domestic corruption, is a relatively new concept, with the World Bank spearheading the approach in 1996. It was noted that international organizations will not start something new unless there is external pressure to do so. Fighting international corruption is a sensitive area. On the one hand, IFIs are not supposed to interfere with the political affairs of their member countries. On the other hand, they have a fiduciary duty to use funds for their intended purpose. It was also noted that corruption is very bad for an organization's bottom line and that research shows a link between high levels of corruption and the rise of terrorism.

There are three units at the World Bank that deal with sanctions issues: The integrity unit (INT) investigates staff who have received bribes, as well as incidences of corruption, fraud or collusion involving a contract financed by the World Bank. In addition to the sanctions process, the World Bank has introduced a settlements process. It was noted that settlement has certain benefits. It provides parties with certainty; it is quicker and can be more efficient than the sanctions process; and it incentivizes respondents to be more cooperative with the investigation, which, in turn, leads to more information for the World Bank to better understand what actually took place.

It was highlighted that international organizations are not governments. Organizations cannot subpoena companies in order to get information. Instead, they rely on the audit clause, which is included in loan agreements with borrowers. International organizations, unlike governments, cannot give whistleblower protection. Instead, they provide confidentiality to witnesses.

The World Bank is obliged to inform relevant country governments (i.e., the host and home countries) if there is evidence of corruption or wrongdoing in connection with a project. It has discretion, however, as to when it informs.

One participant advised that, before an organization makes a referral to a country government, it should know the laws of that country. In other words, it should know what it is getting into, ideally by securing a legal opinion from a reputable local law firm in that jurisdiction. A referral to the French government, for example, will not be received in the same way as a referral to the Swiss government.

The question was raised as to what obligations an organization has to inform a country government in the event a staff member violates a local law, particularly in light of an organization's privileges and immunities. One participant mentioned that, in the rare event this has happened, her organization has cooperated with local authorities, but on a voluntary basis and under certain conditions, such as confidentiality and no subpoenaing of staff. As such, this cooperation did not raise issues of waiver of immunity.

The discussion moved to information disclosure policies and open data initiatives and how international organizations can disclose data in a meaningful and transparent manner. Open data systems can help with decision-making, budget planning, donor coordination and civil society empowerment. One person noted that you can't weed out corruption without open data (i.e., without knowing the nature, location and providers of the development assistance being given).

The panel discussed certain lessons that can be learned from previous open data initiatives, lessons that would be particularly useful for a new organization, such as AIIB. First, a new institution has the enviable position of being able to introduce progressive information disclosure policies into its founding policies, which is much easier than to introduce such policies after an institution has been in existence for a long period and thus accustomed to doing things in a certain way. For an institution like the AIIB, which is commonly seen as an instrument of Chinese power, the lack of transparency can be a real hindrance, preventing it from gaining international legitimacy.

The second lesson is that external signals will matter in an institution's information disclosure and transparency policies. It was recommended that AIIB make its co-financing arrangements transparent and clear, an area in which other institutions struggle.

The third lesson is to define end users. It is critical to understand the demand for information, the entities and individuals that can use the information and how such entities and individuals access such data. One participant noted that mapping dashboards have limited audiences—maps should be accessible to those on the ground in the countries where projects are being implemented, not just to professors and others who may have access to robust bandwidth and wi-fi connections. IFIs should not assume that there is a culture of data use. For example, in Honduras, there is a strong, public distrust of data coming out of certain government institutions, and institutions need to be careful not to taint their data by associating it with local agencies that are distrusted.

The fourth lesson, specific to AIIB, is not to wait. There is tremendous interest in the AIIB, particularly in the US. At the same time, there is not a great deal of English language news on aid coming out of China, which leaves great room for speculation about AIIB and encourages the development of misguided policy stances in the US regarding AIIB. AIIB must proactively combat this information gap and move quickly to develop an information disclosure policy and open data initiative to ensure correct information is released.

It was noted that it is a struggle for an organization to find the right balance between disclosing too much and too little information. An organization must weigh the impact of disclosure against the cost in making such information available. It is important to avoid the "data deluge." At the same time, an organization does not know which information will be valuable to whom, suggesting it is better to err on the side of disclosure.

The discussion shifted to the jurisprudence of international administrative tribunals. Before 1980, there were only several administrative tribunals in operation, including the ILO administrative tribunal and the UN administrative tribunal. Now there are over 15 tribunals. The question arises as to whether decisions across all tribunals are consistent with one another, or whether the expansion of the number of tribunals is leading to a divergence in case law and decisions.

Many commentators posit that tribunals before 1980 generally followed each other's decisions and adhered to the same principle of laws.

An International Law Association report was discussed, which in 2004 noted that there ought to be consistency and coherence in the decisions of these tribunals and encouraged the tribunals to take note of each other's decisions. It is quite uncommon for the ILO tribunal and the former UN administrative tribunal to cite other tribunals' decisions, which may be because each of these tribunals can rely on its own extensive jurisprudence. In contrast, the World Bank, ADB and IMF tribunals do occasionally cite cases from other tribunals, demonstrating that there are general principles of law recognized by these tribunals.

The recognition of general principles of law across international tribunals does not necessarily mean that the decisions of these tribunals are consistent with one another. In certain areas, there is convergence of views across tribunals, while in others divergence, including the abolition of position, the standard of proof used in disciplinary cases, and the rights of victims who lodge complaints of harassment or retaliation.

The question was raised as to whether a new organization ought to set up its own tribunal or use an existing one. On the one hand, there are not many existing tribunals that allow affiliation across organizations, and tribunals each have their own cultural context that may not be appropriate for other organizations. Being a "small fish in that big pond" may not be advisable. On the other hand, it is quite costly for an organization to set up its own tribunal. The ESM was raised as a case in point. It established its own administrative tribunal in 2014. To mitigate costs, the tribunal sits (and judges are appointed) only when there is a case to be heard and cooperates with EFTA for administrative support.

One participant noted that tribunals are not just costly, but they can also engender bad will. It is worth highlighting the numerous resolution mechanisms, such as mediation, that can be exhausted before perhaps reaching the tribunal stage; there is "room for creativity" in how to leverage these pre-tribunal mechanisms.

This discussion concluded with several thoughts. Tribunals are distinct from one another in how they consider and decide cases. Nevertheless, for several reasons, there is far more convergence, rather than divergence, in their jurisprudence. For example, there are a number of individuals who sit on more than one tribunal, bringing their other experiences with them. Litigants before tribunals look for relevant case law across tribunals, which also reinforces the tendency toward commonality. This begs the question, however, as to whether convergence is desirable or appropriate. On the one hand, staff rules across international organizations and issues facing organizations share a lot in common. On the other hand, an emphasis on harmonization may impede an organization's ability to come up with its own solutions based on its own experiences and interests.

6 Plenary: Good Governance and Modern IFIs

The first part of the plenary session focused on the role of General Counsel in an IFI. Three roles, in particular, were highlighted: (i) protect the IFI's charter; (ii) protect the institution (from both external and internal challenges); and (iii) protect the institution's mission. An IFI's mission changes from time to time, and the General Counsel needs to be aware of this. General Counsel should be aware of political issues facing the institution, but such issues should not affect the General Counsel's responsibility to protect the institution's mission. The General Counsel needs to understand and mitigate conflicts of interest and internal conflicts over internal resources, particularly if the institution engages in both public- and private-sector activities.

It was agreed that transparency and accountability are the real drivers of good behavior in public institutions. Even though international organizations view themselves as self-contained, notions of governance are still informed by domestic considerations.

AIIB, for example, was the first IFI established in China. Therefore, how AIIB and the Chinese government resolve issues around privileges and immunities, and, more generally, how China approaches the roles and responsibilities of hosting an IFI on its territory, will likely set an example for future IFIs in China. Because AIIB is in China, the international community may set higher expectations or impose more requirements on it. The best way to address these higher expectations is for AIIB to commit itself to as much transparency as possible, while also avoiding the "document tsunami," which is often associated with greater levels of transparency.

There will always be tension between an IFI and the host country on matters of governance, particularly in the area of privileges and immunities. One representative of an IFI noted that the only people who really understand the specific character and legal status of the IFI is the institution's legal department.

The discussion shifted to the question of whether an IFI should have a resident or non-resident board, whether a non-resident board is only appropriate for a small institution and whether a non-resident board should have the same scope of responsibilities as a resident board. AIIB's view is that the role of the board can be discharged from a distance. The board can be convened when and as needed, as well as on a quarterly basis. It was noted that there is a provision in AIIB's charter to allow the board to delegate project approval to the President.

A representative from another IFI that allows project delegation confirmed it works well, although a common question that arises is the monetary threshold under which the President can approve under his delegation authority. An alternative to setting monetary thresholds is a policy of principles-based delegation. One of the benefits of allowing management to approve projects is that poor management decisions can be ameliorated by removing the management—in contrast, boards cannot be fired for mistaken decisions. Several participants remarked that having a non-resident board mitigates the risk of micro-management and allows management to do its job.

The plenary session concluded with four closing thoughts and questions. First, there is no common view of what good governance means in every context. There are certainly shared experiences across IFIs, but there are differences as well. Differences are not necessarily a bad thing, and departing from what is viewed as "best practice" does not mean that the alternative does not meet the standard of good governance. Second, good practice for IFIs is an evolving standard. There are changes in demands and expectations of those for whom governance arrangements at IFIs exist. Should IFIs anticipate the types of governance that might be required in the future, and act accordingly, or should they continue to use governance structures that work effectively in the present? Third, should IFIs be pro-active in setting standards of governance, or should IFI governance be reflective of what prevails in current domestic governance structures? Put differently, should IFIs be trailblazers or be instrumentalized by their members? Fourth, AIIB would very much like to be part of the continuing discourse on good IFI governance.

www.ingramcontent.com/pod-product-compliance
Lightning Source LLC
LaVergne TN
LVHW020635300926
849161LV00004B/705